CHRISTIAN PERSPECTIVES
ON RELIGIOUS KNOWLEDGE

Christian Perspectives on Religious Knowledge

Edited by

C. Stephen Evans and Merold Westphal

William B. Eerdmans Publishing Company
Grand Rapids, Michigan

Library of Congress Cataloging-in-Publication Data

Christian perspectives on religious knowledge / edited by
C. Stephen Evans and Merold Westphal.
p.   cm.
Includes bibliographical references.
Contents: On knowing that we know / William P. Alston — Divine knowledge /
Alvin Plantinga — Proper function, reliabilism, and religious knowledge / William Hasker —
In defense of Gaunilo's defense of the fool / Nicholas Wolterstorff —
Natural theology and the Reformed objection / Laura L. Garcia —
Empiricism, rationalism, and the possibility of historical
religious knowledge / C. Stephen Evans — Christian philosophers and
the Copernican revolution / Merold Westphal — Zarathustra's songs /
Galen A. Johnson — Persons of flesh / Donn Welton.
ISBN 0-8028-0679-1
1. Knowledge, Theory of (Religion).   2. Philosophical theology.
3. Faith and reason.   I. Evans, C. Stephen.   II. Westphal, Merold.
BT40.C487 1993
230'.01—dc20   93-29151
                                                        CIP

For Arthur Holmes

Contents

Introduction:
Christian Perspectives
on Religious Knowledge

C. Stephen Evans and Merold Westphal

Is "religious knowledge" an oxymoronic phrase? Ever since the Enlightenment, it has often been unquestioned dogma among intellectuals that it is. If religious beliefs have any legitimate place, then that place is not among the things we *know*. The humanists and freethinkers are prepared to dismiss religious belief altogether, as the sort of thing a modern person with intellectual integrity cannot believe in a scientific age. Those who are kinder are more apt to second the words of David Hume's conclusions in his famous essay "Of Miracles": "Our most holy religion is founded on *Faith*, not on reason; and it is a sure method of exposing it to put it to such a trial as it is, by no means, fitted to endure."[1]

Hume seems to assume here that faith and reason are totally distinct human activities. This means both (1) that what is held by faith is not rational and (2) that what is knowable by reason requires no faith. Hume knows, of course, that Christian philosophers in every age and in many different ways have challenged the first assumption. What he fails to notice is that his own theory of knowledge gives us reason to question the second.

On Hume's own analysis, reason is unable to ground all human knowledge on evidence (including self-evidence). Much of our ordinary knowledge is grounded in habitual practices that Hume calls "custom." Some of these habits seem instinctual, while others seem learned, but

---

1. David Hume, *An Enquiry Concerning Human Understanding*, ed. Eric Steinberg (Indianapolis: Hackett Publishing Co., 1977), p. 89.

1

if Hume is right, much of what we ordinarily call "knowledge" is partially rooted in practices that we *bring to* the knowing process — practices that we engage in as whole persons and that certainly are not justifiable as "purely rational." Such practices may not amount to religious faith, but they resemble in some interesting ways those personal commitments which are embodied in what religious communities call faith.

Twentieth-century epistemology, within both the "analytic" and the "Continental" traditions, can be described as the movement away from the Enlightenment view of reason as pure and self-contained to variations on this Humean theme of the indigence of reason. This in turn has created a new context for the philosophy of religion. Perhaps Enlightenment critiques of the reasonableness of religious belief point to defects not so much in religious belief as in the conceptions of knowledge uncritically adopted as the basis of these critiques. Maybe religious knowledge looks dubious because we have the wrong idea about what it is to know something and how we know what we know. In the last thirty years there has been a marked resurgence of Christian philosophy, and this suspicion has developed into a full-fledged assault on Enlightenment epistemologies and those philosophies of religion which rest on them. The present volume embodies some of the fruits of that assault.

Christian philosophy today is pluralistic and properly so. There are Christians who are Thomists and Existentialists, Realists and Idealists, Internalists and Externalists, Foundationalists and Coherentists. There are Christian philosophers who self-consciously do philosophy in the "analytic" style, and those who work in the "Continental" style. Some, though of course not all, of this variety is reflected in this volume. Our authors disagree with each other vigorously and criticize each other freely. However, despite the deep differences in philosophical styles and positions, there are some striking affinities. However much the authors of this volume may disagree with each other, they are united in their conviction that, with a proper understanding of the nature of knowledge and how it is derived, the fashionable Enlightenment dismissal of religious belief as unreasonable is itself unreasonable. In many of the essays, this critique of the Enlightenment suspicion of religion takes the form of a demand for parity. Religion deserves no special protected enclave, no exemption from ordinary standards of rational appraisal. However, religion also does not deserve to be singled out and asked to satisfy standards that other areas of human knowledge do not and cannot satisfy.

More substantively, the authors all believe that a proper understanding of the position of human beings as finite, *created* beings is helpful in coming to see what knowledge is and how humans know. All of the essays embody what may be called an appropriate humility that results from the recognition of this human situation. Though the authors see significant differences in the scope of human knowledge, all seek a middle ground between epistemological arrogance and relativistic skepticism.

This does not mean that all of the essays address the doctrine of creation in an explicit manner; in some of the essays the idea of creation is only tacitly present in the account given of the situation of the human knower. Nevertheless, in the essays one gets a clear sense of human knowers as neither angels nor purposeless chunks of matter, but as finite creatures. To be sure, as we will see, their understanding of the doctrine of creation differs in some interesting ways; there are at least important differences of emphasis in the way they draw out implications of this central Christian claim. However, the fact that creation is a crucial element in the essays gives substance to the claim that these perspectives on religious knowledge are all *Christian* perspectives.[2] An examination of some of the differences, in fact, is one way of highlighting some of the underlying similarities; hence we shall now turn our attention to the individual essays in a manner that will allow for such comparisons.

William Alston's essay, "On Knowing That We Know: The Application to Religious Knowledge," begins by developing some of the implications of reliabilist epistemology for religious knowledge. Reliabilism, which is roughly the idea that knowledge is "true belief that is acquired and/or sustained in a reliable way," is a type of "externalist" epistemology. The externalist, in contrast to the "internalist" who sees knowledge as requiring grounds that are accessible to the knower, sees knowledge as made possible by processes that may go on independently of the will and even of the consciousness of the knower. The internalist, by contrast, believes that for me to know something, my true belief must be supported by adequate reasons of which I am aware, or at least could become aware.

2. This is not to claim that Christians have a monopoly on the theme of God as creator. The point is that in the present context the "significant other" confronted by Christian philosophers is not, for example, Jewish theism, but the variety of nontheistic views that express modernity's secularism. Hence, when they do philosophy of religion, Christian philosophers are concerned with the whole of Christian theism and not just with those features that distinguish it from other theisms.

The internalist view has an apparent initial advantage, in that if I can state the grounds of my belief, it might appear that I not only know, but can know *that* I know. Reliabilism offers no such promise. Since it is possible in some cases that I know without being able to state the grounds or evidence for my belief, in those cases it may well be that I know without knowing that I know. Suppose it is true that the Bible is a reliable revelation from God, when properly interpreted with the help of the Spirit of God. In such a case, according to reliabilism, beliefs formed when the Bible is read and interpreted in this way may amount to knowledge. However, granted that it is *possible* that such beliefs amount to knowledge, are they actually knowledge? It might appear that to know that we know in such a case, we must know that the Bible is indeed a reliable revelation from God, and the internalist will say that we must have some grounds for this knowledge. Without such evidence, it appears that showing that we have knowledge in such a case will be a circular enterprise; on the assumption that reliable processes are at work, then we have knowledge. To know that a process is reliable, however, one must know that it typically or normally gives rise to true beliefs. So it looks as if we must assume that we have some religious knowledge in order to show that we do have some.

Alston argues, however, that the apparent advantage of internalist theories is illusory. It is equally true of internalist theories that they require that we know some things in order to know that we know something. A look at the processes that are accepted as producing "secular" knowledge, such as sense perception, induction, and memory, shows that to know that we have knowledge through these processes we must resort to the same sort of circularity. The human condition implies that "it is a mistake to suppose that we can first determine whether we have knowledge before getting any." So it is not surprising that religious knowledge resembles our knowledge of the natural world; "if God has not already made it possible for us to get quite a bit of first-level knowledge of him, we have no chance to come to know that we have such knowledge." Alston concludes that we should not only accept the human condition but give thanks to God for it. The implicit message here is that if God has chosen to create us as such limited, finite knowers, then it must be good for us to be such.

Alvin Plantinga's essay, "Divine Knowledge," is not primarily directed to the question of the nature of human knowledge at all, but rather to the nature of God's knowledge. However, the account of divine knowledge given depends crucially on a contrast with the account Plantinga provides of human knowledge. Plantinga begins with a puzzle as to how God knows propositions about what free creatures will or could do in the future. Such propositions are termed *counterfactuals of creaturely freedom*. Even if we put aside the worry about whether such knowledge is compatible with freedom, such divine knowledge looks questionable to us, more questionable than God's knowledge of the past or present, or his knowledge of necessary truths. Plantinga suggests that divine knowledge of counterfactuals of freedom looks more dubious to us than other kinds because we understand how we know the other kinds, but we have no idea how we could know about future free actions. Since we don't understand how we could know such things, we are tempted to conclude that we don't know how God could know them either, and consequently we wonder whether he does.

Plantinga admits that we don't know how God could know counterfactuals of freedom, but he argues that this is not a real problem. The fact is that we don't understand how God knows any of what he knows; what we can understand is that we should not be expected to understand, because divine knowledge must be fundamentally different from human knowledge. Human knowledge, on Plantinga's view, must be understood in light of the doctrine of creation: "The basic idea, therefore, is that we are so constructed (so constructed by God) that under certain sorts of conditions we form certain sorts of beliefs; and those beliefs constitute knowledge when they are true and when they result from the operation of the design plan God has implemented for us — more exactly, the operation of those parts of the design plan aimed at the production of true beliefs."

In order for us to know anything, therefore, God had to know something — namely, the design plan and how to implement it. God had to know "how to institute the causal laws and how to create us in such a way that by virtue of the cooperation of our natures with these laws and the conditions under which they operate we would have the sort of knowledge he intended us to have." Human knowledge thus presupposes divine knowledge. It follows from this that human knowledge and divine knowledge are significantly different: my knowledge presupposes my having been given my cognitive faculties by an intelligent designer, but of course nothing like this can be true for God.

The conclusion Plantinga draws is that it is true that we don't understand how God could know the future. However, that fact implies no special problem for divine knowledge of the future. The truth is that we are equally ignorant of how God knows himself or the past. In all cases "all we can really say is that it is a necessary truth that for any proposition p, p is true if and only if God knows it." Once we understand our own creaturely status properly, we understand that it is a mistake to model God's way of knowing on our own ways, and thus we can understand why we cannot be expected to understand how God knows what he knows.

The essay by William Hasker, "Proper Function, Reliabilism, and Religious Knowledge: A Critique of Plantinga's Epistemology," contains an analysis and critique of the epistemology Plantinga employs, and also a case for an alternative theory Hasker wishes to advance. Plantinga's epistemology, termed by Hasker the "Theory of Proper Function," which is briefly summarized by Plantinga in his essay for the purpose of clarifying the difference between divine and human knowledge, regards a belief as *warranted* if it is produced by our epistemic faculties when they are functioning properly in accordance with the relevant portion of the divine design plan. Roughly, when our faculties are designed by God so as to produce true beliefs when operating in a certain environment, then, when they do so operate, the outcome amounts to knowledge.

Hasker, besides mounting some general criticisms of Plantinga's theory, develops at some length what he takes to be a counterexample to the theory. He asks us to imagine Geoffrey, "who, as the result of a random genetic mutation, not directed or planned by anyone," has been "totally blind from birth." However, the mutation that produced this defect has also given Geoffrey an unusual ability. The part of his brain that normally would register visual information now registers in a powerful way the "magnetic fields generated by the earth and its environment." This enables Geoffrey to "determine his location in the neighborhood and to make his way around it with considerable facility."

Hasker wishes to claim that under these circumstances Geoffrey has warranted beliefs about his location, and "indeed that he *knows* where he is." However, Geoffrey's brain is not functioning in accordance with the way God designed the brain to function, which shows that knowledge does not always depend on proper function in Plantinga's sense. Hasker concludes from this that the notion of the design plan is not essential for epistemological theory. We can instead simply understand proper function in terms of "the operation of belief-forming processes in human beings" that contribute "to the survival and maintenance of 'the system as a whole' — that is, the entire human being, and perhaps the family or social group of which the human is a part." These processes do this simply by providing human beings with a supply of true beliefs.

By dropping the notion of a design plan, Plantinga's epistemology is transformed into a version of reliabilism. Such a deletion might appear to undermine the theistic foundations of epistemological theory, and thus Hasker's view looks "less Christian" than Plantinga's. Hasker suggests, however, that although the concept of a "design plan" may not be part of the analysis of proper function, it may still be invoked in the *explanation* of our epistemic practices.

In the last section of his paper, Hasker puts his theory to work by examining whether religious beliefs possess the right kind of warrant. Doubts about this arise because of the inconsistencies among the religious beliefs that claim this sort of "reliable" grounding. Hasker surveys several possible strategies for dealing with this problem, and he concludes with the provocative suggestion that the decisive factor which may make my religious beliefs warranted is the fact that they are grounded in my own first-person experience. Thus, what I know is grounded not only in my finite, creaturely status but also in the fact that I am the particular creature that I am.

Nicholas Wolterstorff has been, along with Plantinga and Alston, an important voice in the development of what has been termed "Reformed epistemology."[3] His essay here, "In Defense of Gaunilo's Defense of the Fool," does not, however, deal head-on with epistemological theory, but rather with the ontological argument developed by Anselm, one of the famous "proofs" for God's existence that have been put forward as natural theology. One of the consequences of "Reformed epistemology," with its insistence that religious beliefs can be "properly basic,"[4] is that the debate about natural theology becomes of much less importance for Christian belief. Reliabilist-type epistemologies, as defended by Alston, Plantinga, and Hasker, imply that religious beliefs can be justified, and even amount to knowledge, even if the believer

3. For seminal essays that develop this theme, see Alvin Plantinga and Nicholas Wolterstorff, eds., *Faith and Rationality: Reason and Belief in God* (Notre Dame: University of Notre Dame Press, 1983).

4. For development of this idea see Alvin Plantinga, "Reason and Belief in God," and Nicholas Wolterstorff, "Can Belief in God Be Rational If It Has No Foundations?" in *Faith and Rationality*, pp. 16-93 and 135-86, respectively.

has no proof of her beliefs, or even access to any evidence at all. Hence, it is not surprising that in his essay Wolterstorff feels no need to defend Anselm's argument, but rather defends Gaunilo, the monk who spoke up on behalf of "the fool," the person who has said in his heart that there is no God. Wolterstorff thinks that Gaunilo made some telling points against Anselm's attempt to prove that the very idea of God implies that God must exist.

Wolterstorff is careful not to argue that no forms of the ontological argument are successful; he knows that Plantinga and others have developed versions of the argument that differ significantly from Anselm's. However, he wishes to side with Gaunilo in the dispute over the soundness of Anselm's original version. Anselm's argument is that God, "a being than which none greater can be conceived," must exist in reality, since if God exists only in the mind as an idea we could conceive a greater being, one that exists in reality as well as in the mind. Gaunilo disputes this by developing a parody of Anselm's argument, a proof that a perfect island exists, "than which none greater can be conceived," for analogous reasons.

As Wolterstorff tells the story, although Gaunilo is not a first-rate thinker and states some of his points in an unclear way, essentially his parody does indeed reveal the weak point of Anselm's argument, the assumption that understanding the meaning of a term is equivalent to understanding the reference of the term. Gaunilo suggests that there is a kind of understanding that does not depend on reference. On Wolterstorff's view, the debate between Anselm and Gaunilo is a precursor of the much later dispute between Meinong, who argued that our ideas of nonexistent objects must refer to something and therefore that those objects must exist in some sense, and Frege, who distinguished between sense and reference and thereby held that it was possible for a term to have meaning without referring to anything. Wolterstorff's sympathies here appear to lie with Frege, and the issue is one with implications far beyond whether Anselm's ontological argument is sound. The breaking apart of sense and reference is in fact a crucial move in making possible the debate between realism and antirealism.

Though Wolterstorff's essay involves a close textual reading, it is important not to lose sight of the forest for the trees. By siding with Gaunilo (and Frege), Wolterstorff arguably is siding with Hume and Kant — certainly not with the details of their epistemologies, but with the broad reminders they offer us about the limits of reason. We can see this point perhaps more clearly if we remind ourselves that modern defenders of what we might call "ambitious" forms of the ontological argument — Descartes, Leibniz, Spinoza, and Hegel — are paradigms of the exaggerated claims for reason's self-sufficiency against which so much contemporary philosophy, including "Reformed epistemology," is directed.

Laura L. Garcia, in her essay "Natural Theology and the Reformed Objection," continues the discussion of natural theology. The "Reformed epistemologists" have stirred up a fair amount of controversy between themselves and defenders of traditional natural theology as practiced by classical thinkers such as Thomas Aquinas. Aquinas has been presented as a "classical foundationalist" who accepts an epistemological standard that is unreasonably severe and who appears to make the legitimacy of religious belief unnecessarily rest on philosophical arguments. On the other side, natural theologians have sometimes presented the Reformed epistemologists as fideists who have abandoned rational defense of the faith. Garcia, writing from the perspective of traditional natural theology, shows that this tension is much exaggerated and that prospects are good for a substantial amount of agreement between natural theologians and Reformed epistemologists.

Garcia sees the aims of Reformed epistemology to lie in the defense of ordinary believers who arrive at faith without philosophical argument, and who do not proportion the strength of their faith to the evidence available to support it. However, she argues that treating belief in God as properly basic doesn't solve all the problems of ordinary believers, since even basic beliefs can be troubled by doubts and counterevidence, and she suggests a number of other problems for the Reformed epistemologist in understanding how properly basic religious beliefs might be "triggered."

Interestingly enough, however, and contrary to what we might have expected, Garcia claims that natural theology is not, on the view of Aquinas, the solution to those problems. Aquinas agrees with the Reformed epistemologist that firm Christian belief is best built on faith that is grounded in God's revelatory actions because of the finitude and sinfulness of human reason. "The deliverances of faith are more certain than the deliverances of reason," says Aquinas, since God's word cannot be false, while the deliverances of reason can be. Aquinas is no "evidentialist" who holds that belief must be proportioned to rational evidence. Natural theology does not provide a way of coming to religious belief that is superior to the way of faith.

Nevertheless, natural theology is a good thing and not to be despised. Although it can be wrongfully used, it can also be beneficial in helping the believer find philosophical arguments for some of the things she believes and "can lead the unbeliever closer to faith by removing certain intellectual obstacles to her belief." On this point the agreement between Aquinas and Reformed epistemology seems substantial indeed. Reformed epistemologists hold that belief in God does not have to be, and typically is not, based on philosophical arguments, but they do not hold that arguments for God's existence cannot be given, nor that they should not be given. On the contrary, Plantinga has himself offered such arguments and frequently in his work suggests that such arguments are possible. Though differences remain between natural theologians and Reformed epistemologists over such issues as whether justified faith amounts to "knowledge" and over the value of "external evidence" that Scripture is a revelation from God, both types of Christian philosophy see the firmness of faith as stemming from the Christian's volitional commitment to trusting God. Catholic and Reformed thinkers are allies, with a common enemy: "evidentialism and positivism, which place unwarranted restrictions on what can be sensibly believed and on what sort of evidence is admissible."

C. Stephen Evans, in "Empiricism, Rationalism, and the Possibility of Historical Religious Knowledge," turns attention away from the question of religious knowledge in general, and the related debate about natural theology, to the question of a specific kind of religious knowledge. He discusses whether historical religious knowledge, involving belief in religiously significant propositions with historical content, is possible. For Christians who hold that the historicity of Jesus' life, death, and resurrection are part of the content of faith, this is a crucial question. At least since the eighteenth century, philosophers have wondered whether such knowledge is really possible.

Many of the worries are epistemological in nature and appear to presuppose an empiricist epistemology: Can we really come to know through empirical evidence that a particular person in the past performed miracles and lived so as to reveal God to us? Can we have enough historical evidence to show something like this? Evans attempts to show that these apparent worries about evidence are often a smoke screen for a rationalist conception of religious knowledge that makes such historical religious knowledge impossible in principle. On this rationalist view, genuine religious knowledge must be of timeless truths that are not grounded in any contingent facts. Though this rationalistic conception of religious knowledge has appeal, Evans tries to show that it is far from self-evident and that even the grounds for its appeal should make it suspect for Christians.

Though there are extreme versions of empiricism that also may rule out historical religious knowledge, Evans argues that reasonable forms of empiricism are open to such a possibility in principle. The question of whether we can learn about God through history is one that must be decided by experience and not in an a priori manner. Once again our finitude as human knowers comes to the fore; we are not godlike beings who know ultimate truth in an a priori fashion, but creatures who must learn by encountering the world of experience.

The pluralistic character of contemporary Christian philosophy comes strongly to the fore in Merold Westphal's essay, "Christian Philosophers and the Copernican Revolution." In this essay Westphal challenges a recent argument by Alvin Plantinga that Christian philosophers should be realists who reject the Kantian view that the world we know is the phenomenal world, the world as it appears to us, not the noumenal world, the world as it is independent of any human observer. Plantinga views this "creative antirealism" as hostile to Christian thought. Westphal distinguishes four variations on the Kantian theme, two theistic and two humanistic, and contends that only one of the four merits Plantinga's blanket rejection, since the theistic versions express important Christian themes and even one of the humanistic versions has important features a theist should appreciate and affirm.

On Westphal's reading, Kant himself is a theist who identifies the noumenal world with reality as it is for God. The whole point of the distinction between the phenomenal and noumenal worlds is to distinguish between human and divine knowledge. We can learn from Kant "that our best theories to date, including our theologies, are fallible, open to critique, and revisable," because the theist is "committed to taking both human finitude and human sinfulness seriously." One of the emphases of Westphal's essay, which is echoed at one point by Garcia, is that Christian philosophy must take account not merely of our finitude as creatures but of our condition as sinful creatures. Antirealism is valuable in pointing to the noetic effects of sin. Humans often do create "gods." Though humans cannot, of course, create the true God, the biblical God, they are inveterate idolaters who continually try to shape God in their own image. Antirealism calls our attention to the possibility and reality of such "phenomenal gods."

The pluralistic character of Christian philosophy is further emphasized by the two concluding essays by Galen Johnson and Donn Welton. Johnson's "Songs of Zarathustra: Faith after Nietzsche" develops a theme that is present in Westphal's essay: that Christian thought can benefit from a purging encounter with radical critiques that demolish unworthy, idolatrous substitutes for the living God. Johnson tries to show that the Nietzschean critique of religious faith is one that Christian philosophers must take seriously. Having passed through the flames, there is nonetheless a type of authentic Christian faith, which Johnson calls tragic faith, that can be resolutely embraced. Together with Westphal, he insists that Christian philosophizing needs to take the fall as seriously as it takes creation.

Johnson reads Nietzsche as developing a skeptical critique of metaphysics as rooted in language, a critique that turns our attention from theoretical arguments about the truth of Christianity to practical arguments. Here Nietzsche forces us to recognize the duplicity and self-deception that affect so much of the religious life, a recognition that should not be entirely a surprise to Christians convinced that even the redeemed are redeemed sinners. Johnson points out that the same "quest for vengeance" that Nietzsche finds in the religious life can be seen in Nietzsche himself. The overcoming of vengeance requires in all of us, Nietzsche and religious believer alike, the renunciation of the "telescopic eye," the "kind of thought that claims to be undertaken from a godlike position of overview, survey, or flight above the earth, not rooted in a position or situation on the earth." Johnson explores this by looking at the wise person as blind, an image that is seen in both Homer and the Old Testament. He concludes by suggesting that authentic Christian faith after Nietzsche will have to be a faith that, like Job, hears a voice that heals though it does not always explain. Authentic Christian faith must be a faith that renounces vengeance and affirms life in the face of suffering. But is this not a legitimate way of describing the passion of Jesus himself?

In "Persons of Flesh," Donn Welton returns us to the creation motif, taking as his starting point René Descartes's understanding of the body. On Welton's view, the problems with Cartesian mind-body dualism, and resulting difficulties for how we come to have knowledge as embodied beings, may stem not from Descartes's understanding of the mind but from his theory of the body. In attempting to develop a scientific theory of the body, Descartes transforms the material world, including the body, into a world of figures, a mathematical world of geometrical shapes, treatable by algebraic rules. The modern world inherited a world that is not so much "material and therefore mathematized" as it is "mathematized and thereby material." Welton sees only a short step from this move to contemporary behaviorist conceptions of the body "as a web of S-R arcs" or to conceptions of the body in earlier theories of cognitive psychology as "a matrix of computational processes."

Welton sketches an alternative conception of the body in terms of which bodies are given to us as *profiles* that are grasped from the point of view of *perspectives*. Such a view can possibly capture how bodies are experienced by us "before" they become mathematized objects. Perhaps if God has created bodies as living beings, then this perspective is closer to the truth about how they really are than the abstract conception that is the result of a mathematical transformation. The materiality of human bodies as living beings constitutes the *flesh* of the body. Such a view leads to an understanding of the body, not as a part of the person, but as the mode of our being as incarnate existers.

Welton concludes with a fascinating treatment of the Gospel of John, where religious knowledge is normally conceived, not as the result of a disembodied soul, but as the achievement of a bodily being. We are encouraged to "eat" the living bread of Christ and to "drink" the living water. This Gospel suggests that spiritual life is not an alternative to embodied existence, but a possibility for an embodied being as embodied. Welton concludes that many of the Enlightenment problems with religious knowledge may be grounded in post-Cartesian mechanistic accounts of the body. A richer understanding of the body may lead to a richer understanding of religious knowledge.

It is quite appropriate that these essays appear in a volume that is dedicated to Arthur Holmes. Holmes, who has taught philosophy at Wheaton College for forty years and has done distinguished work in a number of fields, has been a persistent advocate of Christian philosophy. From Holmes's perspective, it is not enough to have philosophy done by Christians; we need philosophy that reflects the distinctive concerns and convictions of Christians. The group of Christian philosophers represented in this volume have all interacted with Holmes over the years. Several are former students; several others have been significantly influenced by Holmes's life and work.

Besides being an advocate of Christian philosophy, Holmes has been a consistent advocate of pluralism in Christian philosophy. On his view, Christian philosophy is not a monolithic enterprise, reflecting a "party line," but a creative attempt to engage in philosophical reflection and conversation as those who have been shaped by their understandings, always plural and never final, of biblical truth. It is therefore also appropriate that the contributors to this volume are not only Christian but also represent the great variety of Christian philosophers. They include Catholic and Protestant, Thomists and Existentialists, Arminians and Calvinists, analytic and Continental philosophers. A major thrust of Holmes's own work in religious epistemology is his claim that philosophy has a "perspectival" dimension, though Holmes has vigorously fought against the relativism some might see as inherent in such a position. We know as whole persons, and our knowing reflects the perspective we bring to the reflective process. We are therefore delighted that this volume does indeed reflect multiple perspectives. It is our conviction that this pluralism of perspectives allows the commonalities of Christian faith to show through all the more strongly. Christian philosophy can be distinctively Christian without being monolithic.

Our hope is that these essays, taken collectively, both illuminate our situation as created, finite knowers and honor the indefatigable labors of Arthur Holmes in the vineyard of Christian philosophy. Today his vision seems no idle dream but a living reality. With the founding of the Society of Christian Philosophers, an event in which Holmes played a key role, and the establishment of *Faith and Philosophy*, the Christian philosophical community has gathered itself together to challenge the wider philosophical world and to address some of the needs of the church. With the deepest gratitude and respect we offer this volume to Art as a concrete expression of some of the fruits of the vision he has articulated so powerfully for forty years.

On Knowing That We Know:
The Application to Religious Knowledge

William P. Alston

I

In another publication I have defended the possibility of knowledge of God, using a reliabilist account of knowledge for that defense.[1] There I point out that assessments of claims to knowledge of God are usually carried out in terms of an "internalist" conception of knowledge, according to which, in its most popular current incarnation, to know that p is to have a true belief that p that is sufficiently supported by reasons, evidence, or experience that is cognitively accessible to the subject. This has often been put by saying that knowledge is true *justified* belief. To be sure, since the publication of Edmund Gettier's pathbreaking paper "Is Justified True Belief Knowledge?"[2] it has been generally recognized that this is not *sufficient* for knowledge.[3] Nevertheless, it has

---

1. See my "Knowledge of God," in *Faith, Reason, and Skepticism,* Marcus Hester (Philadelphia: Temple University Press, 1991).
2. Edmund Gettier, "Is Justified True Belief Knowledge?" *Analysis* 23 (1963).
3. Put briefly, the Gettier point is that one can have a true justified belief where it is just a lucky accident that the belief is true, so that the subject can hardly be credited with knowledge. Thus (this is not one of Gettier's own examples) suppose that I have a barometer that has worked very well for thirty years, so that I have strong empirical evidence for supposing that its readings are accurate. The current reading indicates that a storm is in the offing, and on this basis I believe that. My belief is true; a storm is in the offing. I have a true justified belief. But in fact the barometer has a hole in it, and the lower level of mercury is due to a leak. I would have had that reading even if a storm were not on the way. Cases like this show that having a true justified belief is not always sufficient for knowledge.

continued to be widely held that true justified belief is *necessary* for knowledge. In that case, and given the internalist conception of justification that requires sufficient support by grounds that are accessible to the subject, one can challenge a given claim to knowledge by challenging the subject to produce her grounds. If she is unable to specify grounds that pass relevant tests for sufficiency of support, it must be concluded that the knowledge claim was unwarranted.

On a reliabilist conception of knowledge, on the other hand, knowledge is construed as true belief that is acquired and/or sustained in a reliable way, in a way that can generally be relied on to yield true rather than false beliefs (together with what it takes to rule out Gettier problems, if that is necessary).[4] If that condition is satisfied, I do really have knowledge, whether or not I can meet internalist requirements by citing evidence, reasons, or grounds that provide sufficient support. I now believe that Rome defeated Carthage in the Punic Wars. Let's say that I formed this belief in a reliable way — by taking this information from a competent authority. Let's also say that the belief has been preserved in a reliable fashion. In that case I do know that Rome won the Punic Wars even if I cannot identify my ground for the belief; perhaps I have no recollection of where or when I learned this or from whom. Again, my true belief (formed before the fact) that a coup directed against Gorbachev in the Soviet Union would fail may have been acquired in a reliable manner, even though it is impossible to show that any reasons I am aware of having for this provide sufficient support. In both these cases there are sufficient reasons for supposing my belief to be true. In the first case those reasons would have to do with the competence of the source from which I acquired the belief, plus facts about my belief storage and retrieval mechanisms. In the second case the reasons would be various facts about the political situation in the Soviet Union, facts that had presumably come within my ken in some way or other, though I did not retain them and perhaps even failed to note them explicitly. There are other conceivable cases in which beliefs are acquired in a reliable way without any such reasons being involved, and also without

---

4. From now on I will tacitly assume that any set of conditions sufficient for knowledge must include some condition that rules out Gettier cases; I will not explicitly specify this in each case. Thus, for example, when I speak of a conception of knowledge as true justified belief, that is to be understood as a conception of knowledge as true justified belief together with whatever is required to rule out Gettier cases.

experiential indications of the truth of what is believed. Thus I may be innately programmed to form the belief every fifteen minutes that fifteen minutes have elapsed since the last such belief was formed. These beliefs just "come to me out of the blue."

Before proceeding further I had better do a bit by way of explicating the notion of reliability I have been using so freely. I will not be able to go into nearly all the important issues involved, but I can at least make a start at unpacking the conception.

To call a belief-forming process reliable is to judge that it will or would yield mostly true beliefs. But over what range of employments? Those in which it has been employed up to now? That would be to identify reliability with a favorable track record, but that can't be right. An unreliable procedure might have chanced to work well on the few occasions on which it was actually employed. Anyone can get lucky. If there have been only five crystal ball readings, all of which just happened to be correct, that wouldn't make crystal ball reading a reliable way of forming beliefs; it might still have a poor record over the long haul. Indeed, we can't identify reliability with a favorable record over all past, present, and future employments. A process or an instrument that is never employed might be quite reliable in that it *would* yield mostly true beliefs in the long run. Thus to call something reliable is to say something about the kind of record it *would* pile up over a suitable number and variety of employments. An actual track record is crucial evidence for judgments of reliability just to the extent that it is a good indication of that. But what makes a run of cases suitable? Briefly, the class of cases must be sufficiently varied to rule out the possibility that the results are due to factors other than the character of the process. Moreover, they must be cases of sorts that we typically encounter. The fact that sensory experience would not be a reliable source of belief in unusually deceptive environments, or in cases of direct brain stimulation, does not show that standard perceptual belief formation is not a reliable process. So, to put it in a nutshell, a belief-forming process is reliable provided *it would yield mostly true beliefs in a sufficiently large and varied run of employments in situations of the sorts we typically encounter.* This is less than perfectly precise (for example, what does it take for a type of situation to be typical for us?), but it has just the kind of looseness we need for the purpose.

Second, what degree of reliability is in question? Reliability is obviously a matter of degree; one instrument, method, or procedure may be more or less reliable than another. I have been speaking of the reliability of a process as amounting to the fact that it would yield mostly true beliefs. But how much is "most"? I won't try to give a precise answer; I don't think there is any basis for doing so. The most that can be said in general is that a "high" degree of reliability is required for justification.[5] But just how high may differ for different processes, depending on the degree of reliability it is realistic to expect. For example, the vision of objects directly in front of one is capable of a greater degree of reliability than is the memory of remote events in one's early years. But we shouldn't want to deny that beliefs generated in the less reliable ways can constitute knowledge.

To return to the main line of the discussion, I have been pointing out that a belief may be formed reliably where internalist constraints on justification are not satisfied. But I don't mean to suggest, of course, that a reliability theory of knowledge applies only where internalist requirements are not satisfied. It may well be that in most cases of reliable belief formation the beliefs are formed on the basis of adequate grounds that the subject can identify by turning his or her attention to the matter. Reliably formed conscious perceptual beliefs are formed on the basis of sensory experience of which the subject is aware, and the subject is normally also aware that the experience is the basis of the belief in question. Beliefs formed on the basis of inference, whether explicitly spelled out or not, are typically such that the subject knows that from which she has inferred that p. If I infer from the fact that the car lights aren't working that the cause of the car's not starting is a run-down battery, rather than a defective starter, I will know from what I gathered this. My point is only that on a reliabilist account of knowledge it is not necessary for knowledge that there be sufficient grounds of the belief in question which the subject can spot on reflection. Hence, the fact that the subject is unable to specify any such grounds does not show that the subject lacks knowledge.

Thus far I have been thinking of the internalist requirement as being only that the subject have access to grounds for the belief that are in fact sufficient. A stronger form of internalism would also require that the subject be cognitively related, in a certain way, to the fact that the grounds are sufficient. This may take the form of a requirement that

5. For some discussion of this issue, see Alvin I. Goldman, *Epistemology and Cognition* (Cambridge, MA: Harvard University Press, 1986), section 5.5.

the subject know that the grounds are sufficient, be justified in supposing this, be able to show that the grounds are sufficient, and so on. This stronger internalist requirement would seem to be satisfied significantly less often than the earlier one. It would seem that people often form perceptual, memory, and inferential beliefs in a reliable way without knowing, justifiably believing, or being able to show that the way is a reliable one. To be sure, this depends on what it takes for such knowledge, justified belief, or showing. But if any of these requires having adequate reasons for a judgment of reliability, it would seem that we often lack any such reasons in cases of reliable belief formation. Even if our normal ways of forming perceptual beliefs are usually reliable, who is in a position to provide cogent reasons for this? Most perceivers are not even capable of properly discussing or thinking about the issue. And even for those who are, the reasons for supposing normal perceptual belief formation to be reliable will undoubtedly themselves draw on what we think we know perceptually, thus raising the spectre of circularity. If I have reason to think that my normal way of forming beliefs about my surroundings on the basis of visual experience are reliable, it is because in the past the expectations I formed on the basis of such beliefs turned out to be mostly correct. But how do I know that they are correct in individual instances except by relying on sense perception to determine this? I won't say any more about this issue here, since circularity of this sort will be a major topic of discussion later on. Here I will only note that it seems reasonable to suppose that if knowing that p requires knowing, justifiably believing, or being able to show that the grounds of that belief are adequate, it is doubtful that we have knowledge in many cases where we confidently suppose ourselves to have it.

The moral of all this is that on a conception of knowledge as justified true belief, where justification is beholden to internalist constraints, we have much less knowledge than we ordinarily, even on careful reflection, take ourselves to have. A great deal of our putative perceptual, memorial, and inferential knowledge would be denied that title. Alleged knowledge of God is in the same boat in this respect. Your typical believer is either not in a position to specify grounds, reasons, or evidence for his beliefs about God that provide those beliefs sufficient support, or at least he is unable to show that those grounds enjoy that status, and presumably does not know (justifiably believe) that they do. But what we have just seen, or would have seen if I had had the space to set out the point in more detail, is that, if a skeptic about knowledge of God uses this conception of knowledge to refute the idea that there is knowledge of God, she will equally be in a position to shoot down much that she would wish to preserve. An argument against knowledge of God that can just as well be used to discredit much of our supposed knowledge of the physical world, the past, and each other raises at least as serious a question about the conception of knowledge involved as it does about the prospects for knowledge in the religious sphere.

II

When we turn to an account of knowledge in terms of true, reliably acquired belief, we get a quite different picture. Ideally at this point I would show that this is the right way to think about propositional knowledge, or at least put forward strong arguments in its defense. But I am afraid that this is not the place for that endeavor.[6] Here I must confine myself to indicating its plausibility and then proceed to the main business at hand: raising some questions about the prospects for knowledge of God, given this way of thinking about knowledge.

Very briefly then, a reliabilist account of knowledge can be recommended on the grounds that it ensures the presence of a fundamental feature of knowledge that distinguishes it from mere true belief — viz., it is "not at all accidental" that the belief is true. If we survey a number of clear cases of true belief that do not amount to knowledge, they would seem to share the feature that the belief just happened to be true. It was a lucky guess, or a conjecture that turned out to be true despite the fact that it was based on insufficient evidence, or it was true despite being based on a reading from a faulty instrument (as in the barometer case in note 3). Thus it is plausible to think that knowing that p requires that it not just be a lucky accident that the subject's belief that p is true. And what better way to avoid accidental truth than for one's belief to be formed in a way that can generally be relied on to lead to true beliefs?

Much more could and should be said, but let that suffice for an indication of the plausibility of a reliability account of knowledge. Our next task is to consider the prospects for knowledge of God on such an

6. For some persuasive arguments in support of this account of knowledge, see Goldman, *Epistemology and Cognition*, Part I.

account. One thing is clear right away. We can't dismiss knowledge of God, just as we can't dismiss familiar putative cases of knowledge of nature and society, on the grounds that the subject cannot exhibit sufficient grounds, reason, or evidence for the belief in question, or on the grounds that the subject cannot show them to be sufficient. For a reliability theory of knowledge imposes no such requirement. So long as the belief is acquired in a reliable way, one that tends to produce true beliefs in the kinds of situations we typically encounter, then, if it is true, it counts as knowledge (pace Gettier problems, as usual). That will be the case whether or not internalist constraints are satisfied. If my belief that a car is parked in my driveway results from normal functioning of my visual apparatus, then, if the belief is true, I know that a car is parked in my driveway, whether or not I can identify a sufficient basis for the belief (there would be no difficulty about that here; I can just advert to my visual experience) and, more to the point, whether or not I know, or can show, that this basis is an adequate one. Again, if my belief that Hungarians are often excitable was formed in a reliable way, then if that is the case I know it to be the case, even if I cannot specify sufficient grounds for the belief (I do not remember enough cases to constitute a suitable sample), or I am not able to show that the basis of the belief is an adequate one.

Passing on to the religious sphere, let's suppose that my belief that God will sustain the faithful by his Holy Spirit was formed in a reliable way. It could be that I acquired this belief from reading a biblical account in which Christ is represented as delivering this message, and God has acted in such a way as to ensure that this communication faithfully represents the truth. Or it may be that God has communicated this to me individually in an experience of his presence. Or it may be that I have accepted this on the authority of the church, which God is guiding in such a way as to preserve it from error on fundamental articles of faith such as this. In any of these cases I acquired the belief in a highly reliable way. What more reliable mode of belief formation could there be than one the accuracy of which is ensured by God? Hence, on a reliability theory, if the belief is indeed true it will count as knowledge. Again, this will hold good even if I cannot specify grounds for the belief that are in fact adequate grounds (I may have forgotten how I came by the belief), and even if I do not know, or cannot show, that the grounds are adequate. Now the sources I have just been mentioning bulk large in the area of religious belief formation. Religious people typically form their beliefs on the authority of their elders, the church, sacred writings, and putative experiences of God. Hence, if these are reliable ways of forming beliefs, as religious traditions typically claim them to be, religious knowledge can be gained in this way.

Let me dwell a bit on the contrast with how things are on an internalist account of knowledge. Such an account, I have noted, requires cognitive access by the subject, usually just on reflection, to what makes for justification of the belief involved. Sometimes it is only required that the subject be able to spot sufficient grounds, reasons, or evidence on reflection; sometimes it is also required that she know, or be able to show, *that* those grounds are adequate. In the religious case there is often no difficulty with the first sort of requirement. Religious people are often clearly aware of what basis they have for one or another belief: it says so in the Bible, or it is taught by the church, or it is borne out by one's experience of God in one's life. But when it comes to showing that such grounds are sufficient for taking the beliefs to be true, that is another story. Even at the most optimistic estimate the average person in the pew, or even the average sophisticated theologian or religious philosopher, would be hard pressed to *show* that the Bible contains revelations from God that carry a divine guarantee of truth, or that the church is guided by the Holy Spirit in its doctrinal pronouncements. At least any claims to be able to show this will be highly controversial. Thus from an internalist justification approach to knowledge, prospects do not look good for satisfying necessary conditions for religious knowledge. But on a reliability account, claims to knowledge of God are relieved of the necessity of satisfying those requirements. If one or another way of acquiring beliefs about God is, in fact, highly reliable, then those beliefs when true can count as knowledge, whether or not the believer is in a position to demonstrate reliability, and, indeed, whether or not the believer has any grasp of the concept of a reliable belief-forming process. Knowing that one's beliefs are reliably formed is no more necessary for their *being* reliably formed and hence their counting as knowledge (on this conception) than knowing that one's food is nourishing is necessary for nourishment to take place.

III

Thus far I have been summarizing what is spelled out in more detail in my earlier essay "Knowledge of God." But now I want to go on to a crucial issue that will long since have been disturbing the reader. Indeed, I can almost hear the exasperation with which the reader has been noting my failure to come to grips with this issue. "You have been pointing out," the reader will say, "that on a reliability account of knowledge one is not prevented from having knowledge of God by one's lack of reflective access to one's grounds and/or their adequacy. It will be sufficient if the way in which one's true belief is formed is a reliable one. And you have sketched out some *possibilities* along this line. Well and good. But all of that only amounts to providing us with possibilities. We are still as far as ever from determining whether anyone does in fact know anything about God. In order for that to be so in a particular case, on a reliability theory of knowledge, at least the following conditions must be satisfied: (1) the belief must be true and (2) the belief must be acquired in a reliable way. But how are we to determine whether these conditions are satisfied? As for condition (1), we would, obviously, have to have the putative religious knowledge in question in order to know that this condition is satisfied. If the belief in question is the belief that Jesus Christ is God incarnate, then to know that condition (1) is satisfied is to know that this belief is true. But since it is true that p if and only if p, that amounts to knowing that Jesus Christ is God incarnate, the very knowledge that was in question all along. In other words, if A is to know that B knows that p, A must himself know that p. Thus we can ascertain that there is religious knowledge only if we already have some. But that raises just the question (of the reality of religious knowledge) with which we started. We are not making any progress."

Before proceeding further, let me note that the problem just raised arises equally for the internalist justification approach to knowledge, and indeed for any (sensible) account of knowledge whatever. Since a fundamental requirement for knowing that p is that it be true that p (be the case that p) I can know that you know that p only if I know that p. This does show something fundamental about knowledge and about knowledge of knowledge. It shows, as I will indicate in more detail shortly, that it is impossible to establish that we have knowledge in a certain area without already assuming some knowledge in that area. By the nature of the case we are unable to provide a purely external demonstration of the reality of knowledge in a certain domain. But this holds for any account of knowledge and has no special application to the reliability theory.

"However," the reader will continue, "the second condition is, naturally, distinctive of the reliability theory, since it has to do with the reliability with which the belief is acquired. And to establish that, in the religious case, would seem to pose at least as great a difficulty. It has already been pointed out that any claims to show that typical grounds of religious belief — the authority of sacred books and of religious institutions and their functionaries — are adequately indicative of the truth of the beliefs they ground will be, at best, highly controversial. Translating this point into the patois of reliability theory, any claim to show that typical ways of forming religious beliefs of the sorts just mentioned are reliable modes of belief formation will be, at best, highly controversial. For the attempt to demonstrate reliability will give rise to just the same issues as the attempt to show that these are adequate grounds for beliefs about God. Indeed, where beliefs are formed on grounds, then, generally speaking and leaving aside weird cases, the belief will be formed in a reliable way if and only if the grounds on which it is formed are adequate, that is, adequately indicative of the truth of the belief. Thus it would seem that, when we try to move from possibility to actuality, prospects for the knowledge of God are no better on a reliability theory of knowledge than on an internalist justification theory. The reliability theory does, no doubt, remove one bar to the possibility of such knowledge — the inability of the subject to show that the grounds of his belief are sufficient. But even on the reliability theory, in order to determine that someone has actualized this possibility we must overcome the same obstacle and show that the grounds of the belief are sufficient (or show what is equivalent to that in reliability theory terms). Thus, why suppose that, in the end, the case for knowledge of God is any better from the perspective of a reliability account of knowledge?"

IV

In responding to this question it will be useful to move back once more to uncontroversial cases of secular knowledge and consider how they look from the standpoint of a reliability theory. In my earlier indication of the troubles an internalist justification account of knowledge has in accommodating much of our supposed perceptual and inferential knowledge, I concentrated on the point that the ordinary unsophisticated knower is usually not in a position to show that the grounds of her belief are adequate (and sometimes is even unable to specify the grounds in question). But I did not, as I did in the religious area, suggest that perhaps no one is capable of showing such grounds to be sufficient. However, there are considerations that encourage such a supposition. To exhibit them I will move over to the reliabilist analogue of the adequacy of grounds, viz., the reliability of the mode of belief formation.

Let's concentrate on sense perception and consider whether it is a reliable source of belief, at least when beliefs about the immediate environment are formed on the basis of sense experience in the ways we typically do. I open my eyes; I see something (or so I unhesitatingly suppose) that looks for all the world like a dog stretched out before a fireplace. I thereby form the belief that a dog is stretched out before a fireplace. We are constantly forming beliefs in this way — a way that can be summarily formulated as *going from what seems to be a presentation of X as Ø to a belief that X is Ø*. The question is, What reasons do we have for supposing that this is a reliable way of forming beliefs, that is, a way that generally yields true beliefs? (We are not asking whether it is an infallible way that never generates falsehoods.)

If we consider the most obvious answers to this question, it will turn out that they all involve a certain kind of circularity. Begin with the most simpleminded response: "We have ample reason to regard sense perception as reliable because it has generally provided true beliefs in the past." But how do we know in each case that the belief provided was true? How do we know in the above case that the dog belief is a true one? Well, we can take another look. We can call or poke the putative dog and see how it reacts. We can ask other people to carry out similar tests. We could call in an expert to assure us that this is indeed a dog and not a wolf or a fox. But in all these cases we are relying on sense perception (our own or other people's) for our evidence. Our reasons for taking sense perception to be reliable will provide sufficient evidence for this only if sense perception is reliable (or alternatively, only if we already have sufficient reason to regard it as reliable). Unless sense perception is reliable (or unless we have sufficient reason for taking it to be reliable), the particular cases of true belief formation we are using for our inductive generalization have no claim to be regarded as such. Since the argument for the reliability of sense perception presupposes, in this way, just what it is attempting to prove, it is guilty of a certain kind of circularity. This is not the most blatant

kind of logical circularity. The argument does not include the conclusion
as one of its premises. Nevertheless, unless we are justified in assuming,
at least in practice, that sense perception is reliable, we have no right
to the premises of the induction, which are based on sense perception.
Since the circularity here consists in the fact that the conclusion has to
be assumed if we are to be *justified* in accepting the premises, we may
term this 'epistemic circularity'.

A somewhat more complex argument is that, by accepting the
deliverances of sense perception and building systems of scientific
knowledge on that basis, we are enabled to predict and control the
course of events to a significant extent. Trusting sense perception proves
itself by its fruits, and that warrants us in regarding it as reliable. But
again, how do we know that in a given case a prediction turned out to
be correct? Someone has to use his senses to find out whether the
prediction was verified. If the prediction was that the milk would be
sour, someone has to taste or smell it, or subject it to chemical tests
and observe the outcome of those tests, etc., in order to determine that
the prediction turned out to be correct. Once more we have to assume
the reliability of sense perception to get our premises for the argument.

There are, of course, much more elaborate arguments for the reliability of sense perception. It has been contended that the reliability of
sense perception is a necessary presupposition of the existence of language, of the learning of language, and of the supposition that the word
'perception' is meaningful. These are all designed to be a priori arguments without any empirical premises. I have argued in my book *Perceiving God* that they all make a covert presupposition of the reliability
of sense perception.[7] Again, it has been argued that our sense experience
— or alternatively, the fact that we have such success in predicting the
course of our sense experience when we take sense perception to be
reliable — is best explained by the supposition that things are, by and
large, as sense perception (and what we have derived from it) takes
them to be. Much ingenuity has been expended in the attempt to show
that the "standard" explanation of these phenomena is superior to any
possible competitors, including the Cartesian demon explanation, the
self-generation of experience explanation, and others. In the work just
mentioned I have contended that, where these arguments are not vitiated in other ways, they too surreptitiously assume what they are

7. See my *Perceiving God* (Ithaca, NY: Cornell University Press, 1991), chapter 3.

seeking to establish. All of this strongly suggests that it is impossible to give an otherwise cogent argument for the reliability of sense perception without falling into epistemic circularity.

If space would allow me to do things properly I would, at this point, embark on an extended defense of the thesis just enunciated. Since this is not possible here, I must refer you to chapter 3 of *Perceiving God*. However, I will provide one sample of the way in which epistemic circularity rears its head in the most unlikely places. This sample consists of an argument for the reliability of sense perception that is based on the Wittgensteinian denial of the possibility of a "private language" — that is, a language that it is in principle impossible for more than one person to understand. The positive correlate of this denial is the view that only "public languages" — that is, languages that are, or can be, used in common by members of a social group (larger than one) — are genuine languages. In such a language, terms mean what they do by virtue of *public* rules for their use.

The argument runs as follows:[8]

> *(1) If (alleged) term 'P' cannot figure in a public language it has no meaning.*

But:

> *(2) If sense perception is not reliable there can be no public language.*

The reason for this is that a public language gets established by way of social interactions in which the participants find out by perception what other participants are saying and doing. Think of this in terms of a neophyte. If this person is to become a functioning user of the language, she must be able to get reliable perceptual information about the linguistic and other behavior of her fellow group members. Otherwise she would be able neither to learn the language (how could she?) nor to use it in communication.

But then, by hypothetical syllogism,

---

8. My inspiration for this argument is some unpublished material by Peter van Inwagen. However, the present formulation is my own, and van Inwagen should not be held responsible for the details.

(3) If sense perception is not reliable no term can have a meaning.

But in raising the issue of the reliability of sense perception, we suppose ourselves to be using language meaningfully. And if we are not using language meaningfully we have failed to raise that issue, whatever we may suppose. Hence,

(4) If no term can have a meaning, we cannot raise the issue as to the reliability of sense perception.

Hence,

(5) If it is possible to raise the issue of the reliability of sense perception, then sense perception is reliable.

Thus there is no real possibility that sense perception is not reliable. If it were not, then there could not so much as be a question of its reliability. If there is such a question, it can have only a favorable answer.

This argument, too, founders on epistemic circularity. Consider the support for premise (2). It consists in pointing out ways in which we have to rely on sense perception in learning a public language. How else can we learn a public language except by getting reliable perceptual information about the linguistic behavior of speakers of the language as that fits onto the physical and social environment? But how do we know that this is the only way? How do we know that we do not have some other cognitive access to the linguistic behavior of others in its natural and social setting? For that matter, how do we know that our mastery of a public language is not innate, in which case it would not have to be learned at all? Obviously, we know all this because of what we have learned about the world, more specifically because of what we have learned about human beings and their resources for learning, for knowledge acquisition, and for linguistic communication. That gives us good reason for denying that human beings can acquire and use a public language without heavy reliance on sense perception. But we have learned this *by relying on our perception of each other in our physical and social environment and by reasoning from that perceptually generated information.* It is not as if we can know a priori that we have no other cognitive access to these matters. Quite the contrary. A priori it seems quite possible that the requisite knowledge should be innate, or that we should have other, nonsensory modes of access to the linguistic behavior of others and to the stage setting of that behavior. Hence, we are relying on sense perception in arguing that a public language presupposes the reliability of sense perception. Epistemic circularity has once more vitiated what looked like a purely a priori argument.

Suppose I am right about the fate of attempts to give a noncircular demonstration of the reliability of sense perception. How widely does this problem extend? In response to this question I will confine myself to reminding the reader of some well-known considerations that suggest that for one or another of our basic sources of belief the prospect of a noncircular demonstration of reliability is not a bright one.

First consider induction, construed narrowly as the inference of a generalization from a number of instances (induction by simple enumeration). We heat numerous samples of lead at sea level and ascertain in each case that the substance melts at (approximately) 327 degrees Celsius. We conclude that lead always melts at sea level at (approximately) 327 degrees Celsius. Since Hume's classic discussion in the *Treatise of Human Nature,* it has been generally recognized that any otherwise effective attempt to show that this procedure is reliable (yields mostly true beliefs from true premises) will be circular. Any track record argument will itself be an induction by simple enumeration; in using it to establish reliability we are, in practice, assuming that argument form to be reliable. Where else can we turn? It is most implausible to suppose that the general reliability of induction is self-evident or otherwise discloses itself to rational intuition, nor have attempts to deduce it from noninductively justified beliefs been successful. Attempts have been made to establish the principle as the best explanation of something or other, but they have not been particularly plausible. There have been many attempts to bypass the issue of reliability by arguing, for example, that it is part of our concept of rationality, or of good inference, or of showing or establishing something, or that the positively evaluative label in question applies to inductive inference; but even if these attempts are successful they most definitely do not show that induction by simple enumeration is reliable. Thus our situation here would seem to be closely analogous to our situation with respect to sense perception.

As for deduction, it quickly becomes obvious that anything that would count as showing that deduction is reliable would have to involve deductive inference, and so would assume the reliability of deduction. Just try it. For example, we can demonstrate the reliability of many inference forms in the propositional calculus by truth tables. But in doing so we are engaging in deduction and presupposing its reliability. We might try an induction from a number of cases in which true premises deductively yield a true conclusion, but for this to be non-circular it would have to be the case that our justification for these attributions of truth rested nowhere on the use of deductive inference, and the prospects for this are not rosy. More specifically, to the extent that we choose our sample with that restriction in mind, the inductive inference is correspondingly weakened by the truncated character of the sample.

Memory presents an interesting case. It looks at first sight as if we can develop a track record argument for the reliability of memory without using memory to get any of our premises. For we do have ways of determining whether p was the case at some past time other than remembering p to have happened. To determine whether our current TV set was delivered on August 6, 1991, we can look at the delivery slip, consult records in the store, and so on. But the delivery slip is good evidence only if this is the slip that accompanied that set; and I have to rely on my memory to assure myself of that, or else appeal to another record with respect to which the same problem arises. More generally, the reliability of records, traces of past events like the disorder in the wake of a party, and so on are themselves things for which we need evidence, and to marshall that evidence we will have to rely on memory at some point. I will have to remember that in the past parties like that one left the house in some disarray; or else I will have to consult diary entries that indicate this in various cases, in which case I have to remember that I made that entry as a record of what I had observed to happen; or I will have to draw on the experience of others, in which case I will be relying on their memories at some point. And so it goes.

Again, consider introspection. Here we would seem not to be in as desperate a situation for independent checks on the subject matter as we are with sense perception. Don't we have third-person ways of determining what a given person is thinking, sensing, or feeling at a given moment? To be sure, these third-person resources are much more limited than the first person's introspective access. They don't give us nearly as much information, and what they do give us is much less certain, liable at every point to be overturned by the subject's own sincere report of her thoughts and feelings. Nevertheless, so far as they go, don't they constitute an independent way of determining the truth value of introspectively derived beliefs? But are they completely independent? Isn't our confidence in these external indications of conscious states ultimately based on correlations with first-person reports? Apart from such correlations do we have any sufficient reason to credit such third-person manifestations? If the answers to these questions are affirmative and negative, respectively, then third-person indications of conscious states have basically the same status as nonperceptual indications of perceivable physical facts; they depend for their epistemic status on connections with the more basic perceptual or introspective access to the subject matter. Hence they don't provide a wholly independent check. This conclusion will be contested by those who suppose some external evidence for conscious states to be "criterial," to have its status guaranteed by the concepts of the conscious states in question. I find this Wittgensteinian position quite unpersuasive, but I can't properly go into that here.

These sketchy remarks suggest that the situation we found to hold for sense perception obtains with respect to all of our most fundamental belief-forming practices, whether the input is taken from memory, introspection, rational intuition, or reasoning of one kind or another. If so, we are confronted with the problem of epistemic circularity over the whole range of our cognitive life. But suppose we are mistaken in this. Suppose that sense perception or introspection or one or another sort of reasoning can be noncircularly shown to be reliable. Suppose that for one or another of these belief sources there is a successful argument for its reliability that takes its premises exclusively from other sources. Even so, we would not have escaped the necessity of dealing with the problem of how to regard doxastic (belief-forming) practices we all engage in without being able to show that they are reliable. Let's say, contrary to our contentions here, that we can noncircularly establish the reliability of sense perception. Suppose that this argument appeals only to rational intuition and deductive reasoning; the argument de-duces the reliability of sense perception from self-evident principles. What about those practices? Consider one of them — rational intuition. Can we mount a noncircular proof of its reliability? If we can't, we have the same problem at a second remove. If we can, then if that proof depends on using sense perception we are involved in a very small circle. If we do not have to use sense perception here, let's consider the practice(s) we do use. Can we give a noncircular proof of its reliability? If not, our original problem has been postponed to this point. And so on. We are faced with the familiar dilemma of continuing the regress or falling into circularity. Whatever the possibilities of a noncircular proof of reliability for one or another source, if we pursue the question far enough one of three things will happen: (1) we will encounter one or more sources for which a noncircular proof cannot be given, (2) we will be caught up in circularity, or (3) we will be involved in an infinite regress. Since the number of basic sources is quite small for human beings, we can ignore the third possibility, and for the same reason any circle involved will be a small one. Thus in practice we can say that, whatever the details of our epistemic situation, either there are some doxastic practices for which we cannot give a noncircular demonstration of reliability, or in giving such demonstrations we involve ourselves in a very small circle.

V

I hope it is clear by now why I embarked on this digression. I was confronted by the complaint that although I had shown the possibility of genuine knowledge of God, assuming a reliability account of knowledge, the prospects looked dim for establishing that that possibility is ever actualized. In thinking about that challenge one is led to think about what it would take to show that a particular way of forming beliefs is reliable or, alternatively, what would count as showing this. To investigate this, I looked at a mode of belief formation that in practice is taken, with maximum confidence, to be a source of knowledge: our normal ways of forming perceptual beliefs about the physical environment. On close scrutiny, so I claim, it turns out that no one — not even the most brilliant philosopher — is able to give a noncircular demonstration (or even strong argument) for the reliability of these ways of forming beliefs. Any otherwise strong argument for that conclusion is subject to the stricture that it assumes what it is trying to establish in taking many of its premises from sense perception, thereby supposing sense perception to be a reliable source of such beliefs. I have even more briefly indicated my conviction that the same situation obtains with respect to other universally recognized basic sources of belief.

Now for the application of all this to our central problem. I was confronted with the question as to how we can determine whether various ways of forming beliefs about God (hereinafter 'theological beliefs') are reliable. It was suggested that no one is able to do so. It seems clear that, when someone puts forward that position, what is judged to be impossible is an *external* demonstration of reliability, one that does not use any theological beliefs in the premises. That would seem to be a reasonable restriction, since if theological beliefs were to figure as premises we would be assuming, in practice, that some ways of forming theological beliefs are reliable, presumably the same ones the reliability of which we are arguing for. If we weren't assuming this, why would we feel entitled to use the outputs of such practices as premises in the argument? And if we are restricted to premises concerning other matters, the suggestion is that we will be unable to show that any ways of forming theological beliefs are reliable. Let's assume that this is so. But what we have seen now is that exactly the same situation obtains with respect to (all?) other belief-forming practices as well, including those in which we have the greatest confidence. That would seem to take the sting out of the "no external validation" situation with respect to theological belief formation. It suggests that this situation is due to something deeply embedded in the human situation, and hence that it does not constitute any special fault of the theological sphere. Let's consider this further.

Speaking most generally, what our consideration of epistemic circularity indicates is that when we look at one of our major areas of belief formation — sense perception, inductive inference, introspection, religious experience — there is no way to give an external proof that we have knowledge in that area. Any argument for this that is sufficiently impressive will draw on putatively known facts in that very area, and so will exhibit epistemic circularity. As noted above, this conclusion follows just from the fact that knowledge requires true belief. I can't know that a belief that *p* is true without knowing that *p*, thus already taking myself to have knowledge in the area in question. But since I have been specially concerned with a reliability conception of knowledge, I have been more concerned with what it takes to show that a particular way of forming beliefs is reliable. Here I have suggested, with references to other work, that if we take large domains of belief formation like those just mentioned, we will not be able to show that the standard practices of belief formation in that domain are reliable without calling on what we take ourselves to have learned in that domain, and so assuming the reliability of those modes of belief formation.

To be sure, we can support the reliability of very specific ways of forming beliefs without assuming their reliability. Thus if it is a question of whether visual identification of dogs (as dogs) at close range in good light, where the visual apparatus is functioning normally, is a reliable mode of belief formation, we can give an effective argument for a positive answer to this question without epistemic circularity, assuming, as seems to be the case, that we have other modes of access to such facts as that X is a dog. But it seems clear that such validation of highly specific modes of belief formation will make use of information gleaned from other perceptual sources. Since the argument for any particular sensory belief-forming mechanism will presuppose the reliability of other such mechanisms — which presupposition will itself be validated, if at all, only by presupposing the reliability of still other ways of forming perceptual beliefs — it seems clear that the whole enterprise is conducted under the assumption of the general reliability of sense perception.

Thus we can say, in general, that the determination of whether we have knowledge in a given sphere is, and must be, an "inside job." We are, in general, incapable of showing that we have knowledge in a particular domain without relying on particular bits of knowledge in that very domain, and hence begging the question. And, as noted earlier, even if that were possible for one or another domain, we would, sooner rather than later, come to other domains for which this is not possible, or else argue in a very small circle. Hence, what appeared to be a difficulty for the claim to knowledge of God is revealed to be a basic feature of the human cognitive situation. By virtue of the nature of knowledge, and of our cognitive situation vis-à-vis the knowable, we are unable to give a satisfactory external demonstration of the existence of knowledge in any large domain of belief. Therefore, the fact that this is impossible in the case of religious knowledge is no ground for a specific complaint against claims to knowledge in that area.

VI

Let's look a bit more closely at the situation with respect to knowledge of religious knowledge. The complaint to which I have been responding is that we cannot show that we have any knowledge of God on purely external, nontheological grounds. Going just by what we know about the natural world from perception, reasoning, and so on, we cannot validate any claim to knowledge of God. I have not made any attempt to deny this charge. To be sure, I have not tried to support it either. I am inclined to think that it is true. This is partly because of what I have discovered in other areas, such as sense perception, in which I have looked into the issues more fully, and partly because I can't see how such an external demonstration would go. But I am not concerned here to settle this issue. If a non-epistemically-circular argument can be given for the existence of knowledge of God, well and good. I choose to proceed here on a "worst case scenario" according to which that is not possible. And my point is that even if it is not possible to give an external validation, that does not constitute a black mark against religious knowledge in particular. It simply indicates that religious knowledge has the same status as other large departments of human knowledge, including those of which we are most confident. One cannot reject knowledge of God on this basis without, in consistency, tossing out all or most other standard knowledge claims as well. The skeptic about religious knowledge must find some other way to make his case.

It will help to put some flesh on this rather abstract point if I say something about the way(s) in which we do or can make use of supposed theological knowledge in supporting the claim that we (some of us) have such knowledge. The most basic point is this: The question of the conditions under which we can reliably form beliefs about God is a theological question, just as the question of the conditions under which we can reliably form beliefs about the physical world is a scientific question. As for the latter point, consider some specific forms it takes. The question of the conditions under which we can reliably form perceptual beliefs about the physical environment is a question for the physics, physiology, and psychology of perception. Or at least any answer to that question will perforce make heavy use of the results of those disciplines. Again, the question of the conditions under which we can reliably form memory beliefs must draw heavily on what we have learned in the psychology and physiology of memory. The conditions under which we can reliably form beliefs by deductive reasoning are largely a question of deductive logic. As for the conditions under which we can reliably form beliefs by nondeductive reasoning, to make progress in answering that we must have recourse to a large proportion, perhaps an indefinitely large proportion, of what we have learned about the world. For the question of whether the evidence on which we (nondeductively) base a certain belief provides a sufficient indication of its truth is to be answered by considering how things are with respect to that department of fact. To illustrate this with a simple case, suppose that I believe that golden retrievers are generally placid and affectionate, on the basis of having observed ten golden retrievers, all of whom markedly displayed these qualities. Clearly the strength of my evidence is not just a function of formal features such as the number of cases and the proportion of positive cases in the whole sample. It also depends on what we know about which kinds of characteristics of dogs are, or tend to be, breed specific and how uniform temperamental characteristics such as these are across a breed.

The theological analogue of these points is that in considering the conditions under which beliefs about God are reliably formed we must take into account what (we think) we know about God, his purposes, his patterns of activity, the way he has set things up for his creation (and more specifically for us), and so on. Just as in the natural world cases, if we do not take such things into account, we will have nothing to go on, or at least not enough to get anywhere. Apart from supposing that we are related to God in certain ways and/or that God has set things up in certain ways, how could we have any basis for taking ourselves to get accurate information about God in one way rather than another? And questions about how we are related to God and how God has arranged things in his creation (and for what purposes) obviously fall within the purview of theology.

If, in our consideration of the sources of knowledge of God, we focus on God's communication with us (using that term in the widest sense) and on our experience of the presence and activity of God in our lives, the above points have long been recognized by theology, though they have not been expressed in just the terminology I have been using. In theistic religions such as Christianity, the main putative sources of knowledge of God consist of God's communications to selected messengers, recorded in sacred writings, and our experience of the presence and activity of God in history and in our individual and communal lives. The question of where in the territory so demarcated we find reliable information about God has long been recognized as a central theological question, or rather set of questions. What is required for the canonicity and/or authority of Scripture, who is competent to determine the interpretation of Scripture, which historical events give us the most penetrating insight into the divine nature, purpose, and intent — these are universally recognized as central theological issues. The same is to be said for issues regarding how to distinguish genuine experiences of God from counterfeits — though in Christianity this topic has been more assiduously cultivated in Catholic theology than in Protestant theology and has been pervasively neglected in both traditions in recent years. The general point is that with respect to modes of cognitive access to God that involve genuine interaction with God, like those currently under consideration, it falls to theology to determine where reliable information about God is to be obtained, since it is within the purview of theology to determine what sorts of divine-human interaction there are, and in which of these interactions, or under what conditions, information is transmitted. Needless to say, the interaction does not have to be direct in each individual instance. Thus, even if my knowledge of God comes from written records of divine communications to persons in the past, or from the way in which such traditions are communicated through the church, I still owe my knowledge to divine-human interaction, even if I do not in my own person engage in dynamic interaction with God.[9]

Natural theology, on the other hand, may seem to present a quite different picture. In natural theology we seek knowledge of God by starting from facts about the natural world and using them as a basis for conclusions about God. Here God is treated, as we might say, as an object of theoretical speculation, and if knowledge of God is attainable in this way it would not necessarily involve a genuine divine-human interaction. To simplify matters for a quick discussion, let's confine ourselves to those stretches of natural theology that argue to God as an *explanation* of certain natural facts — the existence of the physical universe, the teleological order of the universe, moral obligation, or whatever. If the divine explanations of such phenomena are sufficiently superior to all competitors, we may attain knowledge of God in this purely abstract way without the necessity of any real interaction, even of an indirect sort. Similarly, if my only cognitive access to quarks and positrons comes via their function in high-level theoretical explanations of natural regularities, I need not enter into active cognitive interaction — perceptual or otherwise — with quarks in order to find out something about them. Thus it may seem that if we can get knowledge of God via the natural theology route we need

9. To be sure, on some views, when I read the Bible in the right way I am thereby engaged in interaction with God, since the Holy Spirit is actively guiding my understanding and assimilation of the divine word.

not make any theological assumptions about God — his nature, purposes, activities, and modes of interaction with human beings — in order to assure ourselves that we have knowledge of him. It will suffice to determine that our explanatory inferences are sound. And why shouldn't we establish the credentials of those forms of inference by considering how they pan out in science or other modes of reasoning about the natural world? In that case we wouldn't need to bring theological assumptions into the picture at all.

This question raises a number of thorny issues into which I cannot go here. For one thing, there is the question as to whether there really are subject-matter neutral forms or patterns of inference to the best explanation such that one can confidently extrapolate from the success of a given inference form in one domain to its success in a quite different domain. For another, there is, obviously, the question of how strong the arguments of natural theology are when divorced from any suppositions that we know certain things about God already. Bypassing all that, let me say the following: At the most optimistic estimate, natural theology is radically insufficient as a basis for the system of belief of a functioning religion. At best, it does not tell us nearly enough about what God is like, what he has in mind for his creation, what he has done and is doing to carry out his purposes, what he requires of us, what he has in store for us, and other matters that are of central concern to the religious life. Therefore we are forced to have recourse to communications from God and to our experience of God to get some purchase on these matters. The bulk of the putative knowledge of God that one finds in a religious tradition comes from these latter sources. Hence it is eminently right and proper to concentrate on them in illustration of my central thesis. And as far as they are concerned, that central thesis is amply borne out, as I have been noting. We have to rely on our knowledge of God to determine what sources of belief about God are reliable ones. This involves epistemic circularity, but, as I have been pointing out, this doesn't distinguish religious knowledge from other areas of human knowledge, including the most prestigious ones.

VII

To sum up the basic message of this paper in a slightly different way, it is a mistake to suppose that we can first determine whether we have knowledge before getting any. Not only is the determination that we have a certain piece of knowledge itself a piece of knowledge, but to carry out that determination we have to rely on other knowledge we suppose ourselves to have already. Knowledge that we know cannot be the first bit of knowledge we attain, or anywhere near the first. And, I have been arguing, this is not only true in general, but also within each large department of knowledge. We can't get knowledge about our knowledge of the natural world without relying on a lot of what we take ourselves to know about the natural world. And so it is with our knowledge of God. If God has not already made it possible for us to get quite a bit of first-level knowledge of him, we have no chance to come to know that we have such knowledge. Such is the human condition, for which we should, as in all things, give thanks to God.

Divine Knowledge

Alvin Plantinga

Who has directed the Spirit of the LORD,
or as his counselor has instructed him?

Isaiah 40:13

Theists typically hold that God is *omniscient* or all-knowing. This means at least that God knows every true proposition and believes no false propositions. Theists typically add that God is *essentially* omniscient: he is in fact omniscient, and furthermore it isn't possible that he should have the complement of omniscience; he is omniscient in every possible world in which he exists. If, with most theists, you think God is a necessary being and therefore exists in every possible world, you will add still further that God is *necessarily* omniscient — omniscient in every possible world, those being the worlds in which he exists. If this is so, then the proposition that *p* is true, for some proposition *p*, will be equivalent in the broadly logical sense to the proposition that God *knows p*, and also to the proposition that God *believes p*. (Here, of course, we think of belief in such a way that it is not precluded by knowledge: belief, so thought of — as the medievals said — is a matter of thinking with assent.) Charles Taliaferro argues that what we have so far is not sufficient for divine omniscience; no doubt he is right. (There is also the matter of God's knowing how to *do* various things, of his knowing without inference,[1] and

---

1. But see George Mavrodes's paper "How Does God Know the Things He

40

in general knowing in the way that befits a perfect being.) I suppose the majority opinion, however, is that the above requirements (or at least the first of them) are at any rate *necessary* for omniscience.

I. The Problem

But some have seen a problem here. They claim that there are *some* propositions which do indeed have a truth value, but which are nonetheless such that not even God knows whether they are true. (Others might not perhaps be willing to go quite as far as all that, but would still be prepared to say that there is a 'real problem' in God's knowing these propositions.) Examples of such propositions would be, first, 'future contingents', such as *there will be a sea battle tomorrow,* and, more poignantly, propositions specifying free future actions, such as

> *(1) Sam will be free with respect to the action of having lunch tomorrow, and will in fact have lunch tomorrow.*

A second sort of example would be *counterfactuals of (creaturely) freedom:* truths about what free creatures would do or would have done under various circumstances. There are at least two important varieties of counterfactuals of creaturely freedom: first, those that say what some of the free creatures there actually *are* would have done under various circumstances, and, second, those that specify what would have been done by free creatures if there had been free creatures *different* from the ones there actually are. An example of the first kind would be

> *(2) If you had offered to sell Paul your car for $500, he would have (freely) bought it.*

A (slightly more arcane) example of the second would be

> *(3) If God had strongly actualized T(W)^2 (W, a world in*

Knows?" in *Divine and Human Action,* ed. Thomas Morris (Notre Dame: University of Notre Dame Press, 1988), pp. 345ff.

2. For explanation of 'T(W)' see *Alvin Plantinga,* ed. Peter van Inwagen and James Tomberlin (Dordrecht: D. Reidel, 1985), p. 50.

*which there exist human beings distinct from any that exist
in α, the actual world) there would have been an initial pair
of human beings distinct from any that exist in α, who, unlike
Adam and Eve, would not have sinned.*

Or

*(4) Essence E1 is unexemplified and is such that if it had been
exemplified in conditions C, then its instantiation would have
been free to do what is wrong but would have done only what
is right.*

We can arrange these in order of magnitude with respect to the
difficulty there seems to be in supposing that God could know them.
First and perhaps least difficult would be to see that God could know
propositions like (1), propositions about what some presently existing
free creature will in fact freely do. Second and next most difficult would
be propositions like (2), propositions that specify what some free creature would have done, had that creature been free in circumstances
different from those it in fact occupies. Third and most difficult would
be propositions that specify what would have been freely done by free
persons that would have existed, had there existed free persons distinct
from the persons that do in fact exist. (Perhaps, as with [4], we should
think of this in terms of individual essences that are not in fact exemplified.)

Now what is the difficulty with God's knowing (1) through (4)?
Here there are four quite different positions. First, it might be maintained that God doesn't know such propositions because as a matter of
fact there simply aren't any such propositions to be known. There just
aren't any propositions about future free actions; and there just aren't
any counterfactuals of creaturely freedom. There simply is no such
proposition, so the claim goes, as *Paul will freely take part in a sea battle
tomorrow.* But can this really be true? It certainly *seems* that there is
such a proposition; and it certainly seems that someone could believe
it. In fact, I myself often believe, so it seems to me, propositions about
the future free acts of persons, both of myself and of others. That there
is such a proposition as *Paul will freely take part in a sea battle tomorrow*
seems no more initially doubtful than that there is such a proposition
as *Paul freely took part in a sea battle yesterday.* Why think there is a

problem with there being propositions like (1)? And doesn't the same go for propositions like (2)? Knowing Paul, I am inclined to believe proposition (2); could it really be that there simply is no such proposition? The commonsense view, surely, is that there are such propositions; for the contrary view we would need a solid (or at least reasonably imperforate) argument (and we would also need some account of those sentences which seem to express such propositions but in fact, on the view in question, do not). I don't know of any such argument, and for purposes of present discussion I shall simply assume that there are such propositions.

Second, it might be held that, while indeed there *are* propositions of these kinds, they do not have truth values. This is a venerable view, and it has boasted many advocates who are both acute and accomplished. This is not the place to give this view the careful attention it clearly deserves. Instead, let me simply record the fact that I find this view as puzzling as the previous one; it is at best monumentally difficult to see how a proposition could fail to have a truth value. A proposition makes a claim, it says that the world, or some part of it, or something it contains, is a certain way, or has a certain property; such a proposition is therefore true if the thing in question has the property and false otherwise. Suppose I say that Paul (now) has the property of being such that he will take part in a sea battle tomorrow. What I say is true if he has that property and false otherwise. It is false if, for example, there *is* no such property as *taking part in a sea battle tomorrow*. If there *is* such a property, however, then if Paul has it, the proposition is true; and if he doesn't (doesn't *yet*, say), then the proposition is false. How could it possibly fail to be either true or false? An *utterance of a sentence*, of course, can fail to be either true or false. I awake with a slight cold; testing my voice, I say, remembering a scene from last night's TV program but referring to no one, "She's got that funny look again." My utterance is neither true nor false: it fails to express any proposition, on that occasion. An utterance of a sentence is true (false), however, if and only if it expresses a proposition, and the proposition it expresses is true (false). But if you tell me that there *is* such a proposition as *p*, only, as it happens, it is neither true nor false, I will be puzzled. I don't see how it *could* fail to be true or false. I shall therefore also assume that the propositions of these three sorts have truth values.

A third view is restricted to counterfactuals of freedom. This view

holds that while indeed there *are* such propositions and while they do
indeed have truth values, they are all false — in fact *necessarily* false.[3]
Once more, I can't take the time and space here to discuss the matter
properly.[4] Very briefly, however, the reason given for supposing that
these propositions are false — namely, that there is necessarily nothing
that grounds their truth or makes them true — seems to hold for
counterfactuals of divine freedom if it holds for counterfactuals of
creaturely freedom. But won't any theist hold that at least some propositions of the sort represented by

> *(5) If Adam and Eve had not sinned, God would have (freely)
> refrained from forcibly evicting them from the garden*

and

> *(6) If this bit of iron had been heated, God would have (freely)
> upheld it in existence and permitted it to expand*

are true? I shall also, therefore, assume that counterfactuals of creaturely
freedom are not all necessarily false (and indeed that some are true).

The view I really want to discuss is the thought that, while indeed
there *are* true propositions of these three kinds (and some of them are
true), they can't be known by God. Richard Swinburne, for example,
holds that God could know what I will do tomorrow, but he freely
averts his eyes from these propositions in order to shield our freedom.
The idea seems to be that there is indeed a *truth* about what I will
freely do, but if God were to *know* that truth, then I wouldn't do what
I will do *freely*. It therefore follows that there is a truth about what I
will freely do, but God can't know it.

But *why*, on the sort of view in question, can't God know these
propositions? What, precisely, is the problem? One answer for propositions of the first sort would be that they can't be known, because if
God *knows* what you are going to do, it follows that you don't or won't

3. This is the view embraced by Robert Adams in "Middle Knowledge and the
Problem of Evil," *American Philosophical Quarterly* (1977). In the piece in question, he
doesn't explicitly say that these propositions are necessarily false, but only this interpretation fits the rest of what he says, a fact that he has confirmed in personal
communication.

4. See my reply to Adams on this point in *Alvin Plantinga*, pp. 372ff.

do that thing freely.[5] I don't think this does follow.[6] This is not the place to debate the issue, however; let's set this suggestion aside, for the moment, and assume, as seems to me in fact to be the case, that God's knowing that I will do *A* does not entail that I won't do *A* freely. I am instead concerned with the *second* reason for supposing that God does not know such propositions: the view that these propositions — counterfactuals of freedom and/or propositions about someone's future free actions — *simply can't be known*. God is omniscient, all right, but his being omniscient means not that he knows everything (every true proposition) but rather that he knows everything that can be known.

Well, why do such people think these propositions can't be known? The fundamental answer, I think, is that we can't see *how* they could be known. How could God know a thing like that, a thing about the future, or about some counterfactual situation that, so far as logic goes, could go either way? Thus, for example, Jerry Walls: "the basic idea that God knows what is possible through knowledge of His essence is sensible enough as is the claim that the created order in some sense mirrors the divine essence. But *the manner* in which God can know what choices would actually be made by free creatures remains quite mysterious."[7]

I think we must agree that we don't or can't see how God could know a thing like that. He can't know a future free choice by taking advantage of causal laws and causal regularities, for example, because the action in question would be by hypothesis *free;* therefore causal laws and antecedent conditions determine neither that the action would take place nor that it would fail to take place. So he couldn't know that the action will occur by knowing causal laws and present or hypothesized conditions and extrapolating either to the action's taking place or to its failing to take place.

Here the point has to do with counterfactuals of freedom; but a similar point holds for future free actions. God can't know that Paul will (freely) take part in a sea battle tomorrow by knowing causal laws and present conditions, for the action in question is by hypothesis free.

5. See, e.g., Nelson Pike's "Divine Omniscience and Voluntary Action," *Philosophical Review* 74 (Jan. 1965). Pike's seminal piece has generated a veritable cottage industry of objections and replies.

6. See my "On Ockham's Way Out," *Faith and Philosophy* 3, 3 (July 1986): 235-69.

7. Jerry Walls, "Is Molinism as Bad as Calvinism?" (!), *Faith and Philosophy* 7, 1 (Jan. 1990): 89.

Further, I assume that God has a temporal perspective (I realize that there is weighty opinion on the other side); his perspective is similar to ours in that he knows that some things have already happened, some things are at present happening, and other things will happen but haven't happened yet. (These things are no more and no less than the sober truth; hence if God doesn't know them, he isn't omniscient.) Therefore God also does not just *see* these future free actions taking place, because they are not (at present) taking place. You might reply that he just sees that they *will* happen; that seems right, but it reintroduces the alleged problem, which is *how* does he 'see' that they will happen?

So he can't know propositions about future free actions by knowing present conditions together with causal laws and computing how they come out; nor (on the temporalist perspective) does he know them by *seeing* the actions take place, in the way we see what is presently happening. (Of course, he might see that they *will* take place, but that reintroduces the very perplexity at issue.) Furthermore, he can't know (creaturely) counterfactuals of freedom by knowing causal laws and present conditions — nor, of course, by way of seeing the relevant actions take place. (In the case of many counterfactuals of freedom, the relevant actions do *not* take place.) And since we can't think of any other ways in which he might know such propositions, we are inclined to conclude that he couldn't know them.

II. Divine Simplicity to the Rescue?

Bill Mann makes an interesting suggestion here: he believes we can get an answer to the question of how God knows propositions (1) through (4) by drawing on the doctrine of Divine Simplicity (DS). According to this puzzling but popular doctrine, no distinctions whatever can be made in God; his essence is identical with his existence, each of his properties is identical with each of his properties, and he himself is identical with each of his properties, as well as with his essence and his existence. By DS, then, God's *knowledge* of each of the propositions (1) through (4) is identical with his *willing* them; thus God's knowledge that Sam will (freely) have a sardine sandwich for lunch is identical with God's willing that Sam (freely) have a sardine sandwich for lunch. There is no problem, presumably, with seeing how God can know the latter;[8] since the latter is identical with the former, there is also no problem with seeing how God can know the former. Mann restricts his account to *contingent* facts, facts such as that Sam is eating a sandwich, and encapsulates his idea as follows:

> For any contingent situation S, God's knowing that S is the case = God's knowing that he wills that S is the case = God's willing that S is the case = God's knowing himself = God.[9]

This is a bold and interesting suggestion; but I can't see how it can be right. We might note first that Mann's restriction to contingent truths is unnecessary; if DS is true, then for *any* true propositions *A* and *B, God's knowing A* will be identical with *God's knowing B.* Therefore his knowing that Sam will freely have lunch is identical with his knowing that $2 + 1 = 3$; and since there is no problem with the latter, there is none with the former. Still further, on Mann's version of DS *God's knowing that Sam will freely have lunch* is identical with *God's knowing that he wills that Sam will freely have lunch;* but it is also identical with *God's willing that Sam will freely have lunch,* and, indeed, with *God's willing that there be such a person as Adam.* Since there is no problem with seeing how God could will that there be such a person as Adam, there can be none (on the current suggestion) with seeing how he can know that Sam will freely have lunch.

Indeed, the method can be extended much further. Atheologians have claimed that the existence of evil is incompatible with God's being omniscient, omnipotent, and wholly good; and believers in God themselves are sometimes deeply perplexed by the question of why God permits some particularly horrifying evil. For *God's knowing that there is evil* is identical with *God's knowing that $7 + 5 = 12$;* the latter is clearly compatible with his being omniscient, omnipotent, and wholly good; the former entails that there is evil; therefore the existence of evil is compatible with God's being omnipotent, omniscient, and wholly good.

8. In fact, there does seem to be a problem with seeing how he can accomplish the latter: If God *wills* that Sam have lunch, will Sam have lunch *freely?* Perhaps we can mend matters by a change of example: God's knowing that Sam will (freely) have a sardine sandwich for lunch is identical with God's *permitting* Sam to have a sardine sandwich for lunch.

9. Bill Mann, "Epistemology Supernaturalized," *Faith and Philosophy* 2, 4 (Oct. 1985): 452.

Furthermore, God's permitting that horrifying evil is identical with his loving mankind; there is no call for perplexity in the latter; therefore there is none in the former either.

But surely something has gone wrong; I can't sensibly allay my perplexity about God's permitting the Holocaust by noting that *God's permitting the Holocaust* is really identical with *God's loving humankind,* or his creating the world. Of course, one problem here is that all of these arguments are reversible: we could just as well argue that God's creating the world or knowing that 2 + 1 = 3 is perplexing, since each is identical with his permitting horrifying evil, and *that* is perplexing. But perhaps the real problem here is the doctrine of divine simplicity. According to that doctrine, at least as it is understood by Mann, God's permitting horrifying evil is identical with his loving mankind; and each is identical with his knowing that 2 + 1 = 3. This claim is so perplexing and counterintuitive that we should accept it only if there are enormously massive and powerful arguments in its favor. So far as I can see, however, there are no such arguments in its favor; in fact, so far as I can see, there aren't even any *moderately* massive and powerful arguments in its favor.[10] Accordingly, we are left with our original perplexity: How can God know future contingents? More specifically, how can he know such propositions as (1) through (4)? And we are left with our original inclination to doubt or deny that he knows such propositions because we can't see how he *could* know them.

III. The Solution

Now I believe this line of thought — the line issuing in an inclination to deny that God can know propositions like (1) through (4) — is mistaken. For the presupposition here is that, while we don't know how God knows about future free actions, we *do* know something about how God knows things — what *past* free actions have been performed, for

10. See my *Does God Have a Nature?* (Milwaukee: Marquette University Press, 1980), pp. 26ff. For contrary opinion, see William Mann, "The Divine Attributes," *American Philosophical Quarterly* 12 (1975); "Divine Simplicity," *Religious Studies* (1982); and "Simplicity and Immutability in God," *International Philosophical Quarterly* (1983). See also Eleonore Stump and Norman Kretzmann, "Absolute Simplicity," *Faith and Philosophy* 2, 4 (Oct. 1985) and Thomas Morris, "On God and Mann: A View of Divine Simplicity," *Religious Studies* 21, 3 (1985): 299-318.

example, or that 2 + 1 = 3, or that he exists and is omniscient, or that he wills the salvation of all people. But *do* we know how God knows these things? How does he know necessary truths, for example? You might say, "He knows necessary truths by knowing his own nature; propositions are divine thoughts, and necessary propositions are the thoughts God thinks with assent in every possible world. Necessary propositions, therefore, are the thoughts such that it is the nature of God to affirm them; so in knowing his own nature he knows the necessary propositions." Perhaps so; but then how does he know his own nature? And if there is a problem with his knowing future free actions, how does he know past free actions? Why isn't there a problem with his knowing *them?* For that matter, how does God know *present* free actions? How does he know that you are presently and freely (I hope) reading this essay?

The truth, I think, is that we believe we have a pretty good idea of how *we* know things of that kind; as a result, we see no problem in God's knowing them. *He* knows them (we assume) in something like the same way in which *we* know them — or, if that's false, then at any rate we know of a way in which those things *can* be known. We think we know how *we* know them, and as a consequence we aren't bothered by the question of how God knows them.

A. How Do We Know?

I want to argue that this line of thought is imperceptive. Once we clearly see what it is for *us* to know such things (once we clearly see how we know them), then we see two things: *(a)* that God doesn't and couldn't possibly know them in anything like the same way, and *(b)* that what we know about how God does know what he knows gives us no reason for distinguishing among various kinds of truths, taking some but not all to be such that we have a reason for thinking it unlikely that he knows them.

We know an astonishing variety of propositions. God has created us with cognitive faculties designed to enable us to achieve true beliefs with respect to propositions about our immediate environment, about our own interior lives, about the thoughts and experiences of other persons, about our universe at large, about the past, about right and wrong, about the whole realm of abstracta (numbers, properties, propositions, states of affairs, possible worlds, sets), about modality (what is necessary and possible), and about himself. These faculties work with great subtlety to produce beliefs of many different degrees of strength, ranging from the merest inclination to believe to absolute dead certainty. Our beliefs and the strength with which we hold them, furthermore, are delicately responsive to changes in experience — perceptual experiences, of course, but also experiences of other kinds; they are also responsive to what others tell us, to further reflection, to what we learn by way of systematic inquiry, and so on.

How do we know these things? How does our knowledge work? Well, you say, we know different things differently; I know that 7 + 5 = 12 in one way, that all human beings are mortal in another, that I am appeared to redly (or am suffering a mild pain) in still another, and that I was appeared to redly yesterday in yet another way. That is certainly true; but can't we also say something *general* about how we know? From a theistic point of view (and who but a theist would be interested in our problem?) the first thing to bear in mind is that we human beings have been *created,* and created in the image of God. In crucial respects we resemble him. God is, of course, an *agent;* he has aims and intentions and takes steps to accomplish his aims. (Thus he creates the world, sustains it in being, providentially brings good out of evil, institutes a plan of salvation, and so on.) But of course God is also an *intellectual* or *intellecting* being; indeed, he can't be an agent or a practical being without being a knower, an intellecting being. He has knowledge; in fact, he has the maximum degree of knowledge. He holds beliefs (even if his way of holding a belief is not the same as ours). He is omniscient: he believes every truth and believes no falsehoods. He therefore has the sort of grasp of concepts, properties, and propositions necessary for holding beliefs; and since he believes every true proposition, he has a grasp of every property and proposition.[11]

In setting out to create human beings in his image, then, God set out to create beings who could reflect something of his capacity to grasp concepts and hold beliefs. Furthermore (as the whole of the Christian tradition assures us), his aim was to create them in such a way that they

---

11. We can go further: from a theistic point of view the natural way to view propositions, properties, and sets is as God's thoughts, concepts, and collections. See my "How to Be an Anti-realist," *Proceedings of the American Philosophical Association* 56, 1 (1983); Thomas Morris's and Christopher Menzel's "Absolute Creation," *American Philosophical Quarterly* (1986); and Menzel's "Theism, Platonism, and Mathematics," *Faith and Philosophy* 4, 4 (Oct. 1987).

can reflect something of his capacity for holding *true* beliefs, for attaining *knowledge*.[12] This isn't his *only* aim in creating us with that complex, subtle, and highly articulated establishment of faculties we do in fact display. No doubt he also aimed at our being able to make and enjoy and appreciate poetry, art, music, humor, play, adventure, and their like; no doubt he was also aiming at our being able to love each other and him. But among his aims is that of enabling us to achieve knowledge, both for its own sake and for the sake of its connection with these other aims.[13]

God has therefore created us with cognitive faculties designed to enable us to achieve true belief with respect to a wide variety of propositions. These faculties work in such a way that under the appropriate circumstances we form the appropriate belief — better, the appropriate belief is *formed* in us. In the typical case we do not *decide* to hold or form the belief in question; we simply find ourselves with it. The Enlightenment myth of the rational human being proceeding magisterially through life, assessing the evidence for and against the propositions that come to his attention and coolly deciding on the basis of that assessment what to believe, is just that: a myth.[14] Upon being appeared to in a familiar but terrifying way, I believe there is a truck bearing down on me; on being asked where I went for a walk yesterday, I find myself with the memory belief that it was up Mt. Cargill; you tell me about your summer vacation and I acquire beliefs about where you went

---

12. Thus, for example, Thomas Aquinas:

> Since human beings are said to be in the image of God in virtue of their having a nature that includes an intellect, such a nature is most in the image of God in virtue of being most able to imitate God. (*Summa Theologiae* Ia q.93 a.4)

> Only in rational creatures is there found a likeness of God which counts as an image. . . . As far as a likeness of the divine nature is concerned, rational creatures seem somehow to attain a representation of [that] type in virtue of imitating God not only in this, that he is and lives, but especially in this, that he understands. (*Summa Theologiae* Ia q.93 a.6)

13. In C. S. Lewis's novel *Out of the Silent Planet* (New York: Macmillan, 1947), the creatures on Malacandra (Mars) are of several different types, displaying several different kinds of cognitive excellences: some are particularly suited to scientific endeavors, some to art and craftsmanship, and some to poetry, interpersonal sensitivity, and insight.

14. Since the term 'myth' is often used in such a way that it is compatible with truth, let me add that this is a *false* myth.

and what you did. In none of these cases do I either assess evidence or decide what to believe.

Of course, under other circumstances things are less automatic; we take a hand (so to speak) in the operation of our cognitive establishment. Expanding on the topic of your summer vacation, you tell me that you happened to stop in the Grand Tetons and for a lark climbed the Grand in eight hours from Jenny Lake. That sounds a bit unlikely, given your age and shape; recalling other exaggerations on your part, I figure it was closer to twelve hours, if you got to the top at all. I may try to assess the alleged evidence in favor of the theory that human life evolved by means of the mechanisms of random genetic mutation and natural selection from unicellular life (which itself arose by substantially similar random mechanical processes from nonliving material); I may try to see what the evidence is and determine whether it is in fact compelling (or, more likely, such as to render the theory less than totally implausible). Then I may go through a process of weighing the evidence and coming to a conclusion. Even in this sort of case I still don't really *decide* anything; I simply call the relevant evidence to mind, try in some appropriate way to weigh it, and find myself with the appropriate belief. But in more typical and less theoretical cases of belief formation, nothing like this is involved.

Experience, obviously enough, plays a crucial role in much belief formation — a different role in different areas of our cognitive establishment.[15] But there are also areas where experience seems to play only a minimal role — memory, for example, or a priori knowledge. I remember what I had for breakfast this morning; there may be a bit of phenomenal imagery, as of a partial and fragmented glimpse of a bowl of Cheerios; but this sensuous imagery is fleeting, indistinct, variable from person to person, and inessential, since in the case of some persons it seems to be altogether absent. Here, therefore, the role played by experience is small — unless you count as 'experience' the fact that the belief that it was *Cheerios* I had seems somehow right, or fitting, or appropriate.[16] Similar remarks hold for a priori knowledge.[17]

---

15. For details, see chapters 3-9 of my *Warrant and Proper Function* (New York: Oxford University Press, 1993). Cited hereafter as *WPF.*

16. For more on the phenomenology of memory, see *WPF,* chapter 3: "Exploring the Design Plan: Myself and My Past."

17. See *WPF,* chapter 6: "*A Priori* Knowledge."

Of course, there is a certain particular way or range of ways in which our faculties function when they function properly (when there is no cognitive dysfunction) — just as there is a way in which your digestive or circulatory system works when it functions properly. Call this way of working *the cognitive design plan.* The design plan specifies, for a wide variety of circumstances, an appropriate cognitive response. You look at a tree; light of a certain wavelength and energy strikes your retina; if things are working properly, there ensues a fairly complicated chain of events culminating in your being appeared to in a certain way (a way that is hard to describe in detail) and forming the belief that your willow tree needs watering. Accordingly, the design plan specifies how human cognitive faculties work when they work properly.[18] Of course, it is possible, as a result of disease or other causes, for our faculties to work in a way that is out of accord with the design plan: there are blindness and other sensory malfunctions; there are agnosias and psychoses; there are cognitive pathologies of a thousand sorts.[19]

From a theistic perspective, therefore, the central thing to see is that God has created us and our cognitive faculties, and that he has created us in accordance with specifications or a design plan. Indeed, from a theistic point of view, the human design plan is a design plan in the most literal and paradigmatic sense: we human beings have been created by a conscious and intelligent person, and the design plan is the set of specifications in accordance with which he has designed our cognitive faculties to function. Now, how shall we think of knowledge from this point of view? How shall we think of *warrant,* that quality or quantity enough of which distinguishes knowledge from mere true belief? Here is a natural first approximation: a belief has warrant for a person only if his faculties are *working properly,* working the way they ought to work, working the way they were designed to work (working the way God designed them to work) in producing and sustaining the belief in question. An initial necessary condition of warrant, therefore, is that one's cognitive equipment, one's belief-forming and belief-sustaining apparatus, be free of cognitive malfunction; it must be functioning in the way it was designed to function by

18. See *WPF,* chapter 2, for a fuller account of design plans.
19. For a fascinating account of some of these pathologies, see Oliver Sacks's *The Man Who Mistook His Wife for a Hat* (New York: Summit Books, 1984) and *A Leg to Stand On* (New York: Summit Books, 1985).

the being who designed and created us. Of course, this isn't sufficient; the epistemic environment must also be of the sort for which my cognitive faculties are designed. (If I am suddenly transported without my knowledge to a part of the universe where the cognitive environment is quite different, my beliefs might have little by way of warrant, even if my faculties are in fine working order — just as, for example, your automobile won't work well under water.) Still further, the bit of the design plan governing the formation of the particular belief in question must be aimed at the production of true or nearly true beliefs (rather than beliefs useful for survival, or beliefs whose function is to confer comfort or make friendship possible). And finally, it must be the case, if my beliefs are to have warrant, that beliefs produced according to faculties functioning in accord with my design plan are likely to be true.

To put these together:

> A belief B has warrant for a person S if and only if *(a)* S's faculties are functioning properly in an epistemically appropriate environment (the sort of environment for which God designed her faculties), *(b)* the segment of the design plan governing the formation of S's belief B is aimed at the production of true beliefs, and *(c)* the objective probability of a belief's being true, given that its production is governed by that segment of the design plan and that conditions *(a)* and *(b)* are met, is high.

The basic idea, therefore, is that we are so constructed (so constructed by God) that under certain sorts of conditions we form certain sorts of beliefs; and these beliefs constitute knowledge when they are true and when they result from the operation of the design plan God has implemented for us — more exactly, the operation of those parts of the design plan aimed at the production of true beliefs.

B. How Does God Know?

Now God's knowledge can't be at all like this. And it isn't just that God doesn't have the kind of cognitive design plan that we do — doesn't have sense organs, for example. Having our kind of cognitive design plan, after all, isn't essential for knowledge. God could have designed rational creatures according to design plans quite different from ours.

Indeed, perhaps he has. Perhaps he has designed rational creatures with sense organs very different from ours (like the bat's radar, for example, or the pit viper's heat detectors, or the mechanism whereby arctic terns can navigate for thousands of miles without so much as a glance at a map); perhaps he has designed rational creatures without sense organs who nonetheless have knowledge much like our perceptual knowledge, except that it would be caused differently; perhaps he has designed rational creatures that are vastly better at a priori knowledge; perhaps he has designed rational creatures that have ways of knowing we couldn't so much as grasp. The crucial difference between our knowledge and his doesn't lie here.

The real reason his knowledge can't be like ours is twofold: first, he has *designed* us to work a certain way; and second, this design is such that our knowledge follows the causal channels dictated by the causal laws he has established together with the sort of general construction we display — embodied, with a medium-sized body made of brain, flesh, and bone — in the specific sort of environment for which he has designed us. To enlarge a bit on the first, God has so designed me that under certain conditions the belief that I see a horse is caused in me; under those circumstances, furthermore (in the human cognitive environment and for the most part), when I believe that I see a horse, there really is a horse lurking in the nearby neighborhood. God has arranged for a certain harmony between the beliefs I hold, on the one hand, and their truth, on the other; this harmony goes by way of the causal connections between my beliefs and their subject matter. Essential to *my* knowing, therefore, is *his* already knowing a lot of things — how to arrange for that harmony, for example.

This is only a first approximation, of course; for perhaps I could have been created by an angel (who had the created sort of knowledge), and that angel by another, also with the created sort of knowledge, and so on. At some point, however, as Aquinas says in a different connection, the series must terminate in a being who has knowledge of another sort altogether. There must be a first knower, just as there must be a first mover; and it can't be the case that what constitutes *his* knowledge is his having been designed and fashioned by some other being, designed and fashioned in such a way that over a wide variety of circumstances he holds true beliefs. For first of all, of course, God can't have been designed and fashioned at all — either by himself or by some other being. And secondly, God's knowing a given truth can't be dependent upon some *other* being's knowing that truth or another,[20] in the way in which *our* knowing something is dependent upon *his* knowing something.

Suppose we look into these points more concretely. Consider our perceptual knowledge. God has created us with a set of *detectors*, you might say. By way of perception, we can detect the presence of various kinds of light and sound (and smells, etc.); by way of perception we can also detect the presence of such things as plants and animals and other human beings and much else. There is a causal link between things being a certain way — there being a tree before me, for example — and my forming the belief that there is a tree there. This works by way of God's having taken advantage, in designing and creating us, of the causal laws and arrangements he had already set in place. Perhaps he chose the causal laws and structures of the world as he did partly because he intended that there be cognitive beings of the sort we exemplify; in any event, our knowing goes by way of the causal structures and channels he has instituted.

Now of course God knew how to do all this. He knew how to institute the causal laws and how to create us in such a way that by virtue of the cooperation of our natures with these laws and the conditions under which they operate we would have the sort of knowledge he intended us to have. (Perhaps all he had to know, in order to know how to do these things, was this: If I say, "Let it be thus and so," then it *will* be thus and so. Here, perhaps, we see something of what it is for him to have knowledge by way of knowing himself; he knows that he is such that necessarily, if he says, "Let there be a so-and-so," there will be a so-and-so; and he knows that he has said "Let there be a so-and-so.") The point, of course, is that he already had to have knowledge for any of this to work; he couldn't have created me in such a way that I have knowledge, without himself having had knowledge. Accordingly, my knowledge presupposes his: I couldn't have knowledge, or couldn't have the kind of knowledge I do have, if he didn't already have knowledge. We require a first knower here, who knows without having been fashioned or constructed to know, just as, according to some of the theistic arguments, we require a first mover, himself unmoved.

I say my knowledge presupposes God's in the sense that I couldn't know

---

20. Except, of course, in the sort of special case where the truth in question is that some creature knows something or other.

unless he knew something first. This is not simply a matter of its being a necessary truth that God does know, so that my knowing something would trivially entail (strictly imply) or presuppose his knowing something. That is indeed true, but it is not, in the present context, of much significance. (*Everything* presupposes God's knowledge in this way.) It is rather that, given theism, together with the correct account or analysis of knowledge (human knowledge, creaturely knowledge), our knowing something non-trivially or relevantly entails or presupposes his knowing something. An important difference between God and us is that our knowledge presupposes knowledge on the part of someone else; his does not.

More fully, what theism and the correct account of our knowledge entail is that someone has designed us; the right answer to the question "How do we know *p*?" involves a reference to what someone else (the designer) knows. Not so for God's knowledge. For consider: if the above account of knowledge is correct (and if not, why would I be bothering you with it?), our knowledge essentially involves the connected notions of proper function and design plan. You know that all human beings are mortal, on that account, only if the relevant portion of your cognitive equipment is functioning properly in producing that belief in you — only if, that is, that portion of your cognitive equipment is functioning in accord with the design plan for human beings. But the paradigmatic cases of proper function and design plan involve a conscious and intelligent designer. Something functions properly, in the paradigmatic cases, only if it functions in the way it was designed to function by the person or persons who designed it. Your television set, for example, functions properly only if it works the way it was designed to work. If it doesn't work that way — because, for example, you unwisely washed it in the bathtub — then it isn't working properly. Of course, there are various subtleties and complications here. Something might not be designed by any single person, but by a committee, or perhaps by a series of committees over time. The design of a Maori war canoe (or a Chevrolet automobile) evolves, with many different designers adding their contributions, a bit here and a bit there.[21] Nonetheless, what determines proper function in the central and paradigmatic cases is whether the thing in question functions in accord with its design plan, each part of which in some way essentially involves the contribution of a conscious and intelligent agent.

Now it might be argued that in fact it isn't in just the central and

21. For more on these complications, see *WPF*, chapter 2.

paradigmatic cases where this is so; it might be argued that the very notion of proper function and design plan involves a reference to conscious and intelligent design, so that it is a necessary truth that if something functions properly, then it (or an ancestral prototype) has been designed by one or more conscious and intelligent beings.[22] If this were so, then from the fact that we have knowledge it would follow that we have been designed by one or more conscious and intelligent agents; and if *that* were so, there would be a theistic argument lurking in the nearby bushes. In the spirit of Aquinas, we can't go to infinity in a series of knowers, each member being such that its cognitive faculties were designed by the preceding member; if so, there must be a designer of cognitive faculties himself undesigned — and this all human beings call God.

Of course, the argument isn't necessarily coercive or wholly rigorous — even given that proper function entails intelligent design. For one thing, someone who sees that proper function entails conscious design may then deny that there *is* such a thing as proper function for human beings and other natural creatures; it *looks* like there is, but in fact there is not, and to suppose that there is, is really to confuse natural creatures (which really aren't creations or creatures in the original sense at all) with artifacts.[23] For another thing, it could be, so far as the argument goes, that the undesigned designer of cognitive faculties isn't maximally powerful, or didn't create the heavens and the earth, or isn't good. So far as the argument goes, furthermore, it might be that there are *several* undesigned designers, a whole committee, even infinitely many, who collaborate on the design of our cognitive design plan. And of course there are still other even more arcane possibilities. To take these possibilities as invalidating the argument, however, is to forget that any serious argument takes its place in a context, a context where much else is taken for granted. It is to forget what William James taught us about

22. The notion of a design plan doesn't *analytically* entail that of an intelligent designer, in the way in which being a bachelor entails being unmarried. Here I use 'design' and 'design plan' in the way in which, e.g., Daniel Dennett (who is not a partisan of theism) uses it: "In the end, we want to be able to explain the intelligence of man, or beast, in terms of his design; and this in turn in terms of the natural selection of this design. . . ." *Brainstorms* (Montgomery, VT: Bradford Books, 1978), p. 12.

23. Thus John Pollock glumly speculates that "functional and psychological generalizations about organisms are just false and the whole enterprise arises from confusing organisms with artifacts (the latter having explicit designs and designers)." "How to Build a Person," in *Philosophical Perspectives, 1, Metaphysics, 1987* (Atascadero, CA: Ridgeview Publishing Co., 1987), p. 149.

live options. For most of us, these arcane possibilities (that there is a vast committee of undesigned designers, or that the [single] undesigned designer did not create the heavens and the earth) are not live options. So *if* the notion of proper function entails conscious and intelligent design, then we have the materials for a good (even if less than wholly conclusive) theistic argument.

And if the notion of proper function entails conscious and intelligent design, we also have a crucial difference between our knowledge and God's knowledge: *Our* knowledge is such that necessarily, if I know something, then I have cognitive faculties which have been designed by an intelligent person who already had knowledge. Thus my having knowledge presupposes someone else's having knowledge. Furthermore, the right answer to the question "How do I know *p*? How does my knowledge work?" will be in terms of my design plan, and ultimately in terms of the intentions and activity of my designer. The answer will be something like this (for perception): The designer wanted me to be able to have true beliefs about my immediate environment. Taking advantage of his knowledge of the properties of various materials he has created and the causal laws he has instituted, he designed a system that works in such a way that (when it is functioning properly in the environment for which it is designed) I form perceptual beliefs which are for the most part true. But of course none of this can be said for God. He does not in the central and literal sense have a design plan; and if there is a way in which his cognitive faculties function, about all we know about it is given in our knowledge that he is necessarily omniscient — that necessarily, for any proposition *p*, he believes *p* if and only if *p* is true.

But *does* the notion of proper function entail conscious and intelligent design? This is a wholly nontrivial question. A number of thinkers have recently (and not so recently) proposed naturalistic analyses of the notions of proper function, function *simpliciter,* and other allied concepts.[24] As you

24. For example, there are the following earlier efforts: Carl Hempel, "The Logic of Functional Analyses," in *Symposium on Sociological Theory,* ed. Llewellyn Gross (Evanston, IL: Row, Peterson, 1959); and Ernest Nagel, "The Structure of Teleological Explanations," in *The Structure of Science* (New York: Harcourt, Brace and World, 1961), pp. 398-428. There are also the following more recent accounts: Larry Wright, "Functions," *The Philosophical Review* (1973), reprinted in *Conceptual Issues in Evolutionary Biology: An Anthology,* ed. Elliot Sober (Cambridge, MA: MIT Press, 1984), p. 350; Ruth Millikan, *Language, Thought, and Other Biological Categories* (Cambridge, MA: MIT Press, 1984), pp. 17ff.; Christopher Boorse, "Wright on Functions," *The Philo-*

would expect, these analyses typically proceed in evolutionary terms. The central idea, on which there are a number of variations, is that an organ or system is functioning properly when there is a way in which its ancestors functioned, when that way contributed to the survival of creatures of its kind, and when the thing in question functions in that way.

All the accounts of this kind with which I am familiar, however, suffer from a serious — indeed, fatal — problem. Suppose a Hitler gains control of the world. For mad reasons of his own, he sets out to modify the human design plan. He gets his scientists to induce a mutation in some members of the human population; those born with this mutation can't see at all well (their visual field is a uniform shade of light green with little more than a few shadowy shapes projected on it). When they open their eyes and use them, furthermore, the result is constant and severe pain. This pain makes it impossible for them to do anything except barely survive. They are unable to listen to music, or read (or write) poetry or literature; they can't do mathematics or evolutionary biology; they can't enjoy humor, play, adventure, friendship, love, or any of the other things that make human life worthwhile. Their lives are poor, nasty, brutish, and short. Hitler and his henchmen (and their successors) systematically weed out those who do not suffer from this mutation; over the generations the numbers of the non-mutants dwindle. Now consider a pair of human beings a few generations down the road, one of whom has the old-style visual system and the other the new. According to the above kind of analysis of proper function, it is the *new*-style visual system that is functioning properly, for the way it functions has contributed to the survival of the ancestors of its possessors. But surely this is wrong. These new visual systems don't function properly at all. We might even put the example by saying that Hitler and his mad henchmen *hate* proper function (or at least proper function on the part of human visual systems) and are doing their best to stamp it out. On the above analysis, if they do succeed in stamping it out, then it wasn't proper function in the first place!

So far as I know, none of the proposed naturalistic accounts of proper function is anywhere close to satisfactory.[25] That is not to say, of course,

---

sophical *Review* (1976): 70ff.; John Bigelow and Robert Pargetter, "Functions," *The Journal of Philosophy* (1987): 181ff.; Pollock, "How to Build a Person," pp. 146ff.; Paul Griffiths, "Functional Explanation and Proper Functions," forthcoming in *British Journal for the Philosophy of Science;* and Karen Neander, "The Teleological Notion of Function," forthcoming in *Australasian Journal of Philosophy.*

25. See *WPF,* chapter 11.

that a satisfactory naturalistic analysis can't be given; but it doesn't look promising.

It is therefore unlikely that a naturalistic analysis of proper function can be given. If so, then our knowledge does indeed presuppose God's knowledge (in a nontrivial way), and an important difference between our knowledge and his is that ours but not his presupposes knowledge on the part of another.

But suppose that a naturalistic analysis or account of proper function *can* be given. If so, then we can't argue in the above way that my knowing some proposition entails that I or my cognitive faculties have been designed. And then the theistic argument to an undesigned designer would fail. Would it follow that it *is* possible that my cognitive faculties have not been designed? I'm not sure. If theism is true, it is a necessary truth that all contingent beings distinct from God have been created by him — or, if you think that is too strong, it is at any rate necessary that all contingent beings distinct from God have been created* by him, where a thing has been created* by God if and only if it has either been created by God or created by something that has been created* by God. But that is not obviously sufficient to show that God or anyone else has *designed* me. Is the following story possible? God set the stage for evolution by creating elementary particles and the (indeterministic) laws that do in fact hold; from moment to moment he holds these particles in being (and confers upon them their causal powers). Perhaps he permits this process to be driven in the way contemporary evolutionists tell us it *is* driven: by way of random genetic mutation, genetic drift, and other blind sources of genetic variation, acted upon by natural selection. Perhaps he does not *intend* or *plan* or *decree* that this process have the outcome that in fact it does, intending and decreeing only that it have *some* outcome, and knowing what outcome it will in fact have. If this is possible, then the development of creatures like ourselves with the sort of cognitive faculties we do in fact have wouldn't be something God planned or decreed, but something he permitted to happen; and under those conditions it would not be the case that our cognitive faculties have been designed, although they would have been created in the above extended sense.[26]

I don't know whether the above story is possible or not, but I very

---

26. This story is reminiscent of one told by Peter van Inwagen, "The Place of Chance in a World Sustained by God," in *Divine and Human Action*, pp. 211ff.

much doubt it. And even if it is possible, I very much doubt that it is compatible with God's having created us in his own image. But perhaps I am wrong; if so, then perhaps theism does not entail that our cognitive faculties have been designed. But my argument is really independent of this question; the real point here lies in a slightly different direction. For what is important for our question isn't, first of all, whether it's possible (given theism) that there be creatures with undesigned cognitive faculties. What counts instead is this: Our knowledge (in fact, whether or not essentially) is indeed derivative, and it *goes by way of the various causal structures and channels God has established.* To explain how I know something — a perceptual proposition, for example — one retraces an intricate causal web (most of whose details and many of whose major features are completely beyond our ken) that begins with environmental conditions of one sort or another and eventuates in my forming the belief in question. These causal connections and structures have been established by God. But *his* knowledge does *not* go by way of these causal connections (or any other); God's knowledge *precedes* the causal connections in the world. If you think, as I do, that God is in time and that there was indeed time prior to the creation of the universe, the thing to say is that God had knowledge prior (temporally prior) to his establishing these causal connections. If you think that time began with the created universe or that God is not in time, you will have to put the point in some other way; but in any event you will certainly think that God created the universe the way he did create it, establishing the causal relations he did, because he *knew* that by so creating it he could achieve his ends and accomplish his aims. This knowledge, then, cannot have gone by way of the causal channels he instituted.

We therefore don't make much progress, in asking how *God* knows, by taking a look to see how *we* know. So how *does* he know? We can't really say much about it. There are important analogies with our knowledge. First, what he knows is of course true, as in our case, and is something he believes, or at any rate something to which he does something relevantly similar to believing. (When we believe, what we believe is one of his thoughts [so I think]. Here too, then, there is a kind of priority; his thinking the thought is the explanation of the existence of the thought. Not so for us.) Second, in his case as in ours, the explanation of his believing is that the thought in question is *true;* it isn't (in general, anyway) that his thinking the thought with assent is the explanation of its being true. Third, in our case, when we know, there will be certain objective probabilities: there will be a high objective probability that a human belief formed in that way is true. In his case, there will be an objective probability of 1 of the belief's being true, given that it is one of God's beliefs. (That is, the probability of a divine belief's being true is 1.)

There is still another analogy, this one perhaps the most important. God has not been designed and does not have a design plan in the literal or paradigmatic sense; still, there is a way in which (if I may say so) he works cognitively or epistemically. This way is given by his being essentially omniscient and necessarily existent: God is essentially omniscient, but he is also a necessary being, so that it is a necessary truth that God believes a proposition A if and only if A is true. Call that way of working 'W'. W is something like an *ideal* for cognitive beings — beings capable of holding beliefs, seeing connections between propositions, and holding true beliefs. It is an ideal in the following sense. Say that a cognitive design plan P is *more excellent than* a design plan P^* just if a being that works according to P would be epistemically or cognitively more excellent than one designed according to P^*. (Of course, there will be environmental relativity here; furthermore, one thing that will figure into the comparison between a pair of design plans will be stability of reliability under change of environment.) Add W to the set to be ordered. Then perhaps the resulting ordering will not be connected; there may be elements that are incomparable. But there will be a *maximal* element under the ordering: W. W, therefore, is an ideal for cognitive design plans. As Aquinas pointed out, most of our terms apply *analogously* rather than univocally when predicated of both human beings and God; it is by virtue of the above analogies (and others) that the terms 'knowledge', 'proper function', and 'design plan' apply analogically to God.

So there are these analogies and similarities between God's knowledge and ours. But the main point is this: Though there are these analogies, we don't really have any idea at all about *how* God knows. We know that his knowledge doesn't proceed via the causal channels by which our knowledge proceeds; we know further that it doesn't proceed by way of any other causal channels either. But of course that doesn't give us a clue as to how it *does* proceed. What can we say about how he knows what he does, about how his knowledge works? The most natural thing to think here is that there *isn't* any way in which it works — any more than there is a way in which the numbers 1, 2, and 3 work, by virtue of which the sum of the first two is the third.

Here we might explore still another analogy.[27] Suppose Descartes is right: we are embodied immaterial substances. Suppose he is also right on another point: our beliefs (or many of them) about our own immediate experiences are incorrigible for us, where a proposition p is incorrigible for a person S just if it is impossible that S believe p and p be false and if it is also impossible that S believe $-p$ and p be true. (Thus it isn't possible that I believe I am in pain when I am not and that I believe I am not in pain when I am.) Then the way in which God knows what he knows is like the way in which I know these propositions about my own immediate experience: for any proposition p you pick, it is impossible that God believe p and p be false, and it is also impossible that God believe $-p$ and p be true. The difference would be (in addition to the fact that for me this holds at most for propositions about my own immediate experience) that it is necessary that for any proposition p, either God believes p or God believes $-p$.

Accordingly, if in an analogical sense we say that there is a way in which God's knowledge works, then, so far as we can see, that way is given by his being necessarily omniscient — his being such that necessarily, for any proposition p, God believes p if and only if p is true. But then it won't really make sense to object to his knowing propositions like (1) through (4) on the grounds that we can't see how he could know them. We can't see how creatures who know the way we do, or maybe even the way any other creatures *could* know, could know that. The reason we can't see how that could be is that, so far as we can see, there aren't the appropriate causal channels. But God's knowledge doesn't go by those channels anyway. We really know no more about how he knows himself, and his own nature, than about how he knows the future or counterfactuals of freedom. In each case, all we can really say is that it is necessary that for any proposition p, p is true if and only if God knows it. If this is a cognitive mechanism, then the same cognitive mechanism will be involved in *all* of his knowledge; and that mechanism is not such that it is harder to see how it would work for one kind of proposition than for another. We don't *see* that it works or how it works for any kind of proposition (in the way in which we see that [and how] it must be the case that there is no universal set). If we are right we know that

27. And here I am indebted to Philip Quinn. I am also indebted throughout this paper to the other members of the Notre Dame philosophy of religion discussion group, in particular David Burrell, Thomas Flint, Jesse Hobbs, and Eleonore Stump.

this condition holds for God's knowledge; but there aren't any sorts of propositions such that it is self-evident that it is necessary that a proposition of that sort is true if and only if God believes it. (It is not the case that this is self-evident, for example, for propositions about the past but not self-evident for propositions about the future.)

By way of conclusion, it is indeed true that we don't see how God knows or could know such propositions as (1) through (4). That fact, however, doesn't give us a reason to distinguish invidiously among truths, holding that some of them are obviously known by God, but doubting that (1) through (4) are. For we don't really see how God knows *any* of the things he knows; all we know is that necessarily, for any proposition p, p is true if and only if God believes it. But there is no more problem with (1) through (4) meeting that condition than with any other proposition's meeting it.

Proper Function, Reliabilism, and Religious Knowledge: A Critique of Plantinga's Epistemology

William Hasker

Over the past several years Alvin Plantinga has initiated the development of what promises to be a major new epistemological theory.[1] Specifically, his theory is concerned with *warrant*, defined as that which, when added to true belief, yields knowledge. He develops his theory, which may be designated as the Theory of Proper Function (TPF), in contrast with internalist, coherentist, and reliabilist theories of warrant, all of which he criticizes on the grounds that they would ascribe warrant to certain beliefs which we can readily see, intuitively, to be unwarranted.

TPF may be characterized briefly as follows: A belief is warranted if it is produced by our epistemic faculties when they are functioning properly — that is, in accordance with their design plan — in an appropriate epistemic environment. Thus, the notion of "functioning properly" is understood in terms of "design plan," where the latter idea may be initially understood on analogy with the design of a manufac-

---

1. The fullest statement of the theory to date is found in Plantinga's article "Positive Epistemic Status and Proper Function," *Philosophical Perspectives* 2 (1988). (Subsequent citations of this article will be given parenthetically in the text.) An earlier and considerably abbreviated version of this material is found in "Epistemic Justification," *Noûs* 20 (1986): 3-18. "Justification and Theism," *Faith and Philosophy* 4 (1987): 403-26, contains some of this same material and some additional material, including an intriguing budget of research projects for the new theory. Plantinga has in process a three-volume work on epistemology; as of this writing the first two volumes, *Warrant: The Current Debate* and *Warrant and Proper Function*, are forthcoming from Oxford. I have benefited from discussing some of this material with Plantinga and others, but (with one exception) the present discussion is based on the articles listed above.

tured object such as a camera or a computer. For a theist such as Plantinga, the idea of a design plan can be taken quite straightforwardly to refer to the way in which God, in creating human beings, intended for their cognitive faculties to function. He points out, however, that the notion of the "proper function" of an organism and its parts is one we have need of whether or not we are theists, and that evolution can be thought of, albeit somewhat metaphorically, as "designing" the organism in the process of "selecting" favorable genotypes to survive and propagate.

My critique of Plantinga's theory of warrant will proceed in five stages. First, I will present briefly the main outline of Plantinga's theory. Second, I will present and critically evaluate the reasons Plantinga gives for thinking his theory is superior to reliabilism, the type of epistemological theory that is closest to TPF. Third, I will present a counterexample, which shows (as I shall claim) that TPF in the form presented by Plantinga is unsatisfactory. Fourth, I will show how TPF can be modified to avoid this counterexample, being transformed in the process into a particular form of reliabilism. Finally, I shall consider the application of Plantinga's theory to a kind of knowledge that is of particular interest to Plantinga and many of his readers — namely, religious knowledge.

The Theory of Proper Function

Plantinga's theory, as we have already noted, is a theory of *warrant* — that property, whatever specifically it may be, which, when added to true belief (and setting aside Gettier problems), yields knowledge. There are, of course, numerous cases in which our beliefs, though true, have little in the way of warrant. In a great many of these cases, Plantinga holds, the problem is due to some sort of *malfunction* of the cognitive apparatus. And this suggests what Plantinga regards as a crucial condition for warranted belief: A belief is warranted only if the cognitive faculties involved in its production are *functioning properly*. The notion of proper function, however, requires further explication. As Plantinga says,

> So far as Nature herself goes, isn't a fish decomposing in a hill of corn functioning just as properly, just as excellently, as one happily swimming about chasing minnows? But then what could be meant

by speaking of "proper functioning" with respect to our cognitive
faculties? (43)

The answer to this, as we've seen, is in terms of the *design plan* of the
cognitive faculties in question: Those faculties are functioning properly
when they are functioning in accordance with their design plan. And
the notion of design plan can in turn be explicated either literally and
theistically or, perhaps, with some conceptual stress and strain, in terms
of our "design" by evolutionary selection.

Proper function, then, is necessary for warranted belief, but it is not
sufficient. For there are possible situations in which our faculties function according to design plan, yet yield beliefs with little or no warrant.
On a visit to nearby Alpha Centauri, we discover that the cat-like
creatures there

> are invisible to human beings, but they emit a sort of radiation
> unknown on earth, a radiation which works directly on the appro-
> priate portion of a human brain, causing its owner to form the belief
> that a dog is barking nearby. (33)

Clearly, under these circumstances the resulting beliefs about barking
dogs have very little warrant. The problem, however, is not with our
cognitive faculties; the problem, rather, is that "your cognitive faculties
and the environment in which you find yourself are not properly at-
tuned" (33). Your eyes are not equipped to detect Alpha Centaurian
cats, and your brain is liable to produce false and unwarranted beliefs
under the influence of that type of radiation. Our human cognitive
faculties simply do not equip us to operate successfully under every
conceivable kind of circumstances. And so we arrive at a further necessary condition: In order for our beliefs to have warrant, they must be
produced by faculties that are functioning properly *in an appropriate
cognitive environment*, which is to say, in the kind of environment in
which they were designed to function.

Yet a further qualification is needed. There are occasions when our
faculties are functioning properly in an appropriate environment, yet
they seem to produce beliefs whose warrant is dubious.

> Someone may remember a painful experience as less painful than
> it was, as is sometimes said to be the case with childbirth. You may

continue to believe in your friend's honesty long after evidence and objective judgment would have dictated a reluctant change of mind. I may believe that I will recover from a dread disease much more strongly than the statistics justify. (39)

In each of these cases, there are obvious human benefits in our having beliefs that are not strictly in accord with the evidence available to us. And our design plan (whether theistic or evolutionary) takes these benefits into account; thus we tend, under such circumstances, to form beliefs that are deficient in warrant. What we need to see, then, is that "different parts or aspects of our design plan could be aimed at different goals," and "what confers positive epistemic status is one's cognitive faculties working . . . according to the design plan *insofar as that segment of the design plan is aimed at producing true beliefs*" (39).[2]

A final matter that remains to be dealt with is the *degree* of warrant. Not all warranted beliefs are equally warranted, and an account of warrant must also have something to say on the question of degrees. Plantinga's answer to this has an engaging simplicity: The degree of *warrant* a belief has for a person is just the degree to which that person is *inclined to accept* the belief in question, given that the belief is produced by cognitive faculties functioning properly in an appropriate epistemic environment and that the relevant portion of the design plan has truth as its aim.

Plantinga's Critique of Reliabilism

In presenting his theory, Plantinga criticizes internalism, coherentism, and reliabilism, all of which, he alleges, would ascribe warrant to beliefs that we can readily see to be lacking in warrant. Since reliabilism is closest to Plantinga's own theory, his criticisms of it are particularly pertinent. Reliabilism comes in a number of significantly different varieties, but for present purposes we can characterize it simply as the view

2. An interesting consequence of this is that it may sometimes be possible to get closer to the truth by deviating from one's overall design plan than by conforming to it. We may even have actual examples of this: persons who rigorously school themselves to believe only according to the evidence apart from emotional influences are sometimes criticized (perhaps not wholly without reason) as "cold" and "unsympathetic."

that a belief has warrant to the extent that it is the product of reliable belief-forming processes. Plantinga's fundamental objection to this is that there can be beliefs that are so formed, which nevertheless have little or no warrant. One example that shows this is the following:[3]

> There is a rare but specific sort of brain tumor, we may suppose, such that associated with it are a number of cognitive processes of the relevant degree of specificity, most of which cause its victim to hold absurd beliefs. One of the processes associated with the tumor, however, causes the victim to believe that he has a brain tumor. Suppose, then, that S suffers from this sort of tumor and accordingly believes that he suffers from a brain tumor. Add that he has no evidence at all for this belief: no symptoms of which he is aware, no testimony on the part of doctors or other expert witnesses, nothing. Then the relevant type, while it may be hard to specify in detail, will certainly be highly reliable; but surely it is not the case that this belief — the belief that he has a brain tumor — has much by way of positive epistemic status for S. (30-31)

The lesson Plantinga draws from this example, and others like it, is clear: There can be reliably produced beliefs that nevertheless have very little warrant. And if this is so, then reliabilism fails as an account of warranted belief.

While this objection would, if successful, be decisive by itself, Plantinga also finds that reliabilism has a serious problem in dealing with the issue of *degrees* of warrant. What he has to say on this is essentially a version of the Generality Problem that has been urged by Richard Feldman.[4] In brief, the problem is this: If the belief-forming processes featured by reliabilism are construed very broadly (for example, visual perception), then they will include cases that vary widely with respect to degree of warrant. (Compare seeing a familiar object at close range in good light with various sorts of visual perception that occur under less favorable circumstances.) If, on the other hand, the processes are specified narrowly, so as to include only cases that are identical in degree

3. It should be said that this is only one of many examples Plantinga deploys against reliabilism. Many of these examples are similar in important respects to this one, but the interested reader should consult Plantinga's articles to get the full range of examples.

4. See Richard Feldman, "Reliability and Justification," *The Monist* 68 (1985): 159-74.

of warrant, we soon come to processes that in fact have very few instances, and the frequency of success in those instances may bear little or no relation to what we would intuitively take to be the degree of warrant conferred by the processes. So this matter of degree of warrant remains a vexed question for reliabilism, whereas Plantinga, as we've already seen, cuts through these difficulties by stating that degree of warrant is just the degree to which the subject is *inclined to accept* the belief in question, given that the belief is produced by cognitive faculties functioning properly in an appropriate epistemic environment and that the relevant portion of the design plan has truth as its aim.

Are Plantinga's criticisms of reliabilism convincing? I don't think so. With regard to the tumor example (and the same point holds for many of Plantinga's other examples), the difficulty is that the "process" by which the subject comes to believe that he has a brain tumor simply would not be regarded by many reliabilists as an "epistemic process" in the relevant sense.[5] To be sure, there does not as yet exist any clear-cut characterization of an epistemic process that is widely accepted by reliabilists. This is undoubtedly a point on which further work is needed (a not unexpected situation with regard to a theory that is still very much under development). But there are plausible reasons for supposing that the tumor-belief process is not an "epistemic process" in the relevant sense. One might require, for instance, that such a process should be able to deal with a variety of "inputs" and yield as outputs beliefs that are more likely to be true than beliefs that would be formed on the same subjects without the inputs — none of which is true in the example. In any case, an effective counterexample against reliabilism needs to be based on an epistemic process that reliabilists themselves will recognize as such. You can't refute a theory about birds by citing bats as counterexamples.

With regard to the issue of degrees of warrant, the Generality Problem is undoubtedly a difficulty that reliabilism needs to confront. There is no particular reason to think that a solution to this problem is impossible, though it would carry us too far afield to pursue this topic at present.[6] What I do wish to point out, however, is that

5. This point was made by Ernest Sosa in a 1986 American Philosophical Association symposium with Plantinga.

6. Speaking generally, the right approach seems to be this: The epistemic processes should be characterized narrowly, so as to make them homogeneous with respect to

Plantinga's alternative solution is illusory. Plantinga's key move is to assign the task of registering degrees of warrant to our belief-producing capacity itself; if this capacity produces a belief (or a tendency to believe) stronger or weaker than is warranted, then he will say that it isn't functioning properly. The catch in this is the fact that, as Plantinga recognizes, our cognitive faculties may be designed with other aims in addition to the aim of attainment of truth and so may, even when functioning properly, generate degrees of belief that diverge from the degree of epistemic warrant. In his remarks about this, Plantinga seems to assume that the occasions on which this occurs are relatively rare and easily identified. Other philosophers would dispute this; they would allege that, quite apart from any malfunction, our degrees of belief in various propositions are pervasively influenced by value considerations of various kinds. But whether these cases be few or many they do exist, and this means that, even in a properly functioning cognitive system, degree of warrant cannot always be "read off" directly from actual strength of belief. So we need to give an account of degree of warrant in those cases as well. (If we don't, we are saying in effect that the degree of warrant matches the strength of belief produced by a properly functioning cognitive system — except when it doesn't.) So even if it is successful so far as it goes, Plantinga's account of this matter remains seriously incomplete.

But is it even successful so far as it goes? Plantinga's theory entails the following *proportionality thesis:*

> *(PT) When one's cognitive faculties are designed with the aim of producing truth and are functioning properly in an appropriate environment, then any change in the environment that affects the degree of warrant is accompanied by a proportional change in the subject's inclination to believe.*

I see no reason to suppose that (PT) is true, and it is not difficult to generate plausible counterexamples.[7] But if (PT) is false, Plantinga's

---

degree of confirmation, but degree of warrant should then be defined in terms of the *propensity* of the process to produce true beliefs, rather than in terms of its *actual* frequency of success. But while this may be correct so far as it goes, a complete answer to this question depends on the right way of characterizing the epistemic processes in the first place.

7. You are an experienced bird-watcher, and in particular you are very confident

account of degrees of warrant is not merely incomplete; it is radically unsound.

I think it is fair to conclude that Plantinga has failed to show either that reliabilism pronounces beliefs to be warranted that are not, or that TPF is superior to reliabilism in its account of degrees of warrant.

A Counterexample to TPF

We now come to an example which shows, I shall argue, that TPF in the form considered so far is mistaken.[8] The example concerns Geoffrey, who, as the result of a random genetic mutation, not directed or planned by anyone, finds himself in an unusual cognitive situation. On the one hand, Geoffrey has been totally blind from birth, and there is no hope of his ever enjoying any kind of vision. But the mutation that rendered Geoffrey blind also had another result. The portion of his brain that would normally be devoted to processing visual information has now acquired another ability: it registers, in an extremely sensitive way, the magnetic fields generated by the earth and by objects in the environment. Because of this, Geoffrey has the ability, hitherto verified only in certain marine organisms, to locate himself and to make his way around by magnetolocation. As he grows to maturity, he is able to determine his location in the neighborhood and to make his way around it with considerable facility.

Under the described circumstances I think we are obliged to say that Geoffrey's beliefs about his whereabouts are warranted, and indeed that he *knows* where he is. It seems, however, that Geoffrey's cognitive situation is by no means in accordance with his design plan; *that* plan

---

(and appropriately so) in your identification of herring gulls. Unknown to you, however, unusual weather patterns have brought into the area a large number of the extremely similar Thayer's gulls. Under these conditions, your correct identifications of herring gulls enjoy considerably less warrant than they normally would, since there is a significant likelihood of your misidentifying a Thayer's gull as a herring gull. But since you have no knowledge of the incursion of Thayer's gulls, there is no reason whatever to suppose that your subjective confidence in your identifications will vary.

8. This example was first suggested by me in a discussion with Plantinga at the Wheaton College Philosophy Conference in October 1986. Several counterexamples similar to this one have been developed independently by James E. Taylor; see his "Plantinga's Proper Functioning Analysis of Epistemic Warrant," *Philosophical Studies* 64, 2 (Nov. 1991).

calls for that portion of his brain to be devoted to visual perception. So there can be warranted beliefs even when there is not function according to the design plan, and therefore TPF is false.

Fortunately there is no need to speculate about how Plantinga might respond to this objection, since he has included a reply to it in his forthcoming book, *Warrant and Proper Function.*[9] He says, "Now our first thought might be that Geoffrey's beliefs are warranted, all right, but warranted by nothing more arcane than induction." He goes on to note my claim that "the example can be redescribed (focusing on very early examples of Geoffrey's exercise of this faculty) so as to obviate this objection." He replies to this claim:

> But is it at all clear that under these conditions (when we explicitly stipulate that his faculties are not functioning in accord with his design plan) those first exercises of this faculty *do* provide Geoffrey with warranted belief? I think not. Perhaps in those cases what he has isn't warranted true belief, but beliefs true by lucky accident.

So Plantinga is suggesting that *(a)* the early exercises of Geoffrey's faculty confer no warrant on the beliefs they generate, and *(b)* in the later exercises, the warrant comes not from the magnetolocation faculty but from induction.

I have two replies to this line of defense.[10] First, I do think it is possible to describe very early instances of the exercise of the faculty in question (too early for inductive confirmation to contribute to warrant) in such a way that it is extremely plausible that the beliefs in question are warranted.[11] But further (and equally important), the proposal that

9. My thanks to Alvin Plantinga for providing me with a manuscript copy of the relevant chapter. Plantinga was responding to an earlier version of this material, contained in an unpublished paper entitled "Plantinga's Reliabilism."

10. I am indebted to Tom Senor for several suggestions about the Geoffrey example.

11. In his earliest years, Geoffrey is often taken around the town by his family in their horse-drawn carriage, learning in the process the names of various locations visited by his family. One day during his fifth year of life he notices, for the first time, a peculiar, hard-to-describe internal sensation; at the same time he finds himself thinking, and saying aloud, "This is the Post Office," and later, "This is the grocery," "This is the bank," and "This is the Christian Reformed Church." (We will stipulate that his identification of these locations was prompted solely by the internal sensation, and not by ambient sounds, smells, etc.) His older sister listens to all this in stunned silence, but when she returns home she tells the family what has happened and also imparts the information that Geoffrey was *correct* in every one of his identifications. In this

Geoffrey's beliefs are warranted only by induction is highly incongruous coming from a Reidian epistemologist such as Plantinga. To be sure, such a move would not be unexpected on the part of a classical foundationalist such as Descartes or Locke. But one of Reid's major complaints against the foundationalists of his day was that they arbitrarily selected one or two epistemic faculties (such as introspection and reason) and then regarded the deliverances of other faculties as unwarranted unless their truthfulness could be confirmed on the evidence of the "preferred" faculties. Even now, many philosophers take the same attitude toward religious experience, regarding it as evidentially worthless unless it can be independently established that the religious object exists. But of course Reformed epistemologist Plantinga will have none of this — so why should he adopt a similarly prejudiced attitude toward poor Geoffrey?

Apparently Plantinga is not completely convinced by his own suggestion, for after claiming that it is unclear that the early exercise of his faculty provides Geoffrey with warranted belief, he goes on to say:

> But it is equally unclear, I think, that Geoffrey's beliefs *lack* warrant. . . . One of the *purposes* involved in Geoffrey's design plan (i.e., the provision of true beliefs about his location) is still served by his new max plan,[12] although not in accord with the design plan. In a case like that we are pulled in two directions: on the one hand since that purpose is served, we are inclined to think that the relevant cognitive module is functioning properly; on the other hand since it isn't functioning in accord with the design plan we are inclined to think that it is not functioning properly. This hesitation is mirrored, I think, by our hesitation as to whether or not the relevant beliefs have warrant. So the right answer, I think, is that the module in question is not functioning properly in the full or strict sense, but is functioning properly in an analogically extended sense; and in a correspondingly analogically extended sense of 'warrant' his beliefs do have warrant, although they do not have warrant in the

---

scenario induction plays no role — and I think it is extremely plausible to conclude that, under these circumstances, Geoffrey's beliefs do possess warrant.

12. The "max plan" for Geoffrey's cognitive system includes its reaction to *all* contingencies, whether included in his "design plan" or not. In the example, Geoffrey has acquired a new max plan that in certain respects does *not* accord with his design plan.

full or strict sense. Perhaps we should say with Aristotle (who did not have Hasker in mind) "We should perhaps say that in a manner he knew, in a manner not."

Probably something along these lines is the best that can be done in defending TPF against this counterexample. And it may be that from the standpoint of one already firmly committed to TPF this talk of an "analogically extended sense of 'warrant'" (and by implication also of 'knowledge') has some degree of plausibility.[13] I do think I can understand why Plantinga feels "pulled in two directions" by the example. He is inclined to think that Geoffrey's beliefs do have warrant, because that is the way we are naturally inclined to take the story of Geoffrey (a point that is confirmed by other people's reactions to the story). And he is inclined to think that the beliefs do *not* have warrant, because they are acquired in a way that contradicts the Theory of Proper Function. For those who do not come to the example with a strong prior commitment to the theory, the decision may be simpler.

Plantinga's talk of analogical senses is vulnerable to a point often made against other versions of analogy: either the analogical sense shares a core of common meaning with the ordinary sense, in which case it should be possible in principle to characterize this common core in univocal terms, or it does not, and then the analogy becomes mere equivocation. In order to enforce this point, I want to insist on a Yes or No answer to the following question: Does Geoffrey, in virtue of his use of his faculty of magnetolocation, have *warrant* for his beliefs about his location — warrant such that, were it sufficiently strong, and extraneous defeating circumstances lacking, he could *know* where he is on this basis? If the answer is Yes, the counterexample has been conceded. So far as I can see, Plantinga's view requires him to answer No — but in this case the analogy has collapsed into equivocation and has become irrelevant. Apparently the only remaining way out would be for Plantinga to say that the question does not admit of an answer, because the notions of warrant and knowledge are ambiguous in some way that makes a crucial difference to the case. But if that is Plantinga's

---

13. Note, however, that part of Plantinga's defense of this "extended sense" — namely, the point that the new faculty still (like visual perception) provides Geoffrey with true beliefs about his location — is due merely to an accidental feature of the example. It would be easy to construct another example that lacked this feature.

view I think he needs to point out where the ambiguity lies and explain how it is that the rest of us are confused in thinking that the question can be answered.

I have claimed that the example of Geoffrey shows TPF to be an unsatisfactory theory. Some readers may disagree, either evaluating Plantinga's answers more favorably than I have done or holding out the hope that some other, as yet undiscovered, line of defense may succeed. But this much, I think, is clear: If it is possible to formulate a theory that handles such examples easily and naturally — that permits us to follow our inclinations and admit that Geoffrey's beliefs have warrant, and that does not require us to postulate a novel and obscure analogical sense of 'warrant' and 'knowledge' — if it is possible to formulate such a theory, then this theory will have, so far forth, a distinct advantage over TPF. To this task we turn in the next section.

Proper Function and Reliabilism

It is worth noting that if we conclude from the counterexample that TPF is unsatisfactory, not all parts of that theory suffer equally. Geoffrey still, after all, has a cognitive faculty, namely magnetolocation, which is functioning properly in an appropriate environment — one in which the ambient magnetic fields are neither too weak nor too strong, exhibit appropriate variations corresponding to changes in position, and so on. The only part of TPF that must be given up is the reference to the design plan.[14]

This, however, threatens to bring us full circle. For the design plan was originally introduced by Plantinga precisely in order to make sense of the notion of proper function. Are we really forced to give up proper function along with the design plan? Or is there some other way to explain the notion of proper function? I believe that this is indeed the case. To see how, let's return to Plantinga's original introduction of the design plan.

Undoubtedly Plantinga is right in supposing that we do not want to say that a fish decomposing in a hill of corn is "functioning properly." But the introduction of the design plan may not be the best way of

---

14. It was Philip Quinn who first suggested to me that it might be possible to separate the other elements of proper functionalism from the notion of the design plan.

avoiding that unwelcome consequence. Indeed, it is not at all clear that the design plan gives Plantinga what he wants here. For as a theist Plantinga undoubtedly regards the *entire ecosystem* as being designed in the same sense in which this is true of individual organisms; thus, by decomposing and returning nutrients to the soil the fish is indeed doing (part of) what it was designed to do.

I suggest that we may be able to make progress on this issue by considering the way the notion of function operates in biological science. An illuminating discussion of this has been given by philosopher of biology Michael Simon, who argues that

> If functional analysis is understood simply as revealing the mutual adaptedness of parts within a system . . . no connection between function and purpose or intention need be assumed. . . . [T]he connection between serving a function and having been created for a purpose is a contingent one.[15]

He goes on to say:

> Biology employs functional explanations by virtue of the assumption that the parts and processes of living things contribute to the survival and maintenance of the system as a whole, not because it is assumed that these elements were intentionally created to do so.[16]

Apropos of the fish rotting in the hill of corn, he says:

> the reason we do not ordinarily use functional concepts in dealing with such matters as the expansion of water upon freezing is simply that we are not accustomed to regarding inanimate nature as exhibiting a thoroughgoing mutual adaptedness of constituent parts.[17]

If this is correct, then the way is open to explicating proper function without reference to the design plan. We merely have to ask how it is that the operation of belief-forming processes in human beings contributes to the survival and maintenance of "the system as a whole,"

---

15. Michael A. Simon, *The Matter of Life: Philosophical Problems of Biology* (New Haven: Yale University Press, 1971), p. 183.

16. Simon, *The Matter of Life*, p. 183.

17. Simon, *The Matter of Life*, pp. 183-84.

that is, the entire human being, and perhaps the family or social group of which the human is a part. The answer that comes immediately to mind is that it does so by providing the human being in question with a supply of true beliefs. This is, to be sure, far from a complete answer; as Plantinga has pointed out, there are other ways in which our cognitive equipment contributes to "survival and maintenance" besides the provision of true beliefs, and on occasion these other contributions may even take precedence. But there is no reason to doubt that true beliefs *do* contribute substantially to the survival and maintenance of human beings, both as individuals and in groups, and so we are able to say, without presupposing anything about a design plan, that this is one of the "functions" of our belief-forming processes. And when we are engaged in *epistemic* evaluation of our belief-forming system, it is this function rather than any of the others that engages our attention.

As with function, so with proper function. If our belief-forming system has the function of providing us with true beliefs, this entails that it has modes of operation ("epistemic processes") which are successful in providing such beliefs at least a fair proportion of the time. (If the rate of success were negligible, not enough true beliefs would be produced to contribute to survival and maintenance, and this would not be a function of that part of the organism.) When the system actually operates in these modes — the modes in which it tends to produce true beliefs fairly frequently — it is "functioning properly." So there is a conceptual link between proper function and success, in that there could not *be* a function that was not exercised successfully to some degree (barring injury, etc.). But it is important to realize that proper function is not equivalent to success in a particular instance. When I am stalking a deer with bow and arrow, my eyes, nerves, and muscles may function properly and yet I may miss my target — for instance, if the deer springs away just as I release the arrow. Or, a muscle in my arm may spasm at the crucial moment, deflecting the arrow's flight just enough to compensate for the deer's unexpected movement, so that I make a direct hit. In the former case we have proper function resulting in failure; in the latter case, a lack of proper function results in success. The application to cases of belief formation should be evident.

And by now it is clear, if it was not formerly, that our modified proper functionalism is simply a form of epistemological reliabilism. Warrant, we shall say, is conferred by proper epistemic function — that is, by our epistemic equipment functioning in a mode that is such that it reliably produces true beliefs. We may, quite reasonably, go on to suppose that the degree of warrant is somehow connected with the *propensity* of the belief-forming process in question to produce true rather than false beliefs; a process that almost always produces true beliefs confers greater warrant than one that has a significant percentage of failure. Clearly, these ideas need a great deal more elaboration and refinement — precisely, in fact, the sort of elaboration and refinement they are receiving in the ongoing studies of reliabilist epistemology.

It is not altogether easy to say whether the results of this section constitute a gain or a loss for proper functionalist epistemology. On the one hand, our modified proper functionalism handles with ease such cases as that of Geoffrey. Since the belief-forming processes involving magnetolocation contribute to Geoffrey's survival and maintenance by providing him with correct beliefs about his location, the processes have this as their function, and they do confer warrant on the beliefs in question. But the price of this is that the rest of the theory becomes conceptually detached from the notion of the design plan — and in the process, proper functionalism is seen to be, not an alternative to reliabilism, but simply another version of reliabilism. Whether this price is one that Plantinga, and other proper functionalists, will eventually be willing to pay is unknown at present. Also unknown is whether the proper functionalist version of reliabilism will turn out to have significant advantages as compared with other versions of this theory. This question, I suggest, is one that might well be kept in mind by readers of Plantinga's works on epistemology, even though the question is somewhat at variance with Plantinga's own intentions.

It might seem, to be sure, that my revision of proper functionalism would be immediately unacceptable to Plantinga and his allies because it abandons the theistic foundations of his theory. This, however, is not necessarily the case. To be sure, the notion of the design plan is not involved in the *analysis* of "proper function." But the notion of design may still be invoked in the *explanation* of our epistemic functioning — whether to the exclusion of evolutionary explanations or in some sort of combination with them. (Cases like that of Geoffrey do not, after all, appear to be terribly common in practice!) It is hard to see that theism has much to lose in a shift of this kind.

Proper Function and Religious Knowledge

In conclusion, we shall consider the application of proper functionalist epistemology to a particular kind of knowledge, namely, religious knowledge. In order to have a reasonably precise question to investigate, we may pose the issue initially as follows: Do religious beliefs (beliefs about God or supernatural beings) formed on the grounds of religious experience possess epistemic warrant? This question, I believe, is an extremely difficult one to answer, and I shall be able to do no more than suggest some lines of approach to it. We begin with a series of clarifications, leading to the formulation of a second question, one that holds the key to answering the one just stated.

It should be noted, first of all, that this is not the same as the question whether religious beliefs grounded in religious experience can be "properly basic." This latter question, introduced by Plantinga in a series of classic papers,[18] is clearly a question concerning justification in the deontological sense — what is at issue is whether we can hold such beliefs in a basic way without violating any epistemic duties. Now it is characteristic of externalist epistemologies such as Plantinga's to hold that warrant can be affected by circumstances to which the subject has no access and which cannot, therefore, have any bearing on what epistemic duties one has.[19] The question whether such beliefs have warrant is therefore quite a different question than whether holding them violates epistemic duty.

What, then, must we determine in order to see whether these beliefs possess warrant? The answer is that we need to determine whether the belief-forming processes involved — processes that lead to the formation of religious beliefs grounded in religious experience — are reliable producers of true rather than false beliefs. This is so, I maintain, whether we consider Plantinga's original version of proper functionalism or the reliabilist version adumbrated in the last section.

Perhaps this is surprising. One might be inclined to think that, with

18. See the following articles by Plantinga: "Is Belief in God Rational?" in *Rationality and Religious Belief,* ed. C. F. Delaney (Notre Dame: University of Notre Dame Press, 1979), pp. 7-27; "The Reformed Objection to Natural Theology," *Christian Scholar's Review* 11 (1982): 187-98; "Reason and Belief in God," in *Faith and Rationality: Reason and Belief in God,* ed. Alvin Plantinga and Nicholas Wolterstorff (Notre Dame: University of Notre Dame Press, 1983), pp. 16-93; and "The Foundations of Theism: A Reply," *Faith and Philosophy* 3 (1986): 209-313.

19. The bird-watcher cited in note 7 is a good example of this.

Plantinga's original version of the theory, what we need to determine is whether or not the processes in question are in accord with the subject's design plan. Note, however, that function according to design plan is not in itself sufficient to confer warrant; for that the process must also be reliable, as Plantinga now admits.[20] Now it may be in some sense conceptually possible that religious experience should in fact reliably yield true religious beliefs and yet this not be intended by God, so that the beliefs in question would be contrary to the design plan and would be unwarranted. This may, I say, be conceptually possible — but I see no reason whatever to suppose that it is true, and I suspect that no one is likely actually to hold such a position. So for practical purposes, the question that needs to be answered is one of reliability.

Now determining the reliability of such a process depends on our assessment of the truth of particular beliefs formed by the process. But of course, truth or falsity in the cases we are considering can't just be read off from empirical observations, as it might be if we were verifying weather forecasts. So what we must ask is whether it is *reasonable to believe* that such processes are reliable. Furthermore, one's answer to this will itself depend importantly on one's worldview. An atheist or naturalist, disbelieving in the existence of any supernatural entities, will immediately conclude that processes yielding such beliefs are unreliable. The religious believer, on the other hand, is able to be more open on this question, not prejudging it one way or the other.

With these clarifications in hand, we are now ready to formulate our revised question as follows: Is it reasonable for a religious believer to hold that the practice of forming religious beliefs grounded upon religious experience reliably produces true beliefs? One might think the answer to this should be Yes; certainly Plantinga would like to arrive at such an answer as a consequence of his theory. In fact, however, there are serious difficulties standing in the way of an affirmative answer. Probably the most serious of these difficulties is found in the well-known *inconsistencies* between religious beliefs that claim such experiential grounding.[21] As William Wainwright points out, "If visions of celestial Buddhas are veridical, visions of

20. See the relevant chapters in Plantinga's *Warrant and Proper Function.*

21. Other difficulties are found in *(a)* the existence within religious traditions of many warnings concerning the dangers of delusive and misleading experiences, and *(b)* the global critiques of religious experience generated by such thinkers as Marx, Nietzsche, and Freud. For reasons I won't go into here, I do not think either of these challenges is as significant as the one noted in the text.

Krishna or Jesus probably aren't."[22] And this is but the beginning of a list of the types of diverse religious objects people claim to have experienced. There is also, of course, the deep-lying conflict between personalistic and theistic experiences, on the one hand, and impersonal, monistic experiences, on the other. The religious believer, desiring to affirm religious experience as a reliable source of truth, is confronted by a bewildering array of different religious traditions, and along with these traditions a corresponding diversity of religious belief-forming processes endorsed by one or another of them. Without doubt, these conflicting claims furnish at least a prima facie defeater of the claims of reliability.

Our result to this point, then, is as follows: The religious believer is rational in affirming that experientially grounded religious beliefs are warranted if and only if she is rational in affirming a *reliability thesis* to the effect that the processes generating such beliefs are epistemologically reliable. What form might such a reliability thesis take, given the "conflicting claims" problem noted above? I shall discuss three possible versions of a reliability thesis, and then briefly suggest a fourth possibility.

Our first candidate is the *thesis of general reliability*. According to this thesis, religious experience generally *is* reliable in its production of true beliefs about the religious object(s), in spite of the great disparities in the content of these beliefs. Clearly, strong measures are required if this thesis is to avoid immediate defeat by the conflicting claims problem. One way in which this can be done is exhibited in the recent writings of John Hick.[23] According to Hick, Ultimate Reality cannot be described in any literal, straightforward way in human conceptual systems; however, the divine beings of various religions — the Heavenly Father, Buddha, Vishnu, Jesus, Brahman, and so on — are all differing *personae* (or *impersonae*) through which humans grasp the divine. The doctrines and theologies of the various religions, then, are not literally true, but such a doctrine is "mythologically true" to the extent that it "tends to invoke in its hearers a dispositional response which is appropriate to" the Real,[24] resulting in spiritual transformation.

22. William J. Wainwright, *Philosophy of Religion* (Belmont, CA: Wadsworth, 1988), p. 125.

23. See Hick's *God Has Many Names* (Philadelphia: Westminster Press, 1982); *Problems of Religious Pluralism* (London: Macmillan, 1985); and *An Interpretation of Religion* (London: Macmillan, 1989).

24. John Hick, "Response to Mesle," in C. Robert Mesle, *John Hick's Theodicy: A Process Humanist Critique* (New York: St. Martin's Press, 1991), p. 116.

Clearly, a great deal needs to be said in order to come to terms properly with Hick's proposal. In the present context, however, it is not unfair to remark that Hick has simply changed the subject. "Mythological truth" is not truth *simpliciter*, and epistemic processes that produce mythological truth are not thereby rendered reliable; at most, they may be "mythologically reliable." There is, furthermore, the obvious point that Hick's proposal is in sharp conflict with the actual beliefs of the vast majority of religious persons, who hold their own beliefs to be true in some sense that precludes conflicting beliefs from being equally true. Hick, of course, can simply say that these believers are mistaken. But there is a deep irony in this: A project that began with the generous desire to avoid passing a judgment of error on the beliefs held by vast numbers of sincere religious persons ends up by doing exactly that, excepting only the relatively small number of sophisticated believers who will accept as their own Hick's kind of account of the status of their beliefs.

As an alternative to Hick's view, consider the *thesis of tradition-specific reliability*. Here the believer affirms the reliability of the belief-forming processes sanctioned by her own religious tradition. She need not condemn all experiences and beliefs outside her tradition, though she will certainly regard other beliefs as erroneous when they conflict with those of her own tradition. In this way, the conflicting claims problem is obviated. And it is entirely possible that the believer may be rational in maintaining this thesis — provided, that is, that her belief in the truth of the central tenets of her tradition is itself rational.

But there is a price to be paid for this success: it greatly reduces the epistemological significance and value of religious experience. In general, it can no longer be maintained that religious experience is the epistemic ground of the beliefs in question, since the beliefs are presupposed in selecting the experiences. Perhaps one might hold that the experience *confirms* the beliefs, but even this is questionable, because disconfirming experiences are automatically rejected as nonveridical. There is, furthermore, the problem that in order for this thesis to be rationally affirmed the believer must already possess, prior to and independent of the experiences, sufficient rational grounds for holding the beliefs of her tradition to be correct. There is no space here to consider what such grounds might be and what are the prospects of such a project. Clearly, however, those who had hoped to give religious experience itself a prominent place among the grounds of belief will find this approach disappointing.

For our third candidate, consider the *thesis of selective reliability*. In this thesis the believer does not maintain, in the face of conflicting truth claims, that all (or almost all) of the processes in question are reliable. But neither does she simply impose her own tradition as an external selection criterion. Rather, she attempts to decide between conflicting truth claims on the basis of criteria that are in some sense *internal* to the experiences which ground them. For example, theists sometimes argue that theistic interpretations of religious experience are to be preferred to monistic interpretations, on the ground that a personal God can very well be experienced impersonally on some occasions, whereas an impersonal deity cannot veridically be experienced as a Person. They may also argue that the "unitive experiences" which are characteristic of mysticism can reasonably be interpreted in ways that fall short of claiming an identity between the experiencer and God, and that such interpretations are sometimes given even within monistic traditions.[25]

The thesis of selective reliability seems to me to point to lines of research that it is important to pursue. Success along these lines will not be easy, however. The adherents of monistic traditions won't simply yield the point; rather, they will be ready with arguments for the preferability of their own interpretations. Now of course the believer in either tradition need not convince her opponents in order to be rational in her own beliefs. It is necessary, however, that her conclusion in favor of her own tradition be founded on an honest and well-informed encounter with the opposing views, rather than on ignorance, bias, or special pleading. But if success even at this modest level is a condition for rational belief, then the class of rational believers is going to be very small indeed.

On the whole, the results of our survey to this point may seem disappointing. Hick's proposal resolves the problem for those who accept his "mythological" interpretation of religious belief, but it is irrelevant for everyone else. Tradition-specific reliability eliminates conflicting claims, but it also reduces the epistemological significance of religious experience to a degree that many will find implausible. Selective reliability suggests promising lines for research, but success along

25. A good example of this sort of strategy is found in Carolyn Franks Davis, *The Evidential Force of Religious Experience* (Oxford: Oxford University Press, 1989), chap. 7: "The Conflicting Claims Challenge."

those lines is likely to prove difficult. And if success in this enterprise is a condition for rational belief, then the status of a rational believer is one to which few will attain.

At this point I wish to suggest, but not to explore at all fully, another possibility. We've been assuming that, in order to be rational in her belief, our believer must have successfully confronted the conflicting claims problem. But is this really so? Why may she not simply believe, on the basis of her own experience, that things are as they seem experientially to her to be? Consider the parallel case for ordinary perception. You recently saw, not far from your Indiana home, a bird you clearly identified as a golden eagle. You find, however, that no one else in the neighborhood reports seeing an eagle; several others, however, have seen a bird whose description generally resembles your sighting, but which they identified as an osprey. Now it's clear that you aren't entitled to dismiss their reports out of hand; indeed, if anything important hangs on it, you probably have to be willing to investigate the conflicting claims in order to see which is more likely to be correct. But are you lacking in rationality if you continue to believe, pending such an investigation, that you did indeed see a golden eagle? I think not; I think you are perfectly entitled to continue in your original belief, unless and until you find convincing reason to abandon it. But this may seem puzzling. For some of your neighbors may be as skilled in bird identification as you are; shouldn't you, then, regard the matter as indeterminate until the conflict has been resolved? I suggest that you aren't obliged to regard it as indeterminate; I think you are perfectly rational to go on believing you saw a golden eagle, simply because *you are the one who had the experience of seeing a golden eagle.* If this is so, then the "first-person perspective" may play a crucial role in determining what it is reasonable for you to believe. And perhaps something like this is true also in the religious case.[26] But the development of that thought must await another paper; this one must come to an end.[27]

---

26. It's very possible that at this point we have once again come round to the question of whether experientially grounded religious beliefs can be properly basic. But this should be interpreted in terms of *rationality*, not in terms of deontological justification.

27. My thanks for comments on earlier versions of this material to Alvin Plantinga, Philip Quinn, Richard Foley, William Alston, James Taylor, Tom Senor, and the editors of this book.

In Defense of Gaunilo's Defense of the Fool

Nicholas Wolterstorff

I propose saying a good word on behalf of Gaunilo. He has not fared well at the hands of history. While not himself a first-rate thinker — that is clear from the brief text of his which has been preserved — he undertook to debate one of the genius theologian-philosophers of the Western tradition, namely, Anselm. Yet sometimes second- and third-rate thinkers make good points against first-rate thinkers. I shall argue that Gaunilo made some telling points against Anselm — though not, I readily agree, in a first-rate way. Anselm realized the 'tellingness' of these points, so I shall also argue. The sign of his realization, however, is not concession; Anselm does not concede. The sign is rather bluster. Not even the saints are sinless! Anselm's glittering genius has made many reluctant to concede that Gaunilo made any telling points against him; his saintly reputation makes us all reluctant to concede that he concealed when he should have conceded.[1]

Suspicion first arises when, in the course of reading *the whole* of Gaunilo's defense of the fool and *the whole* of Anselm's reply, we look to see why Anselm thinks Gaunilo's argument for the existence in reality of an island, such that none more excellent can be conceived, is not a good analogue to his own argument for the existence of that than which nothing greater can be conceived. It's absurd to suppose that one could in this way establish the existence of such an island. By offering this

---

1. A few assessments concerning the relative strength of the arguments of Anselm and Gaunilo are cited in Jasper Hopkins, "Anselm's Debate with Gaunilo," in Hopkins, *Anselm of Canterbury*, vol. 4 (Toronto and New York: Mellen Press, 1976).

absurd analogue, Gaunilo meant to show that something had gone wrong in Anselm's original argument. To defend himself, Anselm has to point out why the finest conceivable island argument is not a good analogue. He does nothing of the sort. Instead he blusters: "With confidence I reply: if besides that than which a greater can be thought anyone finds for me |anything else| (whether existing in reality or only in thought) to which he can apply the logic of my argument, then I will find and will make him a present of that lost island — no longer to be lost" (*A* 3; 285).[2]

The only additional reference Anselm makes to Gaunilo's analogue occurs a few pages later when he says, with equal sarcasm: "Do you see, then, the respect in which you did rightly compare me with that fool who wanted to assert the existence of Lost Island from the mere fact that its description was understood?" (*A* 5; 293). This remark reads as if it were the conclusion to a passage in which Anselm points out the disanalogy. In fact it is not that.

The passage opens with Anselm claiming that on a crucial point Gaunilo has misunderstood him. Gaunilo, so Anselm says, has interpreted him as working with the formula "that which is greater than all others" *(quod est maius omnibus)*; in fact, says Anselm, he used the formula "that than which nothing greater can be conceived" *(aliquid quo nihil maius cogitari potest)*. The argument does not work if we use the former formula, only if we use the latter. Perhaps Anselm is correct in this charge. But before we conclude that he is, it is worth noting that in Section 1 of his response, Gaunilo, before he used the formula "greater than all others," had used a variant on Anselm's own formula, namely, "some such nature than which nothing greater can be thought." In assessing the significance of his move from this formula to the other, it is relevant to note that at

2. Throughout, I shall be using the translation by Jasper Hopkins, *A New, Interpretive Translation of St. Anselm's Monologion and Proslogion* (Minneapolis: Arthur J. Banning Press, 1986). I do so with some hesitation, since the translation is very interpretive indeed. But all translations are interpretive; and Hopkins has certainly thought through the issues with care. (See, for example, his very combative introduction.) Further, I have no objection to raise against his translation of any of the passages that I cite. References to this translation will be given parenthetically in the text. I shall use "*G*" as an abbreviation for the title of Gaunilo's text, "On Behalf of the Fool," and "*A*" as an abbreviation for the title of Anselm's text, "Reply to Gaunilo." Vertical slash marks within the quotations indicate places where Hopkins added words or phrases to clarify the literal text.

the beginning and end of Section 4 of his response, Gaunilo uses the formula "that which is greater than all others that can be thought" *(illud maius omnibus quae cogitari possunt)*. This suggests that Gaunilo may have intended the formula "greater than all others" *(maius omnibus)* as short for "greater than all others that can be thought" *(maius omnibus quae cogitari possunt)*, rather than as Anselm interpreted it, namely, as short for "greater than all others that are" *(maius omnibus quae sunt)*. But if Gaunilo was not confused about the formula Anselm was using, then at least it seems that he did not fully appreciate the precise role of the formula in the argument; if he had, it seems unlikely that he would have used an abbreviated formula which is so easily interpreted in such a way as to be useless for the argument (as it is for his own analogue). So although Anselm may not successfully have *identified* a deficiency in Gaunilo's understanding, he has at least, we may say, *located* a deficiency.[3]

After observing that he had worked with the formula "that than which nothing greater can be conceived," rather than with the formula "that than which nothing is greater," and that this difference makes all the difference for his argument, Anselm observes that, since that than which nothing greater can be conceived will of course be greater than anything else, by demonstrating the existence of an entity of the former sort one will have demonstrated the existence of an entity of the latter sort. The passage then closes with the sharp ironic words quoted above: "Do you see, then, the respect in which you did rightly compare me with that fool who wanted to assert the existence of Lost Island from the mere fact that its description was understood?" But *why* he cannot rightly be compared to such a fool, Anselm has not said and does not say.

Why would Anselm not have pointed out the disanalogy between his argument for God's existence and Gaunilo's for the existence of a lost island? I can think of just two reasons. One is that the lost island argument is so obviously not a good analogue that it would humiliate Gaunilo and insult the reader to point out the disanalogy; better to let readers discern it for themselves and allow Gaunilo to retain some dignity. The other reason is that Anselm realized that there was no relevant disanalogy to point out.

Most of Anselm's readers down through the centuries have assumed that it was the former of these possible reasons which was the actual

3. In the points made in this paragraph I am following closely J. Hopkins in "Anselm's Debate with Gaunilo."

one; and very many of those of us who are teachers have undertaken to do for our students what Anselm did not do for Gaunilo: We have undertaken to lay out the disanalogy that Anselm had in mind — or what we presume to be the disanalogy that we presume Anselm had in mind. (In the past I have done so as well.) Of course in doing so we presuppose that the disanalogy is not obvious — or that our students are fools indeed!

A successful defense of this line of interpretation will have to overcome two considerations that make it a priori implausible. For one thing, why the bluster? Why the sarcasm? If charity to the befuddled Gaunilo inspired Anselm's silence concerning the point of disanalogy, what inspired his sharp bluster? Anselm remarks that "It is easy even for someone of very little intelligence to detect what is wrong with the other objections which you raise against me on behalf of the Fool; and so, I thought I ought to forego showing this" (*A* 5; 289). But Anselm makes this sharp comment *after* his first reference to the analogue and *before* the second, in neither of which, as we have seen, does he pinpoint the disanalogy. Furthermore, he continues the comment as follows: "But because I hear that they do seem to some readers to avail somewhat against me, I will deal with them briefly."

Thus — and this is the second consideration — Anselm does not refrain from pointing out Gaunilo's errors, be they obvious or not. If one comes straight from the cryptic crispness of chapters 2 and 3 of the *Proslogion* to the paragraph in Anselm's response to Gaunilo in which he blusters, "I will find and will make him a present of that lost island — no longer to be lost," one might with some plausibility regard this as another example of Anselm's cryptic elegance. In fact his response to Gaunilo is as prolix and repetitious as the *Proslogion* is economical and elegant. But if Anselm belabors Gaunilo's errors and presumed errors, why does he leave this error unanalyzed? It makes one suspicious.

Then, too, there is something suspicious about Anselm's opening declaration that he will answer Gaunilo as a Catholic rather than as a fool, a declaration that has its payoff just a bit later when Anselm says: "But I make use of your faith and conscience as a very cogent consideration |in support of| how false these |inferences| are" (*A* 1; 279). "[I]f that than which a greater cannot be thought is not understood or thought and is not in the understanding or in thought, then, surely, either (1) God is not that than which a greater cannot be thought or (2) He is not understood or thought and is not in the understanding or in thought." Of course Gaunilo is not one of the Psalmist's 'fools'; he is a believer. So it would not be appropriate to answer him as a fool. But why answer him as a Catholic, calling on his faith and conscience? Why not answer him as a rational person, calling on his capacity to grasp the self-evident?

Most readers of Anselm do not have these suspicions, whether because they do not read enough of Anselm's text, or because they are bewitched by his towering reputation, or whatever; or, having them, they stifle them. I, having them, propose not stifling them, to see where they lead.

Gaunilo's Interpretation of the Argument

Gaunilo did more than offer an analogue to Anselm's argument whose absurdity was meant to persuade us that something had gone wrong in the original argument. He tried to put his finger on what had gone wrong. Let us begin, then, by looking at how he construed the argument. I have already conceded that Gaunilo probably did not fully see why the argument would not work with the formula "that than which nothing is greater," why it required the formula "that than which nothing greater can be conceived." Gaunilo's apparent lack of perceptiveness on this point is one of the things that lead me to conclude that he was not a first-rate philosopher. But the error does not really make any difference to Gaunilo's main points. So in my statement of his construal of the argument I shall correct for this error.

There is another point on which, so it appears to me, Gaunilo's interpretation is in error, though Anselm does not challenge him on it and though it, too, makes no difference to the Gaunilo/Anselm dialectic. Gaunilo attributes to Anselm the general principle that anything which exists in reality is greater than anything which exists only in the understanding. So far as I can tell, Anselm never appeals to this general thesis — though, for all I know, he accepted it. (If he did, that would account for his silence on the matter.) What he says is just that, since one can think of that than which nothing greater can be conceived as existing in reality, then, if it did exist only in the understanding, in thinking of *it* as existing in reality one would be thinking of *it* as greater than it is. Here, too, in my discussion I will correct for what seems to me an erroneous interpretation on Gaunilo's part.

Gaunilo, I suggest, construed Anselm's argument as the following:

(1) The Psalmist's 'fool' understands the words "that than which nothing greater can be conceived."

(2) If he understands the words "that than which nothing greater can be conceived," then he understands that than which nothing greater can be conceived.

(3) If he understands that than which nothing greater can be conceived, then at least in the understanding there exists that than which nothing greater can be conceived.

(4) It is impossible that that which exists in the understanding, namely, that than which nothing greater can be conceived, should exist in the understanding alone and not also in reality.

(5) Therefore there exists in reality that than which nothing greater can be conceived.

(6) This being cannot even be conceived not to exist.

Did Anselm accept this construal of his argument? He should have — and he did. That Anselm held claims (1) through (3) is clear from chapter 2 of *Proslogion:* When the "Fool hears my words 'something than which nothing greater can be thought,' he understands what he hears. And what he understands is in his understanding. . . . So even the Fool is convinced that something than which nothing greater can be thought is at least in his understanding; for when he hears of this |being|, he understands |what he hears|, and whatever is understood is in the understanding" (*Proslogion* 2; 226-27). In his reply to Gaunilo Anselm reaffirms these points:

And so, in the argument which you criticize I said that when the Fool hears the utterance "that than which a greater cannot be thought," he understands what he hears. (Surely, if it is spoken in a language one knows, then one who does not understand |what he hears| has little or no intelligence |*intellectus*|.) Next, I said that if it is understood, |what is understood| is in the understanding. (Or would what |I claim| to have been necessarily inferred to exist in reality not at all be in the understanding?) (*A* 2; 283)

As to the affirmation of (4) and the move from (4) to (5), there can be no doubt that in the second chapter of *Proslogion* Anselm has also affirmed this and made this inference; in his reply he so repetitively reaffirms it and so repetitively makes the inference again as to become tiresome: "what follows more logically than |this conclusion, viz.|: if that than which a greater *cannot* be thought were only in the understanding, it would be that than which a greater *can* be thought? But, surely, that than which a greater cannot be thought is in no respect that than which a greater can be thought" (*A* 2; 285). We may take the following from Anselm's response as a crisp summary of points (2) through (5): "that than which a greater cannot be is understood and is in the understanding and hence is affirmed to exist in reality" (*A* 5; 293). It is just as clear that in the third chapter of *Proslogion* Anselm affirmed (6). In his reply to Gaunilo he does so again: "anyone who thinks of this |viz., what cannot even be thought not to exist| does not think that it does not exist. Otherwise, he would be thinking what cannot be thought. Therefore, it is not the case that that than which a greater cannot be thought can be thought not to exist" (*A* 3; 287).

One can easily think of analogues of (1) through (3). Here is one: I understand the words "the golden mountain." If I understand those words, then I understand the golden mountain. And if I understand the golden mountain, then in my understanding, at least, there is a golden mountain. Gaunilo's ingenious move was to offer an example that appears to be an analogue, not only of steps (1) to (3), but of (4) and (5) as well: I understand the words "the finest conceivable island." If I understand those words, then I understand the finest conceivable island. And if I understand the finest conceivable island, then there must be the finest conceivable island, at least in my understanding. Now suppose that this finest conceivable island, which I understand, existed only in my understanding. I can conceive of it existing in reality; if it did so, it would then be greater. But that which I understand and which exists in my understanding is the finest conceivable island. So this finest conceivable island, which exists in my understanding, must also exist in reality.

A Point of Terminology

Let us begin with a crucial terminological point that Gaunilo raises. A condition of understanding something is that what is understood exists in reality; from 'S understands x' it follows that 'x exists in reality.' Correspondingly, then, it is proper to *speak* of understanding so-and-so only if one believes that so-and-so exists in reality. If one does not believe that Pegasus exists, then it would be inappropriate to speak of oneself or anyone else as understanding Pegasus. However, it would not necessarily be inappropriate, when in that circumstance, to speak of someone as *thinking of* or *conceiving of (cogitare)* Pegasus. In Gaunilo's words: "in accordance with the proper meaning of this verb |viz., 'to understand'|, false things |i.e., unreal things| cannot be understood *(nequeunt intelligi);* but surely, they can be thought *(cogitari)* — in the way in which the Fool thought that God does not exist" (*G* 7; 275). Perhaps the best way of translating *"intelligere"* in contemporary English, so as to reflect Gaunilo's point, is with the word *know.* One cannot know Pegasus, since Pegasus does not exist; one can, though, conceive of, or think of, Pegasus.

Anselm concedes Gaunilo's terminological point while at the same time giving the impression of believing that nothing of importance hangs on it. Without expressing any disagreement he says, speaking of Gaunilo: You "say that false |i.e., unreal| things cannot be 'understood,' in the proper sense of the word" (*A* 4; 287). And just a bit later, making a different though related point, he says: "even if no existing things could be *understood* not to exist, still they could all be *thought* not to exist — with the exception of that which exists supremely" (*A* 4; 287). It is not to the distinction itself, but to the points Gaunilo makes by using the *intelligere/cogitare* distinction, that Anselm raises his objections. So let us turn to those.

Gaunilo Objects to the End of the Argument

Gaunilo uses his terminological point to object to line (6) of the argument. "But when one says that this Supreme Being *cannot be thought* not to exist, he might better say that it *cannot be understood (nequeat cogitari)* not to exist or even to be able not to exist" (*G* 7; 275). The general principle to which Gaunilo is alluding here can be expressed as follows: Where 'N' is any nominative expression you please, the predicate "understands N to be so-and-so" can be truthfully affirmed of someone only if N is so-and-so, whereas it is possible for the predicate "conceives N to be so-and-so" to be truthfully affirmed of someone even if N is not so-and-so. Specifically then, though the predicate "understands (knows) God not to exist" cannot be truthfully affirmed of anyone, since God does exist, there may well be persons of whom one can truthfully affirm the predicate "thinks of God as not existing." Accordingly, the thing to say, when we arrive at line (6) of the argument, is not that one cannot think of, but that one cannot *understand,* God as not existing. That God exists, and even that God "cannot fail to exist" (*G* 7; 275), can be known; but God cannot be known (understood) to not exist, nor even to possibly not exist *(non esse aut etiam posse non esse),* since God does exist, and necessarily so. Anselm sees clearly what Gaunilo is objecting to in this part of his argument, and he states the objection himself as follows: "As for your claim that when we say that this Supreme Thing *cannot be thought* not to exist we would perhaps do better to say that it *cannot be understood* not to exist or even to be able not to exist . . ." (*A* 4; 287).

However, says Gaunilo, it may be that there is an important limitation on the scope of our ability to conceive of what does not exist and of what is not the case; perhaps we can conceive of what does not exist or is not the case only if we do not *know* that it exists or is the case. For example, perhaps we can conceive of the nonexistence of God only if we do not *know* that God exists. "I do not know whether, during the time when I know most certainly that I exist, I can think that I do not exist" (*G* 7; 275). If our ability to think and conceive is in fact thus limited, then the person who knows that the being than which nothing greater can be conceived exists in reality will indeed find himself or herself unable to conceive or think of God as not existing (conceive or think of the nonexistence of God). But then, says Gaunilo, it must be observed that, contrary to Anselm's claim in *Proslogion* 3 that anything that there is except God can be conceived not to exist, everybody will find the nonexistence of many things inconceivable — specifically, the nonexistence of anything that the person knows exists. Says Gaunilo: "if I cannot |think that I do not exist|, then this |property of not being able to be thought not to exist| will no longer be a unique characteristic of God" (*G* 7; 275). Depending, then, on whether Anselm does or does not accept the suggested limitation on our ability to conceive the nonexistent, he must either concede that God's nonexistence is not unique in its inconceivability, or that we can conceive of God's nonexistence. Anselm cannot have it both ways. What is undoubtedly true, though, is that we cannot *understand* that God does not exist.

In reply to this objection Anselm remarks that it is indeed true that God cannot be known (understood) as not existing: "nothing which exists can be understood not to exist. For it is false that what exists does not exist . . ." (*A* 4; 287). But if this is what he, Anselm, had said, he would have laid himself open to exactly the same objection concerning understanding that Gaunilo cites for conceiving (if the scope of that is limited in the way Gaunilo suggested) — the objection, namely, that in the unknowability of God's nonexistence there is nothing unique. "It would not be a unique characteristic of God not to be able to be understood not to exist" (*A* 4; 287). So the right thing to say is not that the Supreme Being cannot be known not to exist, true though that is; the right thing to say is rather what *was* said, namely, that the Supreme Being cannot be *thought* or *conceived* not to exist — in other words, that its nonexistence cannot be *conceived.* "For if it could be thought not to exist, it could be thought to have a beginning and an end. But this |consequence| is impossible" (*A* 3; 287).

Gaunilo would find this last argument unimpressive. Whether or not the suggested limitation on the scope of conceiving holds, the fool can conceive of God as beginning and ending as well as not existing. And as for us who know that God exists and is everlasting, we too can do so, if the suggested limitation on the scope of conceiving does not hold. (The different point may also be noted that there is nothing contradictory in the concept of a being which has among its essential properties *lacking a beginning* and *lacking an end,* but which yet exists contingently.)

Anselm goes on, however, to reject the limitation on the scope of our power of conceiving that Gaunilo suggested and to propose another in its place. Probably Gaunilo's inclination to accept the suggested limitation on the scope of our power of conceiving was due to confusion on his part, says Anselm. Concerning something that one knows to exist, one cannot conceive *that it does and does not exist;* "we cannot think |it| to exist and at the same time think |it| not to exist" (*A* 4; 289). However, that is a different point from whether we can think of something as not existing while knowing that it exists. But if one confuses the second phenomenon with the first, then one will be led to deny that "many things which we know to exist we think not to exist, and many things which we know not to exist |we think| to exist" (*A* 4; 289). The truth of the matter, so Anselm suggests, is that we can conceive the nonexistence of anything which exists *except for that* which exists "most truly of all and thus most greatly of all" (*Proslogion* 3; 227). All existing things can be conceived not to exist, "with the exception of that which exists supremely. Indeed, all and only things which have a beginning or an end or are composed of parts — and whatever (as I have already said) at any place or time does not exist as a whole — can be thought not to exist. But only that in which thought does not at all find a beginning or an end or a combination of parts, and only that which thought finds existing only as a whole always and everywhere, cannot be thought not to exist" (*A* 4; 287).

How shall we assess the outcome of the attack and defense concerning line (6) of the argument? Gaunilo thinks that we can conceive of anything whatsoever as not existing, or perhaps instead, of anything whatsoever of whose existence we do not know. Either way, so he claims, Anselm is not entitled to say, at the end of the argument, that that than which nothing greater can be conceived is unique in that it alone among existing things cannot be thought (conceived) not to exist. Anselm replies that we can conceive of anything whatsoever as not existing except for that which exists in the highest degree (possible); its nonexistence is uniquely inconceivable. One's estimate of the cogency of the ending of Anselm's argument will depend on one's estimate of the principle concerning the scope of conceiving that he proposes in place of Gaunilo's principle — the principle, namely, that one cannot conceive of the nonexistence of that which exists most truly (and which is, on that account, eternal, simple, and always and everywhere a whole). But since the matters are difficult and complex, and since Gaunilo has more interesting and decisive things to say about other parts of the argument, I propose moving on and not trying to determine whether Gaunilo was correct in this part of his attack.[4]

What is surprising for us in our century is that Anselm did not adopt a different defense — or rather, that he did not phrase this part of his argument differently in the first place. Why did he not speak of its being *impossible* that God not exist rather than of its being *inconceivable* that God not exist? Of the *necessity* of God's existence rather

4. A full consideration of the matter would have to take into account what Anselm says about God's uniqueness in *Proslogion* 13 and 20.

than of the *inconceivability* of God's nonexistence? Rather than claiming in *Proslogion* 3 that "there can be thought to exist something which cannot be thought not to exist; and this thing is greater than that which can be thought not to exist" (227), why did Anselm not instead claim that it is possible to think of a being which exists necessarily; and this is greater than one which does not exist necessarily? Why allow oneself to get into these indecisive arguments about the scope of our power of conceiving? It is often said or assumed nowadays that by "inconceivable" Anselm just meant *impossible*. Not only does the drift of the argument above make that implausible; there are passages in which Anselm clearly distinguishes inconceivability from impossibility: "it is evident that |that than which a greater cannot be thought| neither (1) fails to exist nor (2) is able not to exist nor (3) is able to be thought not to exist" (*A* 5; 291). Moreover, he himself on at least two occasions states the argument in terms of impossibility rather than inconceivability:

> [I]f indeed it can be even thought, it is necessary that it exist. For no one who doubts or denies that there exists something than which a greater cannot be thought doubts or denies that if it were to exist it would neither actually nor conceivably *(nec actu nec intellectu)* be able not to exist. For otherwise |i.e., if it existed but in either respect were able not to exist| it would not be that than which a greater cannot be thought. (*A* 1; 281)

> But it is evident that, likewise, "that which is not able not to exist" can be thought and understood. Now, someone who thinks this thinks of something greater than does someone who thinks of that which is able not to exist. (*A* 9; 299)

Why did Anselm not evade Gaunilo's criticism by preferring *this* argument? I do not know. Perhaps because he was in pursuit of God's uniqueness; and in existing necessarily, God is not unique.

Gaunilo Objects to the Beginning of the Argument, with a Dilemma

Gaunilo also uses his *intelligere/cogitare* distinction to raise an objection to the beginning of the argument. The objection can be put in the form of a dilemma: When Anselm says that "this thing is . . . in my understanding simply because I understand what is said" (*G* 2; 265), he may be using the clause "this thing is in my understanding" as a mere synonym of the clause "I understand what is said" — with consequences to be mentioned shortly. Alternatively, using the word "understanding" in its proper sense (i.e., the sense discussed above), he may be expressing two different propositions with these clauses, and claiming that the proposition expressed by the one is entailed by that expressed by the other. The consequences of this interpretation will also be noted shortly.

Let me pause for a moment to note that what I have interpreted as Gaunilo's posing of a dilemma to Anselm — if you understand *"intelligere"* this way, then this follows, if that way, then that follows — Anselm understands as Gaunilo contradicting himself. On most points, Anselm seems to me an extremely accurate interpreter of Gaunilo; not on this. Here is what Anselm says: "How, I ask, are |these two statements| consistent? — viz., (1) that false things are understood and (2) that to understand is to comprehend, with cognitive certainty, that a thing exists" (*A* 6; 293). But Gaunilo's whole point has been to pose to Anselm a choice between two different uses of *"intelligere."*

Back to the dilemma. Suppose Anselm is using *"intelligere"* in such a way that saying that one understands that than which nothing greater can be conceived, and saying that that than which nothing greater can be conceived exists in one's understanding, are simply ways of saying that one understands the meaning of the words "that than which nothing greater can be conceived." Then what is said with these locutions is indeed noncontroversial; but it will scarcely serve for the argument. The argument depends on persuading us that there is a certain entity which even the fool conceives or understands — an entity distinct, of course, from the words; and then going on to argue that that entity exists in reality and not only in the understanding.

Alternatively, suppose Anselm understands *"intelligere"* in its proper sense. Then, from the standpoint of the 'fool,' point (2) of the argument is just a begging of the question. The 'fool' is in the position of not believing that God exists; hence he will not concede that he *understands (knows)* that than which nothing greater can be thought. One can't first get the 'fool' to agree that he understands this being and then observe that it follows that this being exists in reality; one must first get him to agree that this being exists in reality, then perhaps one can get him to agree that he understands it.

We may assume, however, that the fool would concede that we can *conceive* or *think* of entities that don't exist and of states of affairs that are not actual. Accordingly, the non-question-begging way to proceed would be to try to establish that the 'fool', because he understands the meaning of the words "that than which nothing greater can be conceived," has a *conception* of that than which nothing greater can be conceived; and that done, to go on to try to establish, somehow, that he could not have this conception without that than which nothing greater can be conceived existing in his mind — and bearing to him the relation of being conceived by him, or even of being understood by him.

Before we consider what Gaunilo has to say about this proposed revision of Anselm's argument, a revision designed to avoid begging the question against the fool, let us note that part of Anselm's response to the point made thus far is to offer a *new* ontological argument, this new one formulated in exactly the style which Gaunilo recommended — namely, in terms of *cogitare* rather than *intelligere*, and making no reference at all to things existing in the understanding. The clue that this is what he is doing comes in Anselm's sentences, "Therefore, it is false |to suppose| that something than which a greater cannot be thought does not exist even though it can be thought. Consequently, |it is| all the more |false to suppose that it does not exist| if it can be understood and can be in the understanding" (*A* 1; 281). (It may be noted, parenthetically, that the ontological argument which Alvin Plantinga formulates and defends in his *God, Freedom and Evil* is a variant on this alternative argument, formulated in terms of conceiving, rather than a variant on the original *Proslogion* argument formulated in terms of understanding.) The basic thrust of the new argument can be gathered from this paragraph:

> [W]ith confidence I assert that if it can be even thought to exist, it is necessary that it exist. For that than which a greater cannot be thought can be thought to exist only without a beginning. Now, whatever can be thought to exist but does not exist can be thought to exist through a beginning. Thus, it is not the case that that than which a greater cannot be thought can be thought to exist and yet does not exist. Therefore, if it can be thought to exist, |there follows|, of necessity, |that| it exists. (*A* 1; 280-81)

Gaunilo's Objection to the Non-Question-Begging Variant on the Argument

Let us return to Gaunilo. Gaunilo has suggested that to avoid begging the question against the fool at the beginning of the argument, Anselm should have used something like the following as steps (2), (3), and (4) in the argument:

> (2*) *If one understands the words "that than which nothing greater can be conceived," then one has a conception of that than which nothing greater can be conceived.*

> (3*) *If one has a conception of that than which nothing greater can be conceived, then at least in one's conception (mind) there exists that than which nothing greater can be conceived.*

> (4*) *It is impossible that that which exists in the fool's mind, namely, that than which nothing greater can be conceived, should exist in the mind alone and not also in reality.*

What does Gaunilo wish to say about this non-question-begging variation on the original argument? He wishes to say two quite different things, one of them, in my judgment, indecisive, the other entirely decisive. Let us begin with the indecisive, quoting at some length what Gaunilo says:

|[I]n this way I| also |can| not |think of| God Himself (whom, surely, for this very reason, I can also think not to exist). For neither am I acquainted with this thing itself nor am I able to make inferences |about it| on the basis of some other similar thing; for even you maintain that it is such that there cannot be anything else similar |to it|. Now, suppose that I were to hear something being said about a man totally a stranger to me — |a man| whom I was not even sure existed. Still, by means of the specific or generic knowledge by which I know what a man is (or what men are), I would be able to think of him as well, by reference to the very thing that a man is. . . . But when I hear someone speaking of God or of something greater than all |others|, I cannot have this thing |in my thought and understanding| in the way that I might have that false thing |i.e.,

that unreal man| in my thought and understanding. For although
I can think of that |nonexistent man| by reference to a true |i.e., a
real| thing known to me, I cannot at all |think of| this |supreme|
thing except only with respect to the word. And with respect only
to a word a true thing can scarcely or not at all be thought of. For,
indeed, when one thinks in this way |i.e., with respect to a mere
word|, he thinks not so much the word itself (i.e., not so much the
sounds of the letters or of the syllables), which assuredly is a true
thing, as he does the signification of the word that is heard. Yet,
|the signification is| not |thought| in the manner of one who knows
what is usually signified by this word — i.e., one who thinks in
accordance with the true thing, even if |it exists| in thought alone.
Rather, |the signification is thought| in the manner of one who
does not know that |which is usually signified by the word| but
who thinks only (1) according to the movement-of-mind that is
brought about by hearing this word and (2) in the fashion of one
trying to represent to himself the signification of the word he has
heard. (But it would be surprising if he could ever |in this manner
discern| the true nature of the thing.) Therefore, it is still evident
that in this way, and not at all in any other way, this thing is in my
understanding when I hear and understand someone who says that
there is something greater than all |others| that can be thought.
(G 4; 270-71)

Two distinct lines of thought are interwoven in this passage. The
line on which I shall focus first, the 'indecisive' line, goes as follows:
God cannot be understood by us; neither can we stand to God in the
relation of conceiving God. God is beyond our understanding and
conceiving. But we do in some way understand the words "that than
which nothing greater can be conceived." Accordingly, understanding
those words does not require that one stand to that than which nothing
greater can be conceived in the relation of conceiving of it and understanding it.

What is Anselm's response? Begin with this:

For even if anyone were so foolish as to say that something than
which a greater cannot be thought does not exist, nevertheless he
would not be so shameless as to say that he cannot think or under-
stand what he is saying. Or if some such |impudent person| is found,
not only is his word to be rejected but he himself is to be despised.

> Therefore, with regard to whoever denies the existence of something than which a greater cannot be thought: surely, he thinks and understands the denial he is making. And he cannot think or understand this denial without |thinking or understanding| its parts — one of which is "that than which a greater cannot be thought." Therefore, whoever denies this |viz., that this being exists| thinks and understands |the signification of| "that than which a greater cannot be thought." (*A* 9; 299)

The point Anselm is making is clear, especially from that last sentence: If we understood the words of some definite description, 'the K which is F', then we have a conception of, and understand, the K which is F. But this is the very principle that Gaunilo is calling into question — calling into question, for one thing, because it compromises the doctrine of God's unintelligibility; so far, Anselm has simply reaffirmed the principle without saying anything to answer Gaunilo's scruples.

But let us look farther. What *we* would be inclined to say here is that one may understand the words "that than which nothing greater can be conceived" without there being that entity and without our standing to it in the relation of conceiving or knowing or understanding it. But this reply is not available to Anselm. For it's clear from the passage just quoted that, on his view, if one understands *the words* "that than which nothing greater can be conceived," then one conceives and understands the *being* or *entity* than which nothing greater can be conceived. So this is what he says in place of what we would have said:

> Yet, even if it were true that that than which a greater cannot be thought could not be thought or understood, nonetheless it would not be false that "that than which a greater cannot be thought" can be thought and understood. Nothing prevents our saying |the word| "unsayable," even though that which is called unsayable cannot be said. Moreover, we can think |the concept| *unthinkable,* even though that which it besuits to be called unthinkable cannot be thought. By the same token, when "that than which nothing greater can be thought" is uttered, without doubt what is heard can be thought and understood, even if that thing than which a greater cannot be thought could not be thought or understood. (*A* 9; 298-99)

By itself, this passage is baffling. Anselm appears to want to have it both ways. He wants to affirm that God is beyond our conceiving and understanding; yet it is crucial to his argument that we not just understand the words "that than which nothing greater is conceivable," but conceive and understand *the being than which nothing greater is conceivable.* Or rather, perhaps he thinks of understanding the words *as* conceiving and understanding the being.

Clearly the solution Anselm had in mind is that, though none of us *fully* conceives and understands the being than which nothing greater can be conceived, even the fool conceives or grasps that being well enough to deny of it that it exists — and hence well enough for the purposes of the argument. This is what he says to Gaunilo:

> Don't you think that that thing about which these |statements| are understood can to some extent be thought and understood, and to some extent can be in thought and in the understanding? For if it cannot |be thought or understood|, then the foregoing |statements| cannot be understood about it. But if you say that what is not fully understood is *not* understood and is *not* in the understanding, then say |as well| that someone who cannot stand to gaze upon the most brilliant light of the sun does not see daylight, which is nothing other than the sun's light. Surely, that than which a greater cannot be thought is understood and is in the understanding at least to the extent that the foregoing |statements| are understood about it. (*A* 1; 283)

(In chapter 8 of his response, Anselm goes about trying to show how we could actually arrive at this conception of God, which, while adequate, is not thorough.)

To the 'fool' Anselm must argue, without any appeal to the faith, that if one understands the words "that than which nothing greater is conceivable," then one stands to the entity than which nothing greater is conceivable in the relation of conceiving of it. To the Catholic, however, he can dispense with his theory as to what goes into understanding words and simply argue that it is an implication of the faith that we have a conception (and understanding) of God. This, then, is the significance of his saying that he will answer Gaunilo as a Catholic rather than as a 'fool':

> But I contend that if that than which a greater cannot be thought is not understood or thought and is not in the understanding or in thought, then, surely, either (1) God is not that than which a greater

cannot be thought or (2) He is not understood or thought and is not in the understanding or in thought. But I make use of your faith and conscience as a very cogent consideration |in support of| how false these |inferences| are. (*A* 1; 279)

Anselm clinches the point later: "But if a Catholic makes this denial, let him remember that 'the invisible things of God (including His eternal power and divinity), being understood through those things that have been made, are clearly seen from the mundane creation'" (*A* 8; 297). In short, the Catholic should accept points (2*) and (3*) in the revised argument even if the inferences from (1) to (2*) and from (2*) to (3*) are not acceptable.

It would appear that Anselm has the better of this part of the interchange. Why should it not be that, though our cognitive grasp of God is woefully inadequate when measured against the reality of God, nonetheless it is good enough for us to be able to say and believe things about God? We do not know what Gaunilo thought about this part of Anselm's response; so far as I can see, a 'Catholic' would have to accept it. But Gaunilo has another line of thought up his sleeve; and this, I think, is decisive. Compared to this new line of thought, everything so far has been preliminary skirmishing.

Gaunilo's Decisive Objection: A New Dilemma

The rather lengthy passage quoted from Gaunilo contains, or at least hints at, a line of thought distinct from the one just canvassed. It can be seen as presenting Anselm with a new dilemma, this one a dilemma pertaining to Gaunilo's proposed variant on Anselm's original argument. The presentation of the dilemma requires distinguishing between two different phenomena called "conceiving" ("thinking"). If one understands some expression — in particular, some definite description — then it might appropriately be said of one that one has *a conception;* if I understand the expression "the earth's moon," then I have a conception of the earth's moon. But we must distinguish two different acts, or states, called "conception." The phenomenon sometimes called "conceiving" consists of having a cognitive grip on that which the words signify — or as we in our century would put it, on that which the words refer to, or stand for, or designate. The phenomenon at other times called "conceiving" consists, rather, says Gaunilo, of *imagining* for ourselves, or *representing* to ourselves, a signification of the words. We might call these two kinds of conceiving, respectively, *R-conceiving* (*R* for reality), and *I-conceiving* (*I* for imagination). R-conceiving will not differ, in any way relevant to our discussion here, from understanding. Let me quote that part of Gaunilo's passage which makes this point most directly:

> For, indeed, when one thinks in this way, |i.e., with respect to a mere word|, he thinks not so much the word itself (i.e., not so much the sound of the letters or of the syllables), which assuredly is a true thing, as he does the signification of the word that is heard. Yet, |the signification is| not |thought| in the manner of [*R-conceiving*, that is, of] one who knows what is usually signified by this word — i.e., one who thinks in accordance with the true thing, even if |it exists| in thought alone. Rather, |the signification is thought| in the manner of |*I-conceiving*, that is, of| one who does not know that |which is usually signified by the word| but who thinks only (1) according to the movement-of-mind that is brought about by hearing this word and (2) in the fashion of one trying to represent to himself the signification of the word he has heard. (*G* 5; 271)

Of course, we who come after Frege would want to say that the relevant distinction is not that between *knowing* the referent of an expression and *imagining* a referent, but that between knowing the *referent* of a word and knowing the *sense* of the word. Though Gaunilo is groping in the right direction, he doesn't have a firm hold on that for which he is groping.

But back to Gaunilo's proposed variant on Anselm's argument, with Gaunilo's distinction in hand between two kinds of conceiving. We may agree that if the fool understands the words "that than which nothing greater can be conceived," then he has a corresponding conception. But what shall we understand this conception as being, a case of R-conceiving or a case of I-conceiving? The tacit assumption of the argument is that it consists of conceiving that which the definite description signifies or refers to — namely, that than which nothing greater can be conceived. In short, the tacit assumption of the argument is that it consists of a case of R-conceiving. But why, says Gaunilo, would the 'fool' grant that that is what he is doing? Why would he not insist that, so far as he knows, all he does when he hears the words and understands them is *imagine* a signification? Why would he not insist that, so far as he knows, it is I-conceiving that he is engaged in? We do, after all, speak of thinking about Pegasus, conceiving of the golden mountain, and so on — 'conceiving of things that don't exist'. Such conceiving is not to be analyzed as consisting of standing in the relation of conceiving to what the expression refers to, since the expression doesn't refer to anything. It consists of hearing and understanding the expression and imagining a referent. Thus the issue of whether the entity to which the expression refers exists only in the mind or also in reality does not even arise — since it is not granted that the expression refers to anything.

I suggest, in short, that Gaunilo's fundamental objection to his non-question-begging variant on Anselm's argument is that the kind of conception which the 'fool' will grant that he has is of no use for the argument, and that the kind of conception which is needed for the argument the 'fool' will not grant that he has. The 'fool' will resist the move from (2*) to (3*).

It might be thought that I am overinterpreting what Gaunilo has to say about conception in the passage quoted — or if not that, basing too much on too little. But Gaunilo makes the same point in other passages. Referring to the passage from *Proslogion* in which Anselm says that a painting first exists in the mind of the artist and then is made by the artist to exist in reality, Gaunilo says this: "before that painting is made it exists in the painter's art. And such a thing in the art of the painter is nothing other than a part of the painter's understanding" (*G* 3; 267). Notice that last phrase: *is nothing other than a part of the painter's understanding.* By contrast, when genuine knowledge or understanding takes place, then "whatever true |i.e., real| thing, when heard of or thought of, is apprehended by the understanding: without doubt that true thing is other than the understanding by which it is apprehended" (*G* 3; 267-68). One can indeed say that understanding the words of some definite description 'the K which is F' requires having a conception of the K which is F; but it's not true that the type of conceiving required consists of performing the mental act of conceiving that entity for which those words stand. Thus it is that Gaunilo says: "I do not concede to it any other existence than that |existence| (if it is to be called existence) present when the mind tries to represent to itself a thing completely unknown, |trying to do so| in accordance with a word which it has merely heard" (*G* 5; 271).

We understand the expression "the golden mountain." So we may be described as having a conception of the golden mountain. Thus it may be said that we have conceptions of things that don't exist. But we must not fall into the trap of supposing that there are those things — that there is a nonexistent golden mountain — and that for one to have a conception of the golden mountain is for there to be a golden mountain and for one to stand to that entity in the relation of conceiving it. "How, then, from the |alleged| fact that it is, patently, greater than all |others| does one prove to me that that |which is| greater |than all others| exists in reality? For I still so doubt and deny it to exist that I claim that this greater |than all others| is not even in my thought and understanding even in the way that numerous doubtfully real and uncertainly real things are" (*G* 5; 271). One may understand the words "the present king of France," and have what is appropriately called *a conception of the present king of France*, without there being the present king of France in any mode of being whatsoever.

My use of this example, along with the example of the golden mountain, is obviously meant to suggest that the fundamental topic of dispute between Gaunilo and Anselm has been a topic of dispute again in our own century, between (among others) Meinong and early Russell on the one hand, and Frege on the other. Meinong is the Anselm of the twentieth century, Frege the Gaunilo. A singular term, said Frege, may have a sense without having a reference; and to understand a singular term is, in general, to understand its sense, not to understand its reference. It is not inappropriate to say, of someone who understands the singular term "the golden mountain," that this person has a conception of the golden mountain. But this is to be understood as consisting in grasping the sense of the expression, not in grasping its reference. It has no reference to be grasped. After citing a singular term that has no reference, Michael Dummett, speaking for Frege, says that

> Such an expression has a sense because we have a criterion, perhaps quite sharp, at any rate at least as sharp as for most names having a genuine reference, for an object's being recognized as the referent of the name: but it lacks a reference, because as a matter of fact there is nothing which would identify any object as the referent of the name; there is no object which satisfies the condition determined by the sense for being its referent. What could be more straightforward?[5]

5. Michael Dummett, *Frege: Philosophy of Language*, 2nd ed. (Cambridge, MA: Harvard University Press, 1981), p. 160.

Of course, Gaunilo does not distinguish between the sense and the reference of expressions in the articulate way that Frege does. And Frege would never have said that the grasping of the sense of an expression is nothing other than a part of the understanding itself; the senses of expressions are, on Frege's view, objective features of language. But then, Anselm's alternative account of linguistic understanding and conception was scarcely less primitive than Gaunilo's; it remained for Meinong to develop an ontology in which, of all the entities that there are, some exist in reality and some do not.

Yet, primitive and unacceptable though Gaunilo's account of linguistic understanding and conception was, it was adequate for his polemical question: Why assume that if one understands the words "that than which nothing greater is conceivable," then *there is* that than which nothing greater can be conceived and one stands to it in the relation of conceiving? Other accounts than this can be given of what goes on when we understand singular terms and have conceptions. One doesn't have to suppose that every genuine term has a referent and that to understand the term is to cognitively grasp the referent.

The Upshot

Anselm saw clearly the point in the argument to which Gaunilo was lodging his objection. Here is one among other indications of that: You say that "something than which a greater cannot be thought is in the understanding in no other way than |as something| which cannot even be thought in accordance with the true nature of anything" (*A* 1; 279). We have already seen part of Anselm's reply: To understand the words "that than which nothing greater can be conceived" is to have a conception of that which these words signify (stand for) — namely, that than which nothing greater can be conceived. The rest of his reply goes as follows:

> [F]rom the fact of its being understood, there does follow that |it|
> is in the understanding. For what is thought is thought by thinking;
> and with regard to what is thought by thinking: even as it is thought,
> so it is in |our| thinking. Similarly, what is understood is understood
> by the understanding; and with regard to what is understood by the
> understanding: even as it is understood, so it is in the understanding.
> What is more obvious than this? (*A* 2; 284-85)

The reply is clear; Anselm reaffirms the very principles under dispute and then adds that they are self-evidently true. But what is the *import*, in the polemic, of the reply? I see no other way of interpreting its import than as follows: Gaunilo has uncovered a weak point in Anselm's onto-logical argument, a *crucial* weak point; and Anselm has nothing to say in his own defense. So he reaffirms his conviction that the principles under dispute are self-evidently true, and leaves it at that. He says nothing at all to support his conviction. Not until the twentieth century would the dispute be substantially advanced beyond where Gaunilo and Anselm left it — Gaunilo questioning Anselm's theory of linguistic comprehension and conception and offering suggestions for an alter-native theory, Anselm claiming that the original theory (itself not much more than suggestions) was self-evidently true. But let us be clear on the structure of the polemic: since it was Anselm who gave the argu-ment, the burden of proof was on him. He did not bear the burden.

Let me summarize Gaunilo's major objection, using mainly his own words: "If that which cannot even be thought in accordance with the true nature of anything must |nonetheless| be said to be in the under-standing, then I do not deny that in this |improper| sense it is in my |understanding|" (*G* 5; 271). That is to say: If all you mean by "having so-and-so in the understanding" is *having a conception of so-and-so*, then even things that could not exist can be in the understanding.

> But since from this |concession| its existence also in reality cannot at all be inferred, I still will not at all concede to it that existence |in reality| until |that existence| is proved to me by an indubitable line of reasoning. Now, anyone who says, "that which is greater than all |others| exists, |for| otherwise it would not be greater than all |others|" does not pay enough attention to whom he is speaking. For I do not yet admit — indeed, I even doubt and deny — that that |which is| greater |than all others| exists at all in reality. I do not concede to it any other existence than that |existence| (if it is to be called existence) present when the mind tries to represent to itself a thing completely unknown, |trying to do so| in accordance with a word which it has merely heard. (*G* 5; 271)

And now, finally, what, given Anselm's assumptions, is wrong with this analogous argument? I understand the meaning of the words "an island than which none greater can be conceived." If someone understands those words, then that person understands (or conceives of) an island than which none greater can be conceived. And if someone understands (or conceives of) an island than which none greater can be conceived, then that island exists in the mind. But if that island existed only in the mind, then one could conceive of it as greater. But that one, the one which exists in the mind, is that island than which none greater can be conceived. Therefore it exists in reality.

I submit that the argument is fully analogous to Anselm's, and that the reason Anselm failed to point out the disanalogy is that he realized there was no disanalogy to point out. Anselm displayed an implication of Meinongianism that he liked; Gaunilo, one that everyone finds embarrassing. Of course, there are variants on Anselm's argument to which the corresponding variant on Gaunilo's lost island argument is not a good analogue. But Gaunilo was not offering an analogue to all possible variations on Anselm's argument; he was offering an analogue to Anselm's argument. The analogue is apt. The absurdity of its conclusion shows that something has gone wrong in Anselm's argument. Gaunilo offered a suggestion as to what that was. Anselm reaffirmed the principles to which Gaunilo took exception and declared them self-evident, having nothing to say in their support. The monk from Marmoutiers deserves better from history than he has received. He saw that Anselm's argument in *Proslogion* 2 depended on taking meaning to be reference; and he saw that meaning is not reference.

As for the other parts of Anselm's treatise, they, said Gaunilo, "are argued so truthfully, so brilliantly, |so| impressively, and, indeed, abound with such great usefulness and with such great fragrance (because of an innermost scent of devout and holy affection) that they are not at all to be despised on account of the things which in the beginning parts are rightly sensed but less cogently argued" (*G* 8; 275).

Natural Theology
and the Reformed Objection

Laura L. Garcia

In an influential paper called "The Reformed Objection to Natural Theology,"[1] Alvin Plantinga spells out several reasons why theologians (and philosophers) in the Reformed tradition are suspicious of the project of natural theology. Natural theology is the attempt to demonstrate certain truths concerning God's existence and nature, operating from premises that are knowable by any rational person independently of divine revelation. Plantinga suggests at least four different reasons for rejecting this project: (1) Philosophical proofs are *not the actual source*, for most believers, of their assent to God's existence and his natural attributes; (2) such proofs are *unnecessary* in order for believers to be rationally justified in their beliefs about God; (3) the project of natural theology cannot succeed (or, less contentiously, has not succeeded to date); (4) philosophical proofs are an *improper source* of religious belief, since they will lead to a faith that is unstable and wavering.

On the other side, among the champions of natural theology, we might expect to find a denial of each of these four claims. But this does not appear to be the case. Instead, as I attempt to show below, one of the most prominent defenders of natural theology, St. Thomas Aquinas, would accept both (1) and (2) without hesitation. As regards (3), it is true that he is more sanguine about the success of the project of natural theology than are the Reformed thinkers cited by Plantinga, but this is because Aquinas believes that project to have already succeeded, even

---

1. Alvin Plantinga, "The Reformed Objection to Natural Theology," *Proceedings of the American Catholic Philosophical Association* 54 (1980): 49-62.

in Aristotle's writings, and because he understands the Epistle to the Romans to be claiming that God's existence and power can be demonstrated *a posteriori*.[2] In fact, it is a dogma of the Catholic faith that the existence of God can be known with certainty *from* created things,[3] though there is room for disagreement on the question as to whether this means that it can be *philosophically* demonstrated and on the further question as to whether anyone has succeeded in providing such a demonstration. Thus a defender of natural theology as a legitimate and possible enterprise might even accept the weaker version of (3) above.

I believe the crux of the Reformed objection to natural theology can be found in item (4), the claim that it leads to an unstable and wavering faith, that it will leave the believer susceptible to doubt and to the fluctuating tides of human opinion. Instead, believers are supposed to hold fast to their faith, to resist temptations to doubt, to believe with a kind of assurance or certitude. I see Plantinga's project as in large measure an attempt to preserve this assurance of faith and to show how it can be rationally justified even in the absence of compelling evidence for what believers hold. But I wish to suggest that his adversaries in this project are the evidentialists and positivists he attacks in other essays, and that the defenders of natural theology, especially those who follow Thomas Aquinas, are in fact allies of the Reformed theologians in defending the rationality of religious belief and can accept some version of (4).

Belief in God as Properly Basic

Plantinga argues that the real mistake behind the project of natural theology is that it presupposes a commitment to an epistemological view which Plantinga calls "strong foundationalism." This view includes two claims that Plantinga himself would accept and that make up the

2. Cf. Romans 1:20: "Ever since the creation of the world, his invisible attributes of eternal power and divinity have been able to be understood and perceived in what he has made."

3. The First Vatican Council (1869-70) declared: "The same holy Mother Church holds and teaches that God, the origin and end of all things, can be known with certainty by the natural light of human reason from the things that he created," and Romans 1:20 is cited in support. *The Church Teaches*, trans. J. F. Clarkson, J. H. Edwards, W. F. Kelly, J. J. Welch (Rockford, IL: Tan Books, 1973), p. 27 (no. 58).

core of "weak foundationalism": *(a)* that every rational noetic structure (system of beliefs) has a foundation, and *(b)* that in a rational noetic structure, nonbasic belief is proportional in strength to support from the foundations. But the strong foundationalist adds criteria for what sorts of propositions can properly belong in the foundations, and normally these criteria are such as to prevent religious claims from appearing in the foundations of a rational noetic structure. According to Plantinga, "it is plausible to see Thomas Aquinas, for example, as holding that a proposition is properly basic for a person only if it is self-evident to him . . . or 'evident to the senses'."[4] On this interpretation of Aquinas's view, it seems that belief in God cannot be properly basic, since it is neither self-evident nor evident to the senses, so that if belief in God is to be rational it must be based on other propositions or evidences — that is, it must be the product of a successful piece of natural theology. Unfortunately, this has as a troubling consequence the claim that most believers are irrational in their belief in God, since they have not arrived at this belief via philosophical proofs.

Plantinga and the Reformed thinkers he cites reject this conclusion, and I think rightly so. Plantinga's suggestion is that the problem lies in treating belief in God as a nonbasic belief; instead we should hold that belief in God is properly basic, that it can belong to the foundations of a rational noetic structure.[5] Although Plantinga claims that no *evidence* is needed in order to justify this belief, he says that it is usually formed on the basis of certain experiences that serve to *ground* the belief, similarly to the way in which perceptual experiences ground our belief in the existence of trees. He urges that there is no reason to find religious belief irrational, even if its grounds are nonpropositional and there is no compelling argument which begins from these experiential grounds and concludes to God's existence. After all, even in the perceptual case, we can provide no compelling argument that begins from visual experiences and concludes to the existence of trees. Reformed theologians John Calvin and Herman Bavinck are cited in support of the view that God has planted within every human being an innate disposition to

---

4. Plantinga, "Reformed Objection," p. 56.

5. In fact, it turns out that Plantinga is not opposed to there being criteria for what belongs in the foundations, but that he is opposed to the criteria offered by strong foundationalists so far, since these invariably rule out belief in God as a foundational belief.

belief in God when placed in certain circumstances,[6] just as he has created us with a disposition to believe in trees when placed in certain circumstances.[7]

The claim that belief in God is basic for most religious believers, and properly so, would explain a number of things. It would show why it is that most believers do not come to their beliefs via the arguments of natural theology, and it would explain how they can be justified in this belief independently of such arguments or evidences (see reasons [1] and [2] above for rejecting natural theology). Further, I believe it is meant to solve the problem of unstable or wavering faith, since foundational beliefs normally enjoy a certain immunity from doubt that plagues our higher-order beliefs. This aura of certitude is strengthened by the analogies Plantinga draws between belief in God and belief in the existence of the self, the external world, the past, and other minds, and by his claim that someone who believes in God as a foundational belief can be said to *know* that God exists.

However, even if belief in God is properly basic for some persons in some circumstances, it does not follow automatically that this belief is particularly immune from doubt or criticism, or that it is held with the kind of firmness that believers take to be appropriate to faith. Some

6. Bavinck says, "Spontaneously, altogether involuntarily: without any constraint or coercion, we accept that existence" (*The Doctrine of God,* trans. William Hendriksen [Grand Rapids: Eerdmans, 1951], cited by Plantinga in "Reformed Objection," p. 50). Plantinga quotes Calvin a page later as follows: "There is within the human mind, and indeed by natural instinct, an awareness of divinity. . . . This conviction, namely, that there is some God, is naturally inborn in all, and is fixed deep within, as it were in the very marrow . . . one of which each of us is master from his mother's womb and which nature itself permits no one to forget" (*Institutes of the Christian Religion,* trans. Ford Lewis Battles [Philadelphia: Westminster Press, 1960], 1.3.1; 1.3.3).

7. Although I focus in this essay on Plantinga's work, many others have contributed to articulating and defending this approach to the rationality of religious belief. The work of Nicholas Wolterstorff and William Alston has been especially influential, and some of it can be found in a collection of essays edited by Plantinga and Wolterstorff called *Faith and Rationality: Reason and Belief in God* (Notre Dame: University of Notre Dame Press, 1983). In a more recent collection edited by Robert Audi and William Wainwright, *Rationality, Religious Belief and Moral Commitment* (Ithaca, NY: Cornell University Press, 1986), one finds further helpful essays by Plantinga, Wolterstorff, and Kenneth Konyndyk setting out the Reformed view, as well as a thoughtful critique by Robert Audi. It should be noted that Wolterstorff finds Aquinas more friendly to the Reformed view than does Plantinga. For a collection of essays critical of the Reformed project, see *Thomistic Papers IV,* ed. Leonard Kennedy (Houston: Center for Thomistic Studies, 1988).

of our basic beliefs regarding the external world might be held rather tentatively, and others will be overruled by data that conflict with them. On the other hand, many of our derived beliefs are quite firm and unshakable, such as those higher-level mathematical truths we derive by simple steps from more immediately known premises. It is true that seeing belief in God as properly basic avoids the kind of doubt that can be cast on such belief by undermining its foundations, but it does not ultimately solve the problem of wavering faith. As Thomas Sullivan notes, "being basic does not entail being firm. . . . We have been given no reason not to waver when facing possible defeaters [of our belief in God]."[8]

Placing belief in God in the category of basic beliefs, then, does not by itself solve what Sullivan calls the problem of unqualified assent — how it can be rational to assent to God's existence in an unconditional way, given that (on this view) one has no *evidence* for this belief and has encountered significant evidence or arguments against it. To raise this problem of unqualified assent, or the assurance of faith, is not to side with the evidentialists (W. K. Clifford and others) in thinking that the strength of one's belief in a proposition must not exceed the strength of the evidence one has for the truth of that proposition. But if believers are rationally justified in clinging to their religious beliefs tenaciously in the face of challenges which they recognize to be formidable and for which they have no rebuttal, then this does seem to call for explanation. We all recognize that a stubborn refusal to alter our beliefs in light of new information can be an intellectual vice and can lead us into error, and yet religious believers often praise those who refuse to yield to the temptation to doubt when faced with objections. Is this reasonable, and if so, what makes it so? That is, is it reasonable to hold to propositions that purport to be divinely revealed with the kind of subjective certitude that is characteristic of the act of faith?

The kind of subjective certitude involved in this assurance of faith has to do with the *strength* or *firmness* of our belief, how willing we are to entertain doubts about the truth of the proposition believed. This is to be distinguished from subjective certitude in the sense of the view we hold about the probability of the proposition believed — that is, *our* view as to the strength of the evidence (or grounds) for that proposition.

8. Thomas Sullivan, "Adequate Evidence for Religious Assent," in *Thomistic Papers IV*, p. 85.

Both kinds of subjective certitude must be distinguished from two types of objective certainty, one of which is a claim about the probability the proposition *actually has* on the evidence we possess (whether we assess this rightly or wrongly), while the other is a claim about the probability of the proposition on evidence that is *available* to us, whether we are aware of it or not. I believe it has been shown by others that our beliefs can be rational even when the estimate we have of their probability does not match with their 'objective' probability interpreted in one of these last two ways. But the problem of the assurance of faith is a different one: How can it be rational to hold a belief with a very high level of *firmness* when, even by our own estimate, the evidence we have *for that proposition* does not compel our assent (is not maximally persuasive) and (worse) when the evidence we think we have for a potential defeater of the proposition is relatively strong?[9]

In a recent essay, Paul Draper discusses one of Plantinga's suggested solutions to the problem of the assurance of faith: perhaps the strength of the *grounds* that trigger a given person's belief in God are such as to outweigh any evidence brought against that belief. But it is not at all obvious that this strategy will work for every believer or in every case of conflict.[10] Someone may have arrived at a fairly firm conviction of God's existence as a result of a particularly vivid experience of beauty

9. Here I would like to add that I find this talk about *degrees* of belief somewhat problematic. I am not convinced that we really do believe or assent to some things more firmly than we do to other things; rather, it seems to me that either we believe or we don't. On the other hand, if we think of degrees in terms of our willingness to give up the proposition, here again there seems no all-purpose answer to the question of how willing we are to give up a particular belief — this will presumably vary with the sorts of contrary evidence we are faced with. Similarly, it seems odd to think of ourselves as proportioning the strength of our belief that p to the strength of the evidence we have for p, which suggests that if we have twice as much evidence for p as for q, we should be twice as willing to doubt q as we are to doubt p. Perhaps the evidentialist's maxim here could be taken as the claim that *only* the direct evidence we have for the truth of p is relevant to deciding how willing we ought to be to disbelieve p (except when p is properly basic), while anti-evidentialists claim otherwise. That is, anti-evidentialism might consist not primarily in rejection of certain criteria for proper basicality but in rejection of a tenet that even weak foundationalists are said to embrace: in a rational noetic structure, nonbasic belief is proportional in strength to support from the foundations.

10. Plantinga suggests this strategy in "The Foundations of Theism: A Reply," *Faith and Philosophy* 3 (1986): 298-313, and Draper's critique can be found in "Evil and the Proper Basicality of Belief in God," *Faith and Philosophy* 8 (1991): 135-47.

or danger or guilt or whatever, but in later years she may find the memory of this experience fading and the evidence against God's existence increasingly difficult to ignore. Also, the believer might wonder whether or not her belief was actually caused by the *appropriate* triggering circumstances or was caused instead by some less reliable mechanism. This worry is especially apt to surface in cases where what she believes is something she might plausibly be thought to have accepted on the basis of wholly nonrational causes (wish fulfillment, etc.). Finally, since some believers don't simply find themselves with a belief in God that has maximal firmness, the question remains as to whether *these* believers are justified in their high level of confidence, especially when they are faced with potential defeaters of their beliefs.[11]

Before setting out what I take to be Aquinas's solution to the problem of the assurance of faith, I would like to address the question of whether or not Aquinas would accept the claim that belief in God can be properly basic in Plantinga's sense. Plantinga holds that a believer can be rationally justified in coming to believe, while standing before a beautiful sunset, that there is a God who created this beauty before her, even though she is not inferring God's existence from the existence of beautiful sunsets. The sunset experience is a condition that serves as the occasion for her coming to believe — it triggers that belief — but it is not evidence for it. Still, it would seem that the conditions which trigger belief in God tend to be of a certain predictable sort, and this suggests that there is some logical connection between what is experienced (the effect) and the being believed in (the cause). As Sullivan puts it, "Unless 'grounds' are *cognitive* grounds, unless 'grounds' supply reason with information, having 'grounds' says nothing about the rationality of one's beliefs. If, however, 'grounds' are cognitively grasped data, they would seem to be the very stuff most people call 'evidence.'"[12] Aquinas holds that all human knowledge comes through experience, and that we do not experience God directly but only by way of his effects. Thus, I think he would be inclined to treat Plantinga's 'grounds' as a type of evidence and to hold that those who come to believe in God on the basis of such experiences are not in fact holding that belief as a basic belief but as a derived belief. The derivation or

11. Similar worries are raised by Robert Audi in "Direct Justification, Evidential Dependence, and Theistic Belief," in *Rationality, Religious Belief and Moral Commitment*, pp. 139-66.

12. Sullivan, "Adequate Evidence," p. 84.

inference involved need not be particularly elaborate and may even be in large part implicit, but it is a movement of the intellect from evidence to conclusion nonetheless.[13]

Suppose, however, that Aquinas became convinced that at least some religious experiences qualified as direct experiences of God,[14] or that the absence of an explicitly made inference in the sunset example points to the belief's being basic for that person. Would he hold that such a belief, arrived at in this way, is rationally justified? I believe the answer is clearly yes. Thus, on the definition of "knowledge" as "justified true belief," Aquinas would say that those who believe in God on the basis of the sorts of ordinary experiences Plantinga mentions can be said to *know* that there is a God. However, on *Aquinas's* definition of knowledge, these persons do not know there is a God. For Aquinas, knowledge is of what is self-evident or evident to the senses or in some other way non-gainsayable, obvious to everyone, and of what can be demonstrated on the basis of such universally available truths. What is knowable for Aquinas is always what is provable in principle to any rational person, even if it is difficult or technical and few can actually follow the proof. On this definition of knowledge, a belief in God drawn from a private experience that simply *gives rise* to a personal conviction does not qualify as knowledge. Aquinas would likely place such a belief in the category of *opinion,* which concerns matters for which we have some evidence (or grounds, if you prefer), but which are not demonstrated — the evidence is not sufficient to remove all reasonable possibility of doubt.

While Aquinas's definitions of "knowledge" and "opinion" are unlikely to return to general use, I believe they point to some helpful distinctions

---

13. It is not obvious that Aquinas would say the same thing about belief in the external world or belief in other minds. For a brief summary of one interpretation of Aquinas's theory of perception, see Henry Veatch, "Preliminary Statement of Apology, Analysis, and Critique," in *Thomistic Papers IV,* pp. 5-63. For a detailed critique of the analogy between sense perception and religious experience, see Dennis McInerny's essay in the same volume, "Some Considerations concerning Perceptual Practice and Christian Practice," pp. 101-28.

14. Aquinas does claim that in a type of mystical experience which he calls "rapture" certain persons (e.g., Moses and St. Paul) did see God through his essence. This required a miraculous intervention on God's part, raising the person above his natural powers, and resulted in a kind of intellectual vision of God that is independent of both sensation and imagination. However, Aquinas thinks of this experience as rare and as granted only to those who already have a deep faith in God. See *Truth,* trans. Robert W. Mulligan (Washington, DC: Regnery, 1952), q.13, a.2.

among the many things we would currently say that we know. Some of
these are known in a strong sense, since they can be demonstrated to
almost anyone with a functioning mind, while others are known only in
the weaker sense that they are true, we believe them, and we have some
warrant for them, or in the still weaker sense that we are inclined to believe
them and have no compelling reason not to do so. Many of our rationally
justified beliefs turn out to be false, so that the claim that we *know* (in the
current sense) a certain proposition to be true is corrigible and does not
automatically confer a high level of confidence in the truth of that
proposition. Plantinga wishes to emphasize the Reformers' view that the
person who believes in God in certain triggering circumstances can be
said to *know* that God exists. But this is clearly a weaker claim today than
it would have been for Aquinas. Given Aquinas's definition, there is less
danger of what is *apparently* known turning out to be false, and hence not
known at all. Thus, even the claim that (in today's sense) the believer
knows that God exists does not solve the problem of unconditioned assent
— of how this belief can be affirmed with certitude, given the attacks
upon it that many believers (especially the educated) encounter over time.

And there are further troubling implications of the Reformed
strategy of treating belief in God as basic. One is that it is quite difficult
to specify which triggering conditions will lead to belief in God's existence. Calvin says (following the Epistle to the Romans presumably)
that experiencing the natural world is such a condition, but clearly this
does not do the trick for everyone. Some stand before the natural world
and do not find themselves spontaneously believing that there is a God.
This means that a given person's basic belief in God cannot be easily
confirmed by other persons, since their belief in God may have been
triggered by quite different circumstances or may have failed to mate-
rialize within the same circumstances. I believe these factors serve to
blunt the claim that failing to believe in God is relevantly similar to
failing to believe that your wife or husband exists. In those cases, every
other sane person in the same conditions as you will form the same
belief, but we cannot say the same for belief in God.

A further difficulty with the appeal to basicality is that many believers cannot point to any triggering conditions that created a belief in
God in them; they may feel that arguments and evidences played a
significant role in their belief and that it is nevertheless properly formed
and appropriately held. But Calvin and Bavinck seem to suggest that
every believer comes to belief in God in a kind of utterly spontaneous

way, by instinct, from her mother's womb, etc. Do people who fail to come to belief in God in this way, or who fail to come to it at all, suffer from a kind of intellectual handicap? Plantinga often suggests that they do, that they are "in an epistemically substandard position,"[15] noetically subpar, to be counted among the spiritually challenged perhaps. But it is hard to see why the experience of some believers who have been raised in their faith ought to be taken as normative, rather than the experience of some who have converted; and for converts belief in God (or in more specific items such as the divine origin of Scripture or the church) often seems to them to be a derived (nonbasic) belief.[16] The analogies drawn by Bavinck and Plantinga between belief in God and beliefs about the external world or about other minds create the impression that believing in God is almost entirely a passive affair in which the intellect is driven to assent to God's existence by the presence of the relevant triggering conditions. Says Plantinga, "the appropriate belief is *formed in us;* in the typical case we do not *decide* to hold or form the belief in question, but simply find ourselves with it."[17] Again, I think this conflicts with many persons' experiences of coming to believe in God, where the *will* seems to have played a significant role in the act of assent. Further, it suggests that unbelievers can do nothing much to overcome their epistemological handicap, since their faculties are apparently not functioning properly even when they seem to be standing in circumstances of the relevant kind. How can they be blamed for this involuntary blindness, and how can unbelief ever be properly described as sinful? It could be that these questions are less troubling to certain Reformed thinkers who hold very strong views regarding divine election, since it might be said that those who believe were created to do so while those who persist in unbelief were created differently. But surely many theists, even in the Reformed tradition, would be uncomfortable with this suggestion.

15. Plantinga, "Reformed Objection," p. 52. Plantinga adds: "rather like a man who doesn't believe that his wife exists, or thinks she is like a cleverly constructed robot and has no thoughts, feelings or consciousness."

16. Note that one might agree with an epistemological theory (such as the one Plantinga has been developing) based on the notion of properly functioning faculties, and yet disagree as to how a properly functioning person arrives at belief in God.

17. Plantinga's 1989-90 Stob Lectures, *The Twin Pillars of Christian Scholarship* (published as a pamphlet by Calvin College and Seminary, Grand Rapids, MI, 1990), p. 48. See also p. 51 above.

Perhaps unbelievers are willfully *resisting* a natural impulse to believe in God and are culpable for doing so. But even apart from the fact that this seems phenomenologically false to the experience of many unbelievers, one wonders why it is an obligation to acquiesce in a natural impulse that we have to believe something. If the impulse merely *causes* (though not irresistibly) belief in God, then it is not clear that one should feel confident in yielding to it or that it is not better to seek out evidence instead. Many things that we would like to believe or that we are tempted to believe we recognize as patently false, and we might do well to be antecedently suspicious of beliefs formed in this spontaneous way. This is why it seems preferable to say that the grounds which serve as triggering circumstances for belief in God are not simply causal grounds but are logical or evidential grounds as well, that they provide us with some kind of information which is relevant to the question of God's existence and which leads us to give our assent to the claim that there is a God. However, even this view of the matter leaves open the question as to what level of confidence believers should place in their belief, especially when in subsequent months and years they are faced with apparent defeaters or objections that they cannot easily overcome.

The Role of Natural Theology

Does Aquinas answer this question regarding the assurance of faith by appealing to natural theology? Not at all. At its best, the project of natural theology can indeed produce certainty, but this is the certainty of knowledge, not of faith. When we know something, the evidence moves the intellect to assent to its truth, and since we see that the evidence *proves* the proposition in question, we hold to it with the highest level of subjective certitude and cannot do otherwise. In cases of knowledge (as Aquinas defines knowledge), the will is not operative — we *see* that the proposition is true and we cannot do otherwise than assent to it with great firmness. With respect to our opinions, however, the evidence we have for the proposition in question is adequate but not conclusive, and the intellect assents with less assurance or firmness than to the items that we know; we are more ready to entertain doubts about our opinions. According to Aquinas, faith shares with opinion the lack of conclusive evidence for the propositions believed, but it shares with knowledge a high level of personal confidence or certitude.

This certitude is produced, *not* by the evidence, but by an act of will — one clings to the truths of the faith, and one is extremely reluctant to seriously entertain doubts regarding them, *in spite of the fact* that one has less than conclusive evidence for them. Here Aquinas reveals himself as clearly in the anti-evidentialist camp.

Aquinas defines faith as follows: "The act of believing is an act of the intellect assenting to the Divine truth at the command of the will moved by the grace of God."[18] Faith is believing God, believing that what he says is true, so the primary object of faith is the First Truth, or God himself. What is it to accept *by faith* that God exists? For Aquinas, this could mean one of two things. First, one might come to believe a revealed truth (e.g., that we are meant for eternal happiness) because one believes it is part of a message from God, and *in so doing* one accepts the following presuppositions: *(a)* God exists; *(b)* this message is from God; and *(c)* the message includes the claim that we are made for eternal happiness.[19] Even if the message contains the claim "I am God and I exist," if one assents to it *on God's word*, one still presupposes in that act of assent that God does exist and that this message is from him. However, the presuppositions here need not be believed temporally prior to the assent to the claim that was revealed. An atheist might hear the voice of her conscience (or even, as in St. Augustine's case, children's voices at play) and come to believe that she ought to do what she is being told, while simultaneously coming to believe that there is a God and that this message comes from him. Nevertheless, the will must move the intellect to assent in these cases, since it is *possible* that the message is *not* from God (but from a demonic or psychological source) and, in the mind of the person we've described, it is even possible that God does not exist. The evidence does not compel the intellect to assent either to the revealed claim or to the presuppositions involved in accepting it as a divine message; a choice is involved. A second way of coming to faith in God's existence might involve a movement from *opinion* to *faith*, where one believes (because of various evidences) that God's existence is somewhat probable and then decides

18. Aquinas, *Summa Theologica*, II-II, q.2, a.9.

19. For discussions of what is involved in believing God's existence by faith, see G. E. M. Anscombe, "Faith," included in *The Collected Philosophical Papers of G. E. M. Anscombe*, vol. 3: *Ethics, Religion and Politics* (Minneapolis: University of Minnesota Press, 1981), pp. 113-20, and a more recent essay by R. T. Herbert, "Is Coming to Believe in God Reasonable or Unreasonable?" *Faith and Philosophy* 8 (1991): 36-50.

that it would be good (perhaps because it would be pleasing to God) to give one's full or firm assent to his existence. Both types of coming to believe in God's existence are cases of the intellect assenting (whole-heartedly) to the divine truth at the command of the will, and if they are genuinely cases of coming to faith, Aquinas would say that the will was helped by divine grace.

On the other hand, if one believes that there is a God because one has a sound proof for his existence, then one believes on the basis of the proof and can be said to *know* that he exists. In knowledge, the intellect is moved by the evidence itself and not by the will, whereas in faith the will must come into play. Successful natural theology, then, would provide one with the firmness of assent that accompanies dem-onstrations generally, and it might be apologetically useful in compelling the assent of unbelievers at least to those religious claims that can be proven. Given the certainty afforded by the proofs of natural theology, then, one might expect Aquinas enthusiastically to endorse coming to believe in God via proofs and to recommend it over mere *faith* in God's existence. But the matter is not that simple.

Aquinas argues that it is good and necessary that divine revelation should contain even those truths which could in principle be arrived at through natural reason alone, and he gives three reasons for this claim: first, "in order that man may arrive more quickly at the knowledge of Divine truth," since philosophical proofs take time to master and may not be found until near the end of one's life; second, "in order that the knowledge of God may be more general," since few have the ability or the opportunity to pursue a course of study that would prepare them to appreciate the proofs; and third, "for the sake of certitude. For human reason is very deficient in things concerning God."[20] This last point is of special interest, since it is often thought that the Reformers' mistrust of unaided human reason stands in contrast to the Catholic view of the matter. But Aquinas notes that "philosophers in their researches, by natural investigation, into human affairs, have fallen into many errors, and have disagreed among themselves. And consequently, in order that men might have knowledge of God, free of doubt and uncertainty, it was necessary for Divine matters to be delivered to them by way of faith, being told to them, as it were, by God Himself Who cannot lie."[21]

20. Aquinas, *Summa Theologica*, II-II, q.2, a.4.
21. Aquinas, *Summa Theologica*, II-II, q.2, a.4.

The deliverances of faith are more certain than the deliverances of reason, says Aquinas, since God's word cannot turn out to be false, while the deliverances of reason can.

Given its shortcomings, then, one might be tempted to conclude that natural theology is of no use whatsoever and should be abandoned as a project. But Aquinas does not reach this conclusion. He argues that it can be of use both to the believer and to the unbeliever. It can be helpful for the believer to find philosophical arguments for some of the things she believes, since these can serve as one sort of confirmation of her faith, and it can lead the unbeliever closer to faith by removing certain intellectual obstacles to her belief (if, for example, she thinks that God's existence is impossible or that miracles can't happen). In fact, Aquinas notes that believers are encouraged by St. Peter (in 1 Pet. 3:15) to "Always be ready to give an explanation to anyone who asks you for the reason for your hope," so it is meritorious for a believer when "he loves the truth he believes [and] he thinks out and takes to heart whatever reasons he can find in support thereof."[22] Further, even if the articles of faith are objectively more certain than the deliverances of reason (as coming from an infallible source), we must consider whether or not they are more certain subjectively, that is, relative to us.

Aquinas sees subjective certitude as having two aspects: *firmness of adherence* and *repose of understanding*.[23] Often we gloss over the distinction between these when we refer to certitude as simply a measure of one's willingness (or ability) to doubt what one believes. But Aquinas's point is that when certitude is produced by evidence or proof, then the firmness of adherence *results from* the repose of understanding — the mind rests in the conclusion, it "sees" it to be true, and generally it is not even *able* to entertain serious doubts about its truth. However, in the act of faith, the repose of understanding is absent, and so it is the *will* that produces the firmness of adherence to what is believed (though it is enabled to do so only by grace). And Aquinas's view is that, while faith has the highest possible level of firmness of adherence, it cannot bring the understanding to rest, since we do not see the truths we hold by faith and must accept them on the authority of another. Even when that authority is God, the mind *can* be brought to doubt the truth of what he says, in a way that it *cannot* doubt what it *knows* (in Aquinas's

22. Aquinas, *Summa Theologica*, II-II, q.2, a.10.
23. Aquinas, *Truth*, q.10, a.12.

sense of "knows"). To know a truth is to stand in a relation to it more analogous to the way God knows things; it is to see not just *that* it is true but *why* it is true. Thus, with regard to what Aquinas calls "repose of understanding," science and wisdom are more certain than faith, since "matters of faith are above the human intellect, whereas the objects of the aforesaid three virtues are not," and "the more a man's intellect lays hold of a thing, the more certain it is" (in this sense of "certain").[24] So natural theology, when successful, is a *good* for Aquinas and not an evil; it is a way of grasping *some* religious truths in the way in which we will one day grasp all (or most) of them, a way of acquiring the sort of repose or perfection of the intellect that comes from a complete grasp of the truth. That this fuller way of knowing is preferable can hardly be denied by any believer, I think, and it is in this sense that the knowledge gained by natural theologians is superior to knowing by faith.

However, Aquinas recognizes that there is a wrong use of natural theology as well, and that the attitude with which one approaches this project can be a blameworthy one. This is the attitude of the one who "has not the will, or has not a prompt will, to believe, unless he be moved by human reasons," while Aquinas claims that one ought to "believe matters of faith, not on account of human reason, but on account of Divine authority."[25] The person who thinks she has a sound argument for God's existence does not accept this claim any more on the basis of faith, but she acts rightly, according to Aquinas, as long as she remains *ready* to believe this by faith even if the proof turns out to be flawed. In fact, he suggests that "the wise have greater merit of faith through not renouncing their faith on account of the reasons brought forward by philosophers or heretics in opposition to faith."[26] Thus, the subjective certainty of *faith* (the assurance of faith) does not rest upon the proofs of natural theology for Aquinas. Here, then, I see no substantive disagreement between Aquinas's view and Bavinck's claim that "the so-called proofs are by no means the final grounds of our most certain conviction that God exists: This certainty is established only by faith."[27] I think Aquinas would say that the person who relies on proofs alone for her belief that God exists does have a belief that is likely to

24. Aquinas, *Summa Theologica*, II-II, q.4, a.8.
25. Aquinas, *Summa Theologica*, II-II, q.4, a.8.
26. Aquinas, *Summa Theologica*, II-II, q.4, a.8.
27. Bavinck, *Doctrine of God*, quoted by Plantinga in "Reformed Objection," p. 50.

be unstable and wavering, liable to be undone with the next set of issues from the philosophy journals. Further, much of what believers accept is not at all subject to philosophical proof, and Aquinas is always careful to distinguish between the preambles of faith, which can be demonstrated (in his view), and the mysteries of faith, which cannot. The mysteries of faith must be taken always and by everyone on the authority of God who reveals them, and so the need for faith in the life of the believer cannot be overestimated.

The Assurance of Faith

If natural theology does not produce the confidence of the believer, then, and if Aquinas rejects the view that belief in God is properly basic (or that our confidence in it comes from its foundational status), then what is for him the source of the believer's certainty and why is it legitimate? Given that the articles of faith are above the intellect, what can make it reasonable to believe them at all, much less to hold to them with a kind of subjective certitude? Aquinas's answer is that the Christian revelation tells us that a certain end is possible, namely, eternal happiness, and that there is a way for us to obtain it by God's help. We recognize in ourselves a desire for this end, and so we give our assent to what is revealed because we are told that this is a necessary condition for obtaining the end of eternal happiness.[28] Initially, then, we assent to the truths of the faith, rather than dissenting from them or withholding assent, because we judge that it is *good* to assent, that there is a good to be obtained in assenting which cannot be obtained if we do not (among other things) assent. In this act of assent, we are believing *what* God tells us, and we are believing *that it is God* who is speaking (in Scripture, for example). If we *know* that it is God speaking, then of course it is quite reasonable to accept in an unconditional way what he

---

28. Aquinas's description of the motivation for coming to faith is nicely explicated and defended by Thomas Sullivan in "Adequate Evidence for Religious Assent." Sullivan offers the moral principle: "A person has an obligation to do action A [in this case, an act of religious assent] if that individual has adequate reason to judge that an end E is personally obligatory and action A is indispensable to E" (p. 89). But even if we have an *obligation* to assent, this does not yet solve the problem of *unconditioned* assent, since the obligation might be overridden by others, especially in cases where our initial belief is challenged by new evidence we had not considered.

says, since God cannot lie and he is telling us things we cannot find out on our own. Further, these are things we must believe in order to obtain our highest good, and once we recognize this it would be the height of folly not to believe them. In a sense, then, it is practical reason that tells us that we ought to assent to the articles of faith, although both reason and will are helped along in this process by divine grace, on Aquinas's view.

But how can we decide whether a purported claim to revelation is genuine? How do we recognize that it is God who is speaking? Aquinas's answer is twofold: by the outward evidence of miracles and by the "inward instinct of the Divine invitation."[29] This latter phrase recalls Calvin's "inner testimony of the Holy Spirit," and I believe there is significant agreement between these two thinkers on the importance of this experience in bringing people to the act of faith. Of course, additional evidences might be brought to bear here as well to witness to the divine character of revelation: the nobility of the teachings it contains, the effects of that teaching on those who believe it, the coherence of the teaching with other knowledge and experience, historical evidence for some of its claims, etc. It might seem that faith based purely on the inner experience Calvin and Aquinas describe would be superior, more certain somehow, than faith that is motivated by more external considerations. But given the fallibility of our mental faculties, it's not obvious that the first sort of faith will be any firmer or less subject to doubt than the latter. The initial act of faith, deciding to accept a revelation as from God and to assent to whatever it teaches, may be motivated by any or all of the above considerations, any one of which suffices to make the act of faith *reasonable,* I think. But none of these considerations *proves* that the revelation is from God, so none of them explains why subjective certainty regarding the content of revelation is rationally justified.

In recent essays, Plantinga seems to treat belief in the divine origin of Scripture as another example of a properly basic belief, following some of Calvin's suggestions to that effect.[30] But even if it is, we have

29. Aquinas, *Summa Theologica,* II-II, q.2, a.9.

30. It is common among Reformed theologians to treat God's existence and the Christian revelation as "presuppositions" for all intellectual inquiry. Treating them as properly basic is one way to spell out what this might mean, while avoiding the charge that the "presuppositions" in question are arbitrary or unwarranted. Plantinga quotes Calvin regarding the divine authorship of Scripture as follows: "Since for unbelieving

seen that this will not by itself solve the problem of the assurance of faith, since basicality neither entails nor causally produces subjective certitude. Further, Aquinas would be unlikely to say that the divine character of revelation is something we can *know*, again because we must judge the matter without any direct experience of God himself. Here I think Calvin and Aquinas part company. Aquinas places more emphasis on the external, objective evidence for the divine origin of Scripture, while Calvin is scornful of such evidence and feels that the inner witness of the Spirit suffices for certainty, and indeed for knowledge.[31] Of course, if one genuinely knows that the Scriptures are the word of God, then one similarly knows whatever is contained there, since God cannot lie. While Catholic theologians are often accused of trying to turn faith into knowledge, it seems that on this point Reformed theologians can be more plausibly accused of attempting this sort of epistemic alchemy. Aquinas believes that one cannot strictly speaking *prove* that God speaks in Scripture or in the magisterium of the church, but that the evidence for this claim (whether internal or external) is sufficient to render it highly probable (though not certain). In coming to faith, we assent to these truths, not because they are evident to us (or because they are evidently from God), but because we are attracted by the promise of eternal happiness, we are told that assent to these truths is necessary to obtaining it, and the evidence we do have for their divine origin suffices to make it reasonable for us to choose to believe them. The reasonableness involved here is a product of both cognitive and practical considerations, where the cognitive considerations suffice to make the practical step (the assent itself, moved by the will) reasonable.[32] Nevertheless, I think we will find that these considerations

---

men religion seems to stand by opinion alone, they, in order not to believe anything foolishly or lightly, both wish and demand rational proof that Moses and the prophets spoke divinely. But I reply: the testimony of the Spirit is more excellent than all reason. . . . The same Spirit, therefore, who has spoken through the prophets must penetrate into our hearts to persuade us that they faithfully proclaimed what had been divinely commanded" (Plantinga, *Twin Pillars*, p. 54; citing Calvin's *Institutes*, 1.7.4).

31. See note 28. Plantinga cites Calvin approvingly on this point and adds, "Why suppose that if a belief of mine is a deliverance of faith, it can't also be something I know, a case of knowledge? Why suppose that faith and knowledge are mutually exclusive? . . . Reasoning from [the *Sensus Divinitatis* and the Testimony of the Holy Spirit] in doing scholarship won't have the slightest tendency to bring it about that the result of doing scholarship in that way is not knowledge" (*Twin Pillars*, pp. 55, 56).

32. The view I attribute to Aquinas here seems to have been explicitly endorsed

serve at best only to support the reasonability of assent itself; we do not yet have in hand a justification for the firm, unwavering faith that believers are urged to acquire.

If the believer comes to hold to the articles of faith with full assurance, then, what justifies him in that assurance? It seems the justification cannot be found in evidence, either of an internal or an external kind. One possible answer is that we are *told* (in the Scriptures) to believe firmly and with conviction, and if it makes sense to accept this revelation as from God, it makes sense to follow this command as well — especially since the truths believed are above the human intellect and so we can expect temptations to doubt from time to time. Something about this answer seems correct, since in the act of faith the will must move the intellect, and it is the will that must help the believer "hold fast" (i.e., not easily doubt) the truths of the faith.

On the other hand, there is a hint of utilitarianism about it, as though one is holding firmly to the faith only to achieve a certain end for oneself (however noble the end). I think this can be overcome to some extent by recognizing that the end Aquinas has in mind is not simply a kind of Benthamite bonanza, but the full perfecting of who we are as rational creatures — the full possession of truth and goodness. Ultimately, of course, Christian believers will say that, just as the articles of faith are above our nature and must be bestowed upon us by God, so the movement of the will in committing the intellect wholeheartedly to these claims is a gift of divine grace. If the result is that the intellect holds fast to important truths which illuminate everything else, then the result is not an affront to reason but a great advantage to it. But of course grace can be resisted (on the Catholic view), and objectors might claim that when outward evidence begins to mount against something the believer accepts, he ought to be willing to entertain the possibility that it is false. Not to do so would be intellectually irresponsible.

What is the believer's answer to this? My own sense of the matter is that when believers are actually tempted to doubt something they believe, they often feel that the real reason not to yield to this temptation has more to do with their obligation to *trust God* than with their obligation to do what is prudent. They feel that God should be given the benefit of the doubt, quite literally; where some reason to doubt an

---

by Cardinal Newman and is developed at length by Thomas Sullivan in an essay forthcoming in a volume edited by Linda Zagzebski.

item of faith is presented, they feel that they ought to assume that it will turn out to have flaws, whether or not these flaws are immediately apparent. This kind of trust is not all that different from the situation of a woman who is given some reason to doubt her husband's faithfulness; even if she judges the probability of the proposition that he has been unfaithful to be much greater than zero, and even if she has no reason as yet to disbelieve the evidence of his infidelity, her confidence in his innocence remains very high. This is something for which we would normally praise her, because we think it is appropriate to the relationship she has with her husband, that it is *morally* important for her to trust him even when there is some evidence against his virtue. What this analogy suggests is that, even if the will initially moves the intellect to assent to the truths of faith because of a good to be achieved, the sustained firmness of adherence or assurance of faith derives from the will in a different way, from the will's effort to deepen the level of trust the believer has in the one believed. The good involved in this act of the will is more of a moral good than a practical goal.

Aquinas says that faith is a virtue which is perfected by charity, so that one who believes God comes to know God, and in knowing him comes to love him. Many believers seem to be convinced of their faith, not so much because of the reasons that led them to embrace it in the first place, but because of the many confirmations they have received in their lives of the truth of what it teaches, especially what they take to be their own experiences of the one whom they believe. That is, it seems to them as though God has proved worthy of their trust. This is why the assurance of faith often seems like folly to those who do not believe, since the kind of knowledge and love of God that sustains it cannot be made available to them. Further, I believe that this explains why believers often feel that, as Plantinga puts it, the "nonpropositional warrant enjoyed by [their] belief in God is itself sufficient to turn back the challenge offered by the alleged defeaters."[33] While I agree with Draper that this is a heavy burden to place on the circumstances surrounding one's *initial* belief in God, I think the cumulative experience most believers have of God in their lives is such that they reasonably place a great deal of trust in him and so are untroubled by typical assaults on their faith, whether these are offered by unbelievers or provoked by difficult experiences in their own lives. Along with St. Paul, most Christian believers would say, "I know whom [not just

---

33. Plantinga, "The Foundations of Theism: A Reply," p. 312.

what] I have believed" (2 Tim. 1:12), and it is *this* knowledge that lends certitude to their faith.

This is not to say that the initial act of faith is without reasons of any kind, and we have already mentioned what some of these might be. (Perhaps Reformed thinkers would prefer to call them grounds.) Further, it does not make the apologetic task of responding to attacks on various articles of faith somehow unnecessary. But it does explain, I think, the believer's confidence that such attacks will be successfully repelled, even when the means to do so is not obvious to them or not immediately forthcoming. On the other hand, none of the evidences believers have for the articles of faith, whether these are objective or subjective in nature, yields the kind of certainty (repose of understanding) we can have for the truths of mathematics or for the existence of trees. The articles of faith exceed the ability of the human intellect, and thus they will always be open to doubt in a way that mathematics or direct experience is not. This is why believers, even saints, can be tempted to doubt, and it is why converts normally experience their conversion primarily as a *decision*, rather than as analogous to an act of perception.

Foes of Religious Belief

In spite of the differences we have found between Catholic and Reformed approaches to the act of faith, on matters of the origin of faith and the source of the believer's confidence in God, as well as on the role and limits of natural theology, I find substantial agreement between theologians in the Reformed and Catholic (at least Thomistic) traditions. We can now see why Aquinas, for example, shares the Reformed concern to preserve the rationality of the ordinary believer's faith in God and to promote the authority of God over the authority of fallible human reason.

The differences between these approaches arise in three areas: (1) the question of whether belief in God should be thought of as a basic belief, (2) the importance of public or external evidences for one's beliefs, and (3) the role of the will in the act of faith. On the first point, Aquinas would urge, I think, that even a basic belief has human reason as its source, so that belief based on divine authority (an infallible source) is in *some* ways preferable even to a basic belief in God (whether the grounds for this belief are treated as evidence or simply as causal antecedents). On the second point, Aquinas believes that the internal witness of the Holy Spirit to the voice of God speaking in nature or in Scripture profits greatly from the external witness provided by miracles and other such public considerations, whereas Reformed theologians might see this as an unfortunate reliance on human wisdom — as not simply "beginning from God," in Bavinck's phrase.[34] Finally, while Plantinga cites Calvin to the effect that faith is a species of *knowledge*,[35] Aquinas holds that most believers accept God's existence by faith and that all believers must accept the mysteries of faith by an act of faith, that is, by taking them on God's authority. In this act of faith it is the intellect that assents, but always moved by the will, since the evidence or grounds are in themselves insufficient to cause the mind to assent to what is revealed, and since the claim that the proposed revelation is from God is similarly incapable of proof.

Aquinas's position has the advantage, I think, of allowing for both the action of grace and the contribution of the human will in coming to faith, so that there can be a sense in which faith is praiseworthy and unbelief is culpable. For both Catholic and Reformed thinkers, the major assaults upon the rationality of religious belief come in the guise of certain forms of evidentialism and positivism, which place unwarranted restrictions on what can be sensibly believed and on what sort of evidence is admissible. My hope is that Aquinas will cease to be seen as one of the enemy in the battle for the intellectual respectability of faith and will instead be welcomed as an older (if not wiser) accomplice.

34. Even so, Aquinas faults unbelievers for acting contrary to nature, since "To have faith is not part of human nature, but it is part of human nature that man's mind should not thwart his *inner instinct*, and the outward preaching of the truth" (*Summa Theologica*, II-II, q.10, a.1; emphasis added). If faith in God is not exactly innate, nevertheless Aquinas seems to think that we have a natural tendency to make the relevant inferences to God's existence by looking at the natural world, and this is not very far from what Calvin and other Reformed theologians want to say.

35. Plantinga, *Twin Pillars*, p. 55. Calvin says, "Now we shall possess a right definition of faith if we call it a firm and certain knowledge of God's benevolence toward us, founded upon the truth of the freely given promise of Christ, both revealed to our minds and sealed upon our hearts through the Holy Spirit" (*Institutes*, 3.2.7).

Empiricism, Rationalism, and the Possibility of Historical Religious Knowledge

C. Stephen Evans

Traditional Christians claim that my salvation might depend in part on my believing propositions with historical content, such as that Jesus of Nazareth lived a certain kind of life, instituted the Eucharist, suffered a voluntary but innocent death, and finally was raised from the dead as a bodily being. Such propositions either are part of the content of faith or are beliefs that Christian faith incorporates or presupposes. Many philosophers and theologians have thought that this connection Christianity makes between salvation and history is troublesome. They have worried about whether historical knowledge could ever constitute or be part of religious knowledge. They have wondered whether it is possible for knowledge of events that occur in history at a particular time and place to have essential religious significance.

After all, it does not in general seem to be the case that ultimate religious significance is attached to mere historical beliefs. No one's salvation is thought to depend on what one thinks about Caesar's decision to cross the Rubicon. Obviously, for historical beliefs to have religious importance, they must not be "mere" historical beliefs. They must be beliefs about events that occur in a certain context and that are thought to have a certain significance. The Christian believes, for example, that Jesus' life, death, and resurrection reveal to us the character of God and the path we must take for salvation. It is in this context that the beliefs take on religious significance, and it is quite possible that someone who divorced the relevant beliefs from this context would not find much that is religiously interesting. That, however, is consistent with the claim that within that context the historicity of the events is

134

crucial and that belief in their historicity is part of living religious faith — or is at least presupposed by such faith.

In this essay I do not propose to discuss how historical religious beliefs[1] might get their religious significance, but rather a different problem, one that concerns the epistemological status of such beliefs. It is commonly alleged that if religious faith requires beliefs with historical content, then religious faith will have a shaky epistemological status. Historical beliefs in general carry with them certain risks, and religious historical beliefs may be thought to be especially risky. Religious faith, on the other hand, is often thought to require a kind of finality, absoluteness, and assurance that might be thought to be incompatible with the shaky status of historical beliefs.

There is a significant difference between someone who claims that it is difficult for historical beliefs to count as religious knowledge and someone who claims that this is impossible. The first person claims that, though in principle historical religious knowledge is possible, in practice actual religious historical claims lack sufficient evidence. Let us call this the *weak negative claim* about historical religious knowledge. The second person claims that even very strong historical evidence would not be good enough; historical claims are always too shaky from an epistemological standpoint to be incorporated into religious faith. I shall call this sort of claim about historical religious knowledge the *strong negative claim*.

In this essay I propose to deal only with this strong type of claim, the claim that historical religious knowledge is impossible. My thesis will be that we have no good reason to think that historical religious knowledge is impossible. That, of course, is a long way from the claim that historical religious knowledge is actual.

One might think that the strong negative claim would be an extreme claim, hardly worth refuting. However, we shall see that such claims are more common than one might have thought. Furthermore, by clearing away the extreme claims it will become clearer what problems need to be addressed in order to show that such knowledge is not merely possible but actual. I believe that many discussions of this issue confuse the two different types of positions. I shall try to show that some of the alleged problems with actual historical religious knowledge really

---

1. By a "historical religious belief" I mean a religiously significant belief with historical content — one that makes reference to a datable event, for example.

stem from positions that make such knowledge impossible in principle. Furthermore, some of the genuine problems that make historical religious knowledge difficult have been illegitimately used to argue that such knowledge is impossible.

I. Empiricist and Rationalist Conceptions of Religious Knowledge

What I wish to argue is that the strong negative claim about historical religious knowledge rests, explicitly or implicitly, either on a rationalist conception of religious knowledge or on an extreme, implausible version of empiricism. Plausible empiricist conceptions of religious knowledge, on the other hand, though they may imply that it is difficult to obtain historical religious knowledge and thus support the weak negative claim, are open in principle to the possibility of historical religious knowledge. I shall try to show that epistemological objections to historical religious knowledge that appear to stem from scruples about the empirical evidence for that knowledge often, though not always, rest on covert rationalist assumptions.

In this discussion, I shall not use the terms "empiricist" and "rationalist" to refer to precisely defined epistemological positions, but somewhat loosely to refer to general tendencies to conceive of religious knowledge in particular ways. An empiricist conception of religious knowledge is roughly one that regards religious knowledge as derived from experience. For example, someone who claims to have observed a miracle performed by God is making a claim to know something religiously significant on the basis of experience. Typically, the empiricist regards at least some, though probably not all, religious truths as contingent in nature. The claims that "God called Abram to leave Ur" or that "God delivered Israel from Egypt" or that "God raised Jesus of Nazareth from the dead" would all be examples of such logically contingent religious propositions. Any philosopher or theologian who regards Christianity as subject to empirical confirmation or disconfirmation through historical evidence would serve as an example of someone who holds such an empiricist conception of religious knowledge. Bishop Butler, Richard Swinburne, and Michael Martin all regard Christianity in this way.[2]

2. See Joseph Butler's *Analogy of Religion* (Oxford: Clarendon Press, 1896); Richard

A rationalist conception of religious knowledge, on the other hand, is one that views religious knowledge in the following way: religious knowledge is knowledge of what is timelessly, eternally true. Religious truths are either necessary truths or else resemble necessary truths in important ways. Knowledge of these truths is not dependent on ordinary experience but is gained through a process of reflection. Since theologians sometimes use the word "rationalist" for any philosophical position that sees religious knowledge as needing rational justification, it is important to note that the word "rationalist" here carries as its contrast "empiricist," not "fideist."

For the rationalist (in my sense of the term), religious truths are either self-evident or "recollected" (using the term in a way reminiscent of but broader than Plato's concept of recollection), perhaps by reflecting on universal structures of the world, human life, or experience. Religious truths are not necessarily simple or obvious; gaining such truth may involve an arduous process of reflection. However, once the truth is "seen," it is also seen that this is a truth which is unaffected by empirical evidence of the ordinary sort. Claims that "finite egos are only apparently distinct from the Absolute and are in fact identical with the Absolute" or that "the true being of the human person lies in the person's *potentiality to be*" or that "God is not a being, but the ground of possibility of being" would all be examples of religious knowledge conceived in a rationalist manner. All of these propositions have the following characteristics: If true, they are either necessarily true or what I shall call inescapably true. An inescapable truth is one that is necessarily true given the structure of human nature. Since the features of human nature in question may not be logically necessary, religious truths of this type are not strictly necessary, but they resemble necessary truths in that they cannot be altered unless human beings were altered to become radically different kinds of beings. Their truth cannot depend on whether particular events have occurred, and though a particular experience or set of experiences could be the occasion for someone's coming to realize their truth, they do not seem to be the kind of truths one would normally learn through observation.

It might be thought that such a rationalistic conception of religious

Swinburne's *Revelation: From Metaphor to Analogy* (Oxford: Clarendon Press, 1992); and Michael Martin's *The Case Against Christianity* (Philadelphia: Temple University Press, 1991).

knowledge would not be widely held. Certainly I believe that not many theologians would describe their view of religious knowledge as rationalistic; indeed, they might be surprised to hear someone else thus describe them. Nevertheless, I think that such a rationalistic perspective is fairly widespread.

I shall briefly mention three philosophical examples of rationalist conceptions of religious knowledge — Kant, Wittgenstein, and Hegel — corresponding to three distinct types of rationalism. The first type of rationalism is illustrated by Kant. In his *Religion Within the Limits of Reason Alone,* Kant says very explicitly, "We need, therefore, no empirical example to make the idea of a person morally well-pleasing to God our archetype; this idea as an archetype is already present in our reason."[3]

The early Wittgenstein illustrates a second type of rationalism. In his *Tractatus Logico-Philosophicus,* Wittgenstein appears to view ethical and religious knowledge as a mystical knowledge that is in some way similar to the truths of logic: strictly speaking, such propositions say nothing, though in a mystical way they may "show" us something of great importance. "If there is any value that does have value, it must lie outside the whole sphere of what happens and is the case. For all that happens and is the case is accidental."[4] The same thing is said about God: "God does not reveal himself *in* the world."[5]

Hegel's conception of religion as the more immediate knowledge of the absolute reality that is conceptually grasped in philosophy illustrates a third type of rationalism: "The object of religion as well as of philosophy is eternal truth in its objectivity, God and nothing but God, and the explication of God. Philosophy is not a wisdom of the world, but is knowledge of what is not of the world; it is not knowledge which concerns external mass, or empirical existence and life, but is knowledge of that which is eternal."[6]

Kant, Wittgenstein, and Hegel are of course philosophers and not

---

3. Immanuel Kant, *Religion Within the Limits of Reason Alone,* trans. Theodore Greene and Hoyt Hudson (New York: Harper & Row, 1960), p. 56.

4. Ludwig Wittgenstein, *Tractatus Logico-Philosophicus* (New York: Humanities Press, 1961), 6.41 (p. 145).

5. Wittgenstein, *Tractatus,* 6.432 (p. 149).

6. *G. W. F. Hegel on Art, Religion, and Philosophy* (New York: Harper & Row, 1970), p. 145. (Taken from a translation of *Lectures on the Philosophy of Religion* by E. B. Speirs and J. Burdon Sanderson.)

theologians, but it is significant that they have all had an enormous influence on theology. They represent, I think, three possible strands of religious rationalism. (Other strands may be possible as well, but I see these three as prominent.) One strand, represented by Kant, attempts to reduce religious truth to moral truths, knowable by reason. So if someone objects that we have no reliable historical knowledge of Jesus as an object of faith, one may simply reply that what is really important are the moral possibilities embodied in Jesus' life. Noted theologian Don Cupitt, in responding to the charge that our critical-historical knowledge of Jesus is limited, takes exactly this stance:

> [T]he core of a religion does not lie in the biography or personality of the founder, but in the specifically religious values to which, according to tradition, he bore witness. By these values I mean possible determinations of the human spirit whereby it relates itself to the ultimate goal of existence. . . . How can we depend upon the uncertainties of historical tradition for knowledge of, and our power to attain, a history-transcending truth?[7]

The second strand of rationalistic impulse, illustrated by Wittgenstein, lies in seeing religious truth as mystical rather than moral, some type of truth that really cannot be expressed in human language at all. Paul Tillich's claims about "the God beyond the God of theism," who is not a being but the Ground of Being or Being-itself, might be an example of this tendency.[8]

This second strand may resemble and shade over into the third strand, illustrated by Hegel, which I would describe as metaphysical/speculative rationalism, for here religious truth is identified with speculative truths derived from reflection on the human condition. Besides neo-Hegelian theologians, many of the claims of Buddhism and Hinduism could serve as examples of this metaphysical/speculative rationalism. For rationalists in general, there is a tendency to transform the historical materials of a religious tradition into archetypes with a universal validity, mythology with a universal meaning, or illustrations of necessary moral truths.

7. Don Cupitt, "A Final Comment," in *The Myth of God Incarnate,* ed. John Hick (London: SCM Press, 1977), p. 205.

8. See Paul Tillich, *The Courage to Be* (New Haven: Yale University Press, 1952), pp. 184-90.

II. The Confusion of Rationalist
and Empiricist Objections

I have claimed that the strong negative claim about historical religious knowledge typically rests on a rationalist conception of religious knowledge. Empiricist conceptions of religious knowledge, on the other hand, except for extreme and implausible versions of empiricism, are open in principle to such knowledge. This seems intuitively right to me. It is certainly in keeping with the spirit of empiricism that one should say that whether or not we have any historical religious knowledge is a question for experience to decide; we cannot say a priori that such a thing is impossible. Furthermore, it seems plausible that someone who says that such knowledge is in principle impossible must root that claim, at least ultimately, in an a priori conception of the nature of religious knowledge or of historical knowledge or both.

Kant and Wittgenstein are certainly clear about where they stand on these issues. Not all Christian theologians have been so clear, however. I think the reason for this is that, though theologians find the type of perspective of Kant or Wittgenstein attractive, as Christian theologians they wish in some way to maintain the importance of history, and thus there is a tendency either to be unclear about whether faith includes belief in historical propositions or to be downright inconsistent on this issue. Van Harvey, for example, criticizes Rudolf Bultmann at just this point. He maintains that Bultmann's theological position ought to lead him to regard historical claims about Jesus as unimportant:

> As I have argued in the preceding chapter, this reference to a decisive act of God in Jesus Christ seems gratuitous within the framework of Bultmann's theology. For him, Jesus is merely the historical cause *(das Dass)*, which initiates faith. The figure of Jesus does not inform in any way the content *(das Was)* of faith. Moreover, this reference to Jesus not only seems unnecessary but contradictory, since it is impossible to reconcile with Bultmann's basic premise that faith is a possibility for man as man.[9]

9. Van A. Harvey, *The Historian and the Believer* (New York: Macmillan, 1966), p. 165.

To use my language, Harvey accuses Bultmann of illegitimately dragging in empirical content when his operative understanding of religious knowledge is rationalist.

What I shall try to show is that *critics* of historical religious knowledge often make a similar mistake. They raise objections to historical religious knowledge that are apparently empirical in nature, and thus presuppose an empiricist conception of religious knowledge that is open in principle to such historical knowledge. When we look more deeply, however, we find that these empirical objections are a smoke screen for covert rationalist presuppositions. Legitimate empirical problems then lend unwarranted support for the covert rationalism. Alternatively, the covert rationalism is employed to portray the empirical difficulties as being insuperable, impossible to overcome, instead of simply being difficulties. This kind of confusion is present, as we shall see, in a seminal theological discussion of this problem, Gotthold Ephraim Lessing's famous essay in which he raised the issue of how he could make the transition from historical beliefs to religious knowledge, seeing this as a barrier to becoming a Christian: "That, then, is the ugly, broad ditch which I cannot get across, however often and however earnestly I have tried to make the leap."[10] Lessing's ditch is not one ditch, however, but several ditches confusedly rolled together, as Gordon E. Michalson has convincingly shown in a recent book.[11]

III. Apparently Empiricist Objections to Historical Religious Knowledge

Consider first what might be called the *empiricist* problem, which in turn comes in two versions. Someone with empiricist epistemological leanings might worry whether historical beliefs could ever acquire the

10. Gotthold Lessing, "On the Proof of the Spirit and of Power," in *Lessing's Theological Writings*, ed. and trans. Henry Chadwick (Stanford: Stanford University, 1957), p. 55.

11. Gordon E. Michalson, Jr., *Lessing's "Ugly Ditch": A Study of Theology and History* (University Park, PA: Pennsylvania State Press, 1985). Michalson distinguishes between the temporal ditch, the metaphysical ditch, and the ditch of appropriation, each of which in turn comes in various versions. While I found his work illuminating and helpful, I find it more useful for my purposes to employ a somewhat different taxonomy of the types of problems that beset religious knowledge seen as historical knowledge.

kind of epistemological credentials needed to be certified as religious knowledge. This person might reason as follows: "Perhaps if I had been a contemporary of Jesus and had first-hand experience of him performing miracles, then I could know with some degree of confidence that he is divine and that my salvation depends on my relation to him.[12] But how can I possibly know this when I must depend on historical testimony? Isn't historical knowledge always somewhat uncertain?" Essentially, the worry here is that the historical beliefs in question can't be religious knowledge because they can't be *known* at all.

Let us call this position that views historical knowledge as religiously inadequate because of the inaccessibility of the past that of the *naive empiricist*. The name is not meant to be prejudicial. Lessing's essay nicely illustrates the position of the naive empiricist: "If I had lived at the time of Christ, then of course the prophecies fulfilled in his person would have made me pay great attention to him. If I had actually seen him do miracles . . . I would have believed him in all things in which equally indisputable experiences did not tell against him."[13] Unfortunately, Lessing says, he lives in the eighteenth century, in which miracles no longer occur, and he must therefore rely on the "inducements" of historians, which are "infinitely lesser" than the firsthand experience available to the contemporary generation.[14]

It is important to distinguish the weak negative claim from the strong negative claim being made here. It is the strong claim that Lessing seems to make in the above quotations, for he is willing to allow for the sake of argument that the historical evidence for Christianity is as good as can be imagined.

Why, then, would someone like Lessing suppose that historical knowledge in principle can never amount to religious knowledge? Someone who thinks that historical knowledge can never be evidentially adequate as religious knowledge obviously has a particular epistemological standard for religious knowledge in mind. Religious knowledge

---

12. Here and in succeeding cases I use Christianity for my illustration. This is appropriate because, although the problem of the relationship between historical knowledge and religious knowledge is a properly philosophical one, it is a problem that is especially important for Christianity. It doesn't appear to me that this is a problem at all for Hinduism, Buddhism, Confucianism, and Taoism, and if it is a problem for Judaism and Islam, it is not so severe as in the case of Christianity.

13. Lessing, "On the Proof of the Spirit," pp. 51-52.

14. Lessing, "On the Proof of the Spirit," p. 53.

seems to such a person to require a level of certainty that historical knowledge cannot reach. But why not? Unless we are historical skeptics, some past events appear to be known with a high degree of certainty. Though I suppose I can imagine it being the case that Abraham Lincoln never existed, I don't think I am detectably less certain of this historical fact than anything else I believe very strongly. And clearly there are many beliefs I have, based on my present experience, that are much less certain than some historical ones. So it does not seem to be the case that historical beliefs are always less certain than beliefs grounded in firsthand experience. Perhaps the problem with historical religious beliefs lies not in their historical character but in their uncertainty, a characteristic of empirical beliefs in general, not simply historical ones.

Though I think the naive empiricist objection, which has to do with the difficulty of apprehending the past, is felt very strongly by many ordinary people, some theologians, impressed by the type of reasoning of the last paragraph, regard it as superficial. I will call this theologian the *sophisticated empiricist*, and his problem is the second type of empiricist objection to the possibility of religious knowledge. The sophisticated empiricist thinks that the contrast drawn between firsthand experience and belief based on historical evidence is not that important. Maybe the problem with historical knowledge lies, not in the fact that it deals with past events, but simply with its empirical character. Even firsthand experience involves the application of concepts and introduces the possibility of error, and such error seems especially possible when the concepts involved include such predicates as "miracle" and "sent from God." Even if I had been a contemporary of Jesus and had seen him perform miracles, would this necessarily imply that I could know that he is divine or that my salvation depends on my relation to him? Is this something I could know by experience at all? So the main issues now are seen as the general uncertainty of empirical knowledge and perhaps the special uncertainties arising from the attempt to treat such knowledge as religious in character. Perhaps some further difficulties accrue from the fact that the empirical facts which are in question are inaccessible to present experience, but those difficulties are not the really fundamental ones.

This sophisticated empiricist problem, like the naive form, seems to be generated by a certain conception of religious knowledge. Religious knowledge requires certainty; the problem is generated by the fact that historical knowledge in particular (for the naive empiricist) or empirical knowledge in general (for the sophisticated empiricist) is always uncertain. However, in the two cases the real problem does not lie with historical knowledge or empirical knowledge. It is true that if we are skeptics and deny that empirical knowledge is possible, then no historical or empirical religious knowledge can be gained, but so what? In that case religious knowledge of a historical or empirical kind will be no worse off than any other kind of knowledge. If we reject skepticism, on the other hand, then empirical knowledge in general is possible, and so if empirical *religious* knowledge is impossible, this must be due to a special difficulty arising from the character of religious knowledge.

I can think of two kinds of difficulty that might arise. First, someone might think that religious knowledge cannot be empirical because religious knowledge requires a special degree of certainty to which empirical knowledge cannot attain. Second, one might think that empirical knowledge cannot amount to religious knowledge because the application of religious predicates to experience generates special uncertainties not generally applicable to other kinds of empirical knowledge. In both of these cases, ironically, it appears to me that the empiricist position in some sense "deconstructs," to use a currently fashionable phrase. That is, it seems to me that we have in both of these cases the kind of "reversal" that Hegel delighted in, for in both cases the empiricist objection has been transformed into a rationalist objection, as I shall now try to show.

A *rationalist* problem with historical religious belief on the surface looks very different from the empiricist problem. An initial characterization of the rationalist problem might go something like this: Religious knowledge must have the character of universal, necessary truth; historical knowledge necessarily lacks this character. Religious knowledge is not knowledge of this or that event, but knowledge of what holds true eternally and necessarily. Religious knowledge appears to be a different *kind* of knowledge than historical knowledge, and it is not easy to see how the latter could be transformed into the former. Lessing, who begins his essay on this issue by raising empirical objections, very swiftly reveals that it is this rationalist conception of religious knowledge which really generates his difficulty: *"Accidental truths of history can never become the proof of necessary truths of reason."*[15] Here Lessing could be taken as suggesting that empirical knowledge cannot be the ground of

15. Lessing, "On the Proof of the Spirit," p. 53.

religious knowledge because religious knowledge must be of necessary truths, truths of reason. Historical knowledge, being empirical, can only be of contingent "accidental" truths.

The true empiricist thinks the problem lies with the empirical evidence; if we just had better evidence, then empirical knowledge could amount to religious knowledge. The rationalist believes that no matter how good the empirical evidence, historical knowledge could never amount to religious knowledge; it just isn't the right *kind* of knowledge. When Lessing objects to historical religious knowledge on the grounds that historical propositions are contingent, then his initial claims that his problems have to do with the character of historical evidence can't be taken seriously. Despite his claims that if he had been an eyewitness to the miracles of the New Testament he would have been a believer, it now appears that empirical propositions, however well attested, simply don't have the right kind of character to count as religious knowledge for Lessing. The worries about the uncertainties of history are a confusing red herring, since Lessing's real objection to historical religious knowledge would count just as strongly against firsthand experiential knowledge. If I experienced a miracle, the knowledge I thereby gained would still be knowledge of a contingent and not a necessary truth.

Let me summarize the direction of the argument so far. When we think hard about the naive empiricist worry about historical knowledge, it turns out that the ground of the problem has little to do with history per se; instead, it has to do with the uncertain nature of empirical knowledge generally, thus transforming itself into the sophisticated empiricist version of the problem. The problem of linking empirical knowledge with religious knowledge in turn is rooted in a particular conception of religious knowledge. Either religious knowledge requires a peculiar kind of certainty that empirical knowledge cannot possess, or else religious knowledge requires the employment of distinctive predicates that generate a peculiar kind of empirical uncertainty. In both cases, I will try to show that the underlying conception of religious knowledge the "empiricist" is presupposing has close affinities with the rationalist conception of religious knowledge. To do this I must examine each of the two cases more closely.

IV. Religious Faith as Requiring
Unattainable Empirical Certainty

In the first case the worry is that religious faith requires a level of certainty and commitment that empirical knowledge cannot in principle provide. It is alleged that my assent to an empirical truth is (or at least should be) proportional to the evidence, tentative in nature, subject to being over-turned by further evidence. Religious faith, on the other hand, is supposed to have an absoluteness and finality about it that is incommensurable with this empirical openness. Sometimes this point is made with respect to what philosophers call the "ethics of belief" and what Van Harvey has referred to as the "morality of knowledge."[16] The essential idea here is that if one incorporates empirical beliefs about historical facts into one's religious faith one is intellectually dishonest or violates a standard of intellectual integrity. I should not believe historical facts unreservedly or with all my heart, yet this is exactly what religious faith requires.

Kierkegaard's remarks in *Concluding Unscientific Postscript* about the difficulties involved in grounding faith in a "quantitative approximation" are often cited as support for this point of view.[17] He there maintains that even the greatest conceivable historical evidence would be inadequate as a basis for religious faith: "If all the angels in heaven were to put their heads together, they could still bring to pass only an approximation, because an approximation is the only certainty attainable for historical knowledge — but also too little to build an eternal happiness upon."[18] Faith for Kierke-gaard involves infinitely interested passion, but if faith is directed to what can never be more than an approximation, we get fanaticism.[19] "There is an essential incommensurability between it [an approximation] and a personal infinite interest in one's eternal happiness."[20]

16. See Van Harvey, *The Historian and the Believer*, esp. chap. 4.

17. In reality, of course, these remarks are not Kierkegaard's but those of his pseudonym Johannes Climacus. The relation between Kierkegaard and the pseudonym will not be considered here.

18. Søren Kierkegaard, *Concluding Unscientific Postscript* (Kierkegaard's *Samlede Værker*, 1st ed., vol. 7, p. 19); the English translation here is my own but is modified from the old Swenson-Lowrie version (Princeton: Princeton University Press, 1941), p. 31.

19. Kierkegaard, *Concluding Unscientific Postscript*, *Samlede Værker* 7:20; English edition, p. 32.

20. Kierkegaard, *Concluding Unscientific Postscript*, *Samlede Værker* 7:13; English edition, p. 26.

I believe that this Kierkegaardian point is at least part of the motivation for theological accounts of faith that make faith essentially independent of history. Such accounts have been common in twentieth-century Protestant theology. Paul Tillich's view on this point may seem extreme, but I believe Tillich is simply representing in a clear and consistent way a widespread tendency:

> Faith does not affirm or deny what belongs to the prescientific or scientific knowledge of our world. . . . The knowledge of our world (including ourselves as a part of our world) is a matter of inquiry by ourselves or by those in whom we trust. It is not a matter of faith. The dimension of faith is not the dimension of science, history or psychology. The acceptance of a probable hypothesis in these realms is not faith, but preliminary belief, to be tested by scholarly methods, and to be changed by every new discovery.[21]

I take Tillich to be saying here, not merely that faith concerns itself with personal beliefs that are not the result of scholarship, but that faith does not contain any empirical content whatsoever. Faith does not include *belief*.[22] However, I believe that those who agree with Tillich about this have misunderstood Kierkegaard's point. They are in the grip of a rationalist assumption about the nature of religious knowledge that Kierkegaard would reject.

The removal of faith from the "dimension of science, history or psychology," that is, from the empirical realm altogether, seems designed to insulate faith from the possibility of being disproved or refuted by empirical knowledge. Tillich says explicitly that the conflicts between faith and knowledge are rooted in the mistaken view that faith involves this kind of empirical content. If religious faith has no empirical content, then it cannot come into conflict with science or any kind of empirical scholarship. On Tillich's view, my faith will be safe from the risk that scholarship will show it to be mistaken, because my faith involves no commitments on any matters on which scholarship is competent to pass judgment.

Now from a Kierkegaardian perspective the insulation of faith from risk has a dubious ring about it. Kierkegaard maintains, in fact, that since faith involves passion, and passion thrives on uncertainty, that risk

21. Paul Tillich, *The Dynamics of Faith* (New York: Harper & Row, 1957), p. 33.
22. Tillich, *Dynamics of Faith*, p. 31.

is an essential element of faith.[23] Furthermore, Kierkegaard maintains strenuously that belief in the historical incarnation of God as a human being, paradoxical and scandalous as such a claim may appear, is essential to genuine Christian faith. In *Philosophical Fragments*, Kierkegaard (or, to speak precisely, his pseudonym Johannes Climacus) maintains that if Christian beliefs about Jesus as the God-man are merely mythology, then Christianity would not differ essentially from pagan philosophy.[24] What is genuinely different about Christianity is the claim that human beings are sinful and lack saving Truth; therefore this Truth must be brought to us by God himself in the form of a human being.[25] If this is a story human beings have made up, or are even capable of making up, then human beings do *not* lack the Truth and Christianity is false.[26] The Christian is committed to a set of beliefs that are uncertain in the same way that all empirical, and especially historical, beliefs are uncertain, but that in addition have hanging on them the enormous uncertainty generated by the paradoxicalness of the alleged events.[27]

The incommensurability Kierkegaard claims to perceive between faith and empirical inquiry by no means leads him to empty faith of empirical content. Kierkegaard thinks, rightly or wrongly, that one should not try to base faith on historical scholarship, but he does not think this means that faith must be emptied of historical content. There is no reason to do this, since faith thrives on the risk that the Tillich maneuver seems designed to avoid. And there is every reason not to do this, since if Christian faith is emptied of historical content, then it simply is no longer Christian.

Those who assume that to free faith from the contingencies of empirical scholarship one must free it from empirical content have failed to recognize that it might be possible to have an empirical belief that is not based on empirical evidence. For example, as some Reformation thinkers maintained, my belief that Jesus is God might be rooted in an awareness of sin in my life — an awareness that is the work of the Holy

---

23. Kierkegaard, *Concluding Unscientific Postscript, Samlede Værker* 7:18; English edition, p. 30.

24. Søren Kierkegaard, *Philosophical Fragments* (Princeton: Princeton University Press, 1985). See esp. chaps. 1 and 2. (Readers wishing to consult the Danish will find the pagination of *Samlede Værker*, 1st ed., vol. 4, in the margins of this edition.)

25. Kierkegaard, *Philosophical Fragments*, pp. 13-18, 30-34.

26. Kierkegaard, *Philosophical Fragments*, pp. 21, 35-36.

27. Kierkegaard, *Philosophical Fragments*, pp. 87-88.

Spirit in my life.[28] Perhaps if this awareness of sin is present, then the amount and quality of historical evidence available become unimportant. Rightly or wrongly, Kierkegaard thinks this is the case. He thinks such an awareness of sin will lead to a faith that is not tentatively awaiting the results of the next scholarly conference, a faith that will be maintained regardless of the amount of historical evidence that I have available. My purpose here is not to argue that Kierkegaard is right or wrong about this.[29] My point is rather that there is a big difference between the claim that faith is not a direct result of empirical *evidence* and the claim that faith has no empirical *content*. Someone who shares Kierkegaard's worry about making faith dependent on scholarship need only make the former claim and not the latter. Actually, even the former claim may not be necessary; there may be other ways of dealing with the problem of faith and the tentativeness of scholarly inquiry.[30]

The incommensurability between empirical scholarship and faith that Kierkegaard alleges leads at best to the claim that faith is not a direct result of scholarship. To go further and claim that faith must be emptied of empirical content one must show that beliefs with empirical content can only be properly arrived at on the basis of empirical scholarship, a claim that I predict will be very difficult to support. After all, in my ordinary life I surely have many beliefs with empirical content that are in no meaningful sense the product of scholarship. I believe, for example, with a high degree of assurance, that my wife loves me, that the world I live in is more than five minutes old and will still be around for the next few minutes, and that the students I teach are not cunningly contrived robots. None of these matters is a proper subject for scholarly inquiry.

The urge to insulate faith from empirical content stems, I believe, not from Kierkegaardian qualms about making faith dependent on scholarship, but from rationalist intuitions that faith must not be the

---

28. Kierkegaard himself asserts this clearly in *Practice in Christianity* (Princeton: Princeton University Press, 1991), p. 67. This position is, however, recognizable in Calvin and, as Kierkegaard himself says, in Luther as well.

29. For a critical evaluation of Kierkegaard's claim, see my *Passionate Reason: Making Sense of Kierkegaard's "Philosophical Fragments"* (Bloomington: Indiana University Press, 1992), chap. 9.

30. For an example, see Robert Adams's critical treatment of Kierkegaard, "Kierkegaard's Arguments Against Objective Reasoning in Religion," *The Monist* 60, 2 (1977); reprinted in *Contemporary Philosophy of Religion*, ed. Steven Cahn and David Schatz (Oxford: Oxford University Press, 1982), pp. 213-28.

sort of thing one could be mistaken about. If religion concerns ultimate truth, the rationalist mind says, then surely it cannot be concerned with anything so risky as beliefs with empirical content. It must be concerned with what is truly certain: necessary truths, or self-evident truths, or universally accessible, timeless truths. Even if I have to work hard to recognize these truths — by meditation, prayer, contemplation, or philosophical dialogue — once I hit on them I surely have hit on something that must be far more certain than mere empirical propositions.

Unfortunately for the rationalist, the claim that ultimate religious truth must be self-evident is itself far from self-evident. Nor is it a necessary truth that ultimate religious truth must consist of necessary truths. Perhaps these rationalist claims can be argued for, but I see no reason for the Christian theologian to accept such claims a priori. Rather, the message of Christianity is that we are profoundly historical beings, not timeless, godlike beings who already possess ultimate truth. Sin is historical, and so is redemption, and it should not be surprising that our redemption hinges on something that occurred in history. Nor should it be surprising that it is important for us to know about what has occurred.

So I conclude that worries that faith cannot include empirical content, because empirical beliefs can never be "certain," are at bottom the expression of a rationalist and not an empiricist attitude. Furthermore, this is an attitude that Christians have no particular reason to accept as correct.

V. Religious Faith as Generating Empirical Uncertainty

I have considered at length and criticized as resting on a covert rationalism the claim that empirical knowledge is religiously inadequate because religious knowledge requires a high degree of certainty. The other possible reason for thinking that empirical knowledge in general is religiously inadequate, it will be recalled, is that religious knowledge *generates* an especially high degree of empirical uncertainty. Perhaps the problem is not that religious knowledge needs to be specially certain, but that religious knowledge creates a particular kind of uncertainty.

It is often claimed that all empirical knowledge is subject to uncertainty. Even the eyewitness of an event may be mistaken, for a whole host of standard reasons. The eyewitness may see what she was expecting to see or what she hoped to see or what she feared to see instead of what happened. The observer's judgments may be mistaken because she lacks the concepts to describe accurately what is happening, or perhaps misapplies those concepts. These kinds of problems are endemic to empirical knowledge generally, and there are good reasons to think that specially severe kinds of problems arise when the object of the perception is something regarded as religiously ultimate. (In what follows I shall call this the "religious object.")

Whether the religious object be construed as God, the Absolute, the Tao, or Nirvana, almost all the great religions have thought that the religious object cannot be identified with a particular object in the spatio-temporal world. When we couple this claim with the thesis that our language was developed precisely to describe and act in this spatio-temporal world, then it seems to lead naturally to the claim that it will be difficult to describe the religious object in human language. Indeed, many religious thinkers have maintained that it is impossible. In this context, I am not interested so much in the adequacy of human language to describe the religious object as in the problems generated for empirical knowledge by the *application* of our concepts to what is religiously ultimate.

The problem is essentially this: If we lack adequate concepts to describe the religious object, or if the application of those concepts is problematic, then even if God or what is divine appeared in the empirical order, it is no simple matter to see how this might generate empirical knowledge. For empirical knowledge, at least the kind that can be the object of a propositional attitude, requires concepts and the correct application of those concepts. To go back to a Christian framework, even if God appeared to me, could I reliably recognize and describe God? If God performs a miracle before my very eyes, perhaps I can empirically recognize that something profoundly strange has occurred. However, to classify the event as a miracle is to attribute it to God, and it has appeared to many thinkers that this would be difficult to know empirically.

Of course, some thinkers have held that it is impossible to use human language to describe God, and thus that it is impossible empirically to recognize divine action. In effect, they claim that human concepts simply cannot be successfully applied to the divine. There are versions of empiricism, such as twentieth-century logical positivism, that rule out any meaningful reference to anything beyond sense data. However, it seems to me that these versions of empiricism are extreme and implausible positions. However, it isn't necessary to hold such an extreme position and make such a strong claim in order to say that recognizing the presence of God in human experience presents special problems.

Once again theologians have appealed to Kierkegaard to buttress this point, for Kierkegaard maintains strongly that God cannot be directly or immediately perceived in the natural world, for if God were so perceived, then in effect God would simply be an object in the natural world. According to Kierkegaard, the claim that God can be directly recognized is simply paganism, which lacked an adequate understanding of the transcendence of God.[31] Kierkegaard applies this same reasoning to the incarnation. Jesus may be God in human form. He may have performed miracles, taught profoundly, and lived a remarkable life. But it does not follow logically from these observable facts that Jesus was in fact God. Jesus appeared to be an ordinary human being, and his divinity was not *immediately* recognizable, but was rather apparent only to the eyes of faith.[32] Many people saw Jesus perform miracles, if the Gospels are accurate, without coming to faith; others seem to have arrived at faith without much in the way of empirical evidence.

This worry that empirical religious knowledge is problematic and uncertain does appear to be a genuinely empiricist worry, since it appears to be rooted in an empiricist theory of concept formation. It is difficult to apply our language to God because our language is developed to deal with sensory perceptions of objects in the spatio-temporal world. However, it makes a great deal of difference how we conceive of this problem. Specifically, is the problem one that is potentially solvable? Is it merely difficult to recognize God in human experience or is it impossible? If it is impossible, how do we know that it is impossible? In other words, does this difficulty support the strong negative claim or merely the weak negative claim?

I think the answer to this depends largely on what version of empiricism one holds. Strong versions of empiricism, such as logical positivism or logical empiricism, probably do support the strong negative claim. However, as I said above, it seems to me that these versions of empiricism are the least plausible ones.

---

31. Kierkegaard, *Concluding Unscientific Postscript*, *Samlede Værker* 7:205; English edition, p. 218.

32. Kierkegaard, *Philosophical Fragments*, p. 102.

As I read Kierkegaard, his thesis is not that it is impossible to have an experience of God, but rather that to have such an experience certain subjective conditions have to be satisfied. That is, he does not claim that it is impossible to experience God or recognize Jesus as God, but that this experience is not one that occurs *immediately*. Jesus can be recognized as God, but the recognition is not a *direct* one. What precisely Kierkegaard means by this is of course a matter of interpretation, but I find it very plausible to read the claims in this way: God cannot be perceived or recognized without the right kind of spiritual qualities being present in the perceiver. Kierkegaard's own term for the appropriate kind of spiritual qualities is "subjectivity." The claim is not that Jesus cannot be recognized as God, but that the recognition is mediated by the subjectivity of the perceiver. The claim is not that God cannot be perceived, but that, since God is a spirit, to recognize God at work the individual must be spiritually developed. "When the individual is spiritually developed, it becomes possible to see God everywhere."[33]

Now the claim that certain subjective conditions must be present for something to be experienced is compatible with plausible forms of empiricism. Only the crudest kind of empiricism ignores the subjective qualities of the perceiver. Not everything in the world is as easy to perceive as a color patch, and it is a commonplace of theories of perception today that accurate perception requires the perceiver to have certain subjective qualities. The perceiver must understand the relevant concepts, have mastered the relevant skills, be willing to look for the right things. To "see" a bubble-chamber photograph as a record of subatomic particles, one must be a highly qualified observer. One becomes such an observer by becoming part of the scientific community, absorbing its values and acquiring the skills and conceptual repertoire needed. So I don't see the Kierkegaardian claim as creating an insuperable problem for the claim that there could be empirical religious knowledge. Kierkegaard simply wants to emphasize the fact that the objects of our perception in this case are not objects like trees or pieces of paper but spiritual and religious in character, and thus the relevant personal qualifications will also be religious and spiritual in character. This implies that gaining such knowledge may be difficult, but it certainly does not imply that it is impossible. In principle, such knowledge

33. Kierkegaard, *Concluding Unscientific Postscript, Samlede Værker* 7:207-8; English edition, pp. 220-21.

may be attainable, and if we are good empiricists we will leave the question as to whether it is actually attained by anyone for experience to decide and not legislate a priori that it is impossible. A plausible version of empiricism therefore supports only the weak negative claim, not the strong claim. Applying our human concepts to God in our experience may be difficult and tricky, but we have no good reasons to suppose it is impossible.

The claim that it is impossible for anyone to experience God or God's activity does not seem to follow from any plausible version of empiricism. Rather, it reflects a priori convictions about the character of the divine and the relation of the divine to the natural world. Someone who insists that empirical religious knowledge is impossible seems to know a priori that religious knowledge has as its subject matter something that could not appear in space and time, or something that could not be recognized if it did. However, such an a priori conviction does not stem from the genuinely empirical spirit, but reflects a rationalist mind-set. Why should we assume that whatever religious knowledge takes as its object must be timeless, eternal, or wholly other in such a way that it can't manifest itself in the natural world at all? While it may be a genuinely empiricist claim to say that empirical religious knowledge is difficult to attain or can only be attained under certain conditions, empiricism provides no real support for the thesis that empirical religious knowledge is impossible. Once more we appear to have a dogmatic rationalist claim that is not self-evident or necessarily true, one that Christianity has traditionally rejected, and which therefore stands in need of argument.

VI. Can the Rationalist Conception of Religious Knowledge Be Defended?

Perhaps some support is provided for the rationalist conception of religious knowledge by what might be termed the *problem of particularity*. If religious knowledge is tied to historical events, then it will necessarily be tied to particular events at a particular place and time, known to some people, perhaps, but not to others who unfortunately were blocked from this knowledge by the accidents of history and geography. If religious knowledge concerns some timeless inner truth, then it would be equally available to all human beings, at least in principle, and it might be argued that such equality is what we would expect from God if God is good. Once more, Kierkegaard can be cited in favor of this idea: "Would the god allow the power of time to decide whom he would grant his favor, or would it not be worthy of the god to make the reconciliation equally difficult for every human being at every time and in every place. . . ."[34]

Curiously, Kierkegaard can also be cited on the other side of this issue. Speaking of Christianity, he says that "[t]he blessedness which is tied to a historical situation excludes all who are outside this situation, and of them countless numbers are not excluded by their own fault but by the accidental circumstance that Christianity has not yet been preached to them."[35] I am not sure how to reconcile these two Kierkegaardian texts or indeed whether it is possible to do so.[36] However, I think several points are necessary to put the issue into perspective.

First, the problem of particularity should not be conflated with the problem of the ultimate status of those who are non-Christians. To see this, one has only to point out that universalism is compatible with the claim that ultimate religious truth contains a historical component. I might hold that Jesus' life, death, and resurrection are the ultimate revelation of God and God's love, and that a knowledge of Jesus is thus the key to salvific knowledge of God, while simultaneously holding that ultimately everyone will have that knowledge. So the claim that the ultimate religious truth is historical does not entail, at least without further premises, that those who lack this revelation in this life are eternally damned. It entails at most that those who presently lack this revelation lack the relevant knowledge of God at this time. To conclude that they will lack it eternally one must also hold that a person who lacks a knowledge of Jesus in this life can never gain such knowledge.

Of course, one might respond to this that universalism is inconsistent with the spirit, if not the letter, of historical religious knowledge. Historical religious knowledge seems linked to the idea that human beings are historical in a deep and profound sense. What happens in this life really matters, and thus both salvation and perdition are achieved through historical processes. Universalism, on the other hand,

34. Kierkegaard, *Philosophical Fragments*, p. 106.
35. Kierkegaard, *Concluding Unscientific Postscript*, *Samlede Værker* 7:508; English edition, p. 516.
36. See chap. 9 of my *Passionate Reason* for discussion of ways to resolve this tension.

seems to imply that history really doesn't matter ultimately, since in the end we all arrive at the same place.

Someone impressed by this line of reasoning might reject universalism but still hold that no one is excluded from the possibility of salvation by the accidents of time and geography. One might hold that not everyone is saved, but still believe that after death a kind of clarification is provided for those who have not had the opportunity to make a meaningful choice, enabling them to do so. Furthermore, history might matter to such a choice, because it is perfectly plausible that the choice a person makes would reflect the kind of person she has become in this life.

Another alternative would be to say that some are saved by Christ and in some sense have faith in Christ without realizing that it is Christ they are following. Just as saints in the Old Testament looked forward trustingly to God's redemption, and so in some sense trusted in Christ who is that redemption, without clearly understanding the form that redemption might take, so those who in later times and today lack a clear understanding of what God has done in Christ might look trustingly to God to provide salvation in some form. Perhaps they are in fact enlightened by Christ, the *logos* who enlightens every person who comes into the world.

These two ideas, that at death some receive a clarification and that some follow Christ in this life without realizing that it is Christ whom they are following, may even be combined. At death the people who have trusted Christ without realizing clearly who he is might receive a clarification in which they recognize that their faith is in fact faith in Jesus. However, my point here is not to argue for such soteriological theories but to point out that the question of whether religious knowledge might be historical must be distinguished from the question of the ultimate fate of those who do not respond to that revelation in this life for "accidental" reasons.

One other clarification is also in order here. The possibility of a historical revelation and thus of historical religious knowledge must be distinguished from the question of the exclusivity of such a revelation. The claim that God has revealed himself in the history of the Jewish people and in Jesus of Nazareth is not equivalent to the claim that God has revealed himself solely through this history. Of course, some Christians, mistakenly in my opinion, have wished to assert such exclusivity, but that is a separate, additional claim. Exclusivity is an even stronger claim than a claim of finality and supremacy, which many more Christians have wished to assert in some sense, but finality and supremacy are also logically distinct from the simple claim that historical religious knowledge has been provided. This is illustrated by the work of John Hick, whose position seems to be that God has revealed himself in a variety of places and times through a variety of "prophets," and that these multiple revelations are roughly equal in religious truth.[37] Once the possibility of historical religious knowledge is granted, the questions as to the relations among various claimants to be historical religious knowledge come to the fore, and it certainly must be considered whether one set of such claims could have some sort of superiority to others. However, that discussion is logically distinct from and should not preclude the primary discussion as to whether historical religious knowledge is possible at all.

Once the questions of the "fate of the heathen" and of exclusivity and revelational superiority are laid to one side, the problem of particularity is somewhat clearer but not necessarily solved. One might still wonder why God should reveal himself at one place rather than another, at one time rather than another, to one people rather than another. The proper answer to such musings is, I suspect, to confess that we don't know why God should do these things. However, I don't see why we should know. If God is indeed a personal being, then it seems reasonable that his actions, like those of all other persons we know, should have specificity. Perhaps it makes sense to say that God might be expected to act in particular ways at particular times. But I don't see why we humans should expect to know why God performed *this* particular action at *this* particular place and time.

The rationalist view that ultimate religious truth is a timeless truth which is in some sense equally available to all human beings does have a certain attractiveness. However, I wonder if it does not owe that attractiveness to the flattering picture it presupposes of human nature. To use the language of Kierkegaard in *Philosophical Fragments*, this picture is essentially one that sees human beings as possessing the Truth in some Socratic/Platonic sense. Kierkegaard, in fact, reflecting on the *Phaedo*, says that the Platonic doctrine of recollection implies the immortality and thus divinity of the soul, and that recollection is simply

---

37. See John Hick, *God and the Universe of Faiths* (New York: St. Martin's Press, 1973), and many of his later publications.

knowledge of the god.[38] Perhaps ultimate religious truth is not consciously recognized by everyone, but every human being possesses the essential ability to grasp that Truth. Here human beings and ultimate reality are seen as being on good terms, as having a natural affinity. According to Kierkegaard, Christianity, with its doctrine of sin, presupposes that human beings lack this Truth. We not only lack a conscious understanding of the Truth but even lack the ability to gain such an understanding if we must rely solely on our natural resources. That is precisely why a historical revelation is necessary. If God cannot be accurately known in our "inner consciousness," then God must break in on that consciousness. We need, Kierkegaard thinks, God to break in on us from "outside" that consciousness. We need to know God as God really is, not as we imagine him or want him to be. Human history has the right kind of "objectivity" about it. What has happened in history has happened, whether I like it or not. In other words, though Kierkegaard is far from claiming to know why God became incarnate in first-century Palestine rather than in second-century North America, he does think that the claim that God has appeared in a *particular* time and place makes sense, given the Christian picture of human nature.

Of course, it is obvious that human beings can and do interpret historical events, and so even a historical revelation allows plenty of room for people to try to make God in their own image. To this end one may call as evidence the plethora of "lives of Jesus" in which Jesus always seems to embody just those qualities the author admires. Still, if God has really appeared in human history, there is a sense in which God is really *outside* our preconceptions. God is really *other*, to use a currently fashionable category. Moreover, that otherness may show itself in the shock of recognition manifested in the testimony of those who encountered God in Jesus, a shock that continues to be felt as others encounter God through that testimony.

Kierkegaard thinks that this Christian picture will naturally be perceived by humans as offensive, at least until they have been transformed by God's revelation and have responded to that revelation in faith. After all, if we think we "have God within us" then the Christian picture is a kind of insult. It is a challenge to our pride and self-sufficiency. If

---

38. See the discussion of recollection in Kierkegaard's *The Concept of Irony* (Bloomington: Indiana University Press, 1968), pp. 96ff., and also p. 87 in *Philosophical Fragments*.

Kierkegaard is right about this, then the natural attractiveness of the rationalist picture of religious knowledge may not stem from the truth of that picture but from its psychological appeal. In this respect the common charge that religious belief is rooted in wish fulfillment may be less applicable to Christian belief than to some other religious beliefs. It is probably for this reason that Kierkegaard claims that a lack of concern for truth is one of the biggest reasons why people do not become Christians; most people, he says, would rather believe what is comforting and flattering than what is true, and the Christian picture of human nature and the human task is anything but comforting and flattering.[39]

I conclude that, though the claim that God has revealed himself in history may be surprising and even upsetting, we have no good reason to think that such a revelation is impossible. Particularity may be troublesome, but it should not be thought to rule out a historical revelation unless we have some good reason to think that the rationalist conception of religious knowledge is true. The "problem of particularity" is a problem that *rests on* a rationalist conception of religious knowledge; it will only be regarded as a severe problem by people who already accept the rationalist conception of religious knowledge, together with its underlying optimistic view of human nature. It therefore cannot settle the question of whether religious knowledge can be historical and particular by providing support for that rationalist conception.

VII. Conclusions: Further Work to Be Done

I have attempted to show that the strong negative claim about historical religious knowledge typically rests on a rationalist conception of religious knowledge and not on any plausible empiricist conceptions of religious knowledge. Though the objections are sometimes couched in a manner that makes them appear to be empiricist, when we examine the problems closely we find that they are not. Furthermore, that rationalist conception of religious knowledge does not appear to be intuitively obvious or self-evident. It stands in need of argument. Perhaps

---

39. See Kierkegaard's *The Sickness Unto Death* (Princeton: Princeton University Press, 1980), pp. 42-43. This edition, like the others in the *Kierkegaard's Writings* edition, contains in the margins the pagination of the *Samlede Værker*, 1st ed.

there are good arguments for it that I have not considered. If so, they need to be brought onto the table and examined. In the meantime, I conclude that we have no good reason to rule out the possibility of historical religious knowledge.

Of course, the claim that historical religious knowledge is possible is far from a claim that it is actual. To claim that it is actual, the weak negative thesis must be dealt with, and that may be more troublesome. To establish that such knowledge is actual and not merely possible, I think a number of questions must be addressed, including the following: (1) Must historical religious beliefs be based on evidence? (2) If historical religious beliefs are based on evidence, what kind of evidence is needed and how should it be assessed? (3) If historical religious beliefs are based on evidence, must the quality of the belief be in some way proportionate to the strength of the evidence, and is such an "ethic of belief" consistent with the attitude of authentic religious faith? These questions are certainly difficult and daunting, but I see no reason to think that plausible accounts of belief and knowledge cannot be found that make historical religious knowledge a real and not merely a logical possibility.

Christian Philosophers and the Copernican Revolution

Merold Westphal

O ne of my most interesting experiences as a teacher was in a Philosophy of Mind course I taught some years ago at a Christian college. As we began to explore Descartes's *Meditations,* I asked the students whether someone coming to them as a Christian should be biased in favor of his dualistic account or against it. Those students who were able to see any possible connection between the two thought a Christian reader should be sympathetic to Descartes.

I suggested the opposite possibility on two grounds. First, it might seem that Descartes is saying that I am my mind but not my body and that this might be hard to reconcile with biblical conceptions of creation, especially if it carried any Platonic-Pythagorean disparagement of the body as evil or as the source of evil. Second, I noted that for the biblical writers the body was so essentially part of who I am that the only form of life after death that inspires their hope is the resurrection of the body, and I reminded the students that the Apostles' Creed affirms the resurrection of the body and not the immortality of the soul.

This suggestion disturbed one of the students, who mentioned the matter to her father. He was disturbed enough to discuss it with their pastor, who assured him that I was probably a Jehovah's Witness. In the meantime, the student polled the members of the religion department, only to discover that without exception they were also Jehovah's Witnesses with the same curious addiction to creation, the resurrection of the body, and the Apostles' Creed.

I love to find excuses to tell this story. In the present context my excuse is that it enables me to introduce the kind of question I want to discuss in this essay, the question regarding whether one's Christian faith should dispose one to be sympathetic or unsympathetic toward this or that philosophical position. There have been times and traditions, medieval and modern, that have been uncomfortable with such a question on the grounds that philosophical reflection as such takes place in a theologically neutral medium and that any propensities arising out of religious faith must be severely bracketed. The boarding area from which the owl of Minerva takes her flight is guarded by devices designed to detect all such biases, dispositions, and propensities and to assure that they are not allowed on board.

The view of human reason presupposed by this view of a presuppositionless, neutral medium of thought has become highly dubious; and, in fact, the closest thing to a philosophical consensus today is that this view of reason is fatally flawed. (There is, of course, no consensus about where to go from that conclusion.) Because I believe this consensus to be on the right track (though I shall not argue that here), I am not uncomfortable with questions of the sort specified above. In fact, the purpose of this essay is to ask such a question and propose an answer to it.

Should Christian philosophers be favorably or unfavorably disposed toward Kantian idealism? I want to suggest that they should be favorably disposed and that there are important affinities between Kantian idealism and Christian theism, important resources in the former for expressing themes essential to the latter.

This is not a majority report. Christian philosophers, both Catholic and Protestant, have often felt a strong need to be realists and have exhibited a correspondingly strong allergic reaction to Kantian idealism in all its forms. No student of Art Holmes is likely to say that there is only one way to be a Christian philosopher; and so I do not wish to deny that realism has resources that can be put to good use by Christian thinkers. I only wish to suggest that the instinctive distrust of Kantian idealism is unfortunate and in need of being overcome.

A recent renunciation of Kant and all his works can be found in Alvin Plantinga's 1989-90 Stob Lectures, *The Twin Pillars of Christian Scholarship*.[1] In disputing that repudiation of Kant, my quarrel is not

---

1. Alvin Plantinga, *The Twin Pillars of Christian Scholarship* (published as a pamphlet by Calvin College and Seminary, Grand Rapids, MI, 1990). Cited parenthetically in the text as *TP*.

with Plantinga in particular but with a widespread tendency among Christian philosophers to which he has given a powerful, simple, and typically witty expression.

Rejecting the view that human reason is worldview neutral, Plantinga claims that philosophical conflict is one form in which the battle between the *Civitas Dei* and the *Civitas Mundi* takes place. In the Western intellectual world at present he sees two primary opponents to Christian theism: (1) perennial naturalism, with its ancient roots in Epicurus, Democritus, and Lucretius, and (2) creative antirealism, with its ancient roots in Protagoras and his claim that man *(sic)* is the measure of all things. But he makes it clear that the real locus classicus for this second major modern threat to Christian theism is Kant's *Critique of Pure Reason* (*TP* 10, 14-15).

The reference to the First Critique is important, for the Kantian idealism at issue is not the views of ethics, politics, and religion developed by Kant in subsequent writings but the epistemological core of the First Critique, to which he gave memorable expression in the second edition preface by calling it a second Copernican Revolution. Realism has assumed that "all our knowledge must conform to objects." His idealism will explore the alternative, "that objects must conform to our knowledge" (B xvi). Plantinga identifies precisely this move as the essence of creative antirealism: "But the fundamental *thrust* of Kant's self-styled Copernican Revolution is that the things in the world owe their basic structure and perhaps their very existence to the noetic activity of our minds" (*TP* 15).

I want to suggest that there are four fundamentally different kinds of Kantianism, and that only one of these merits the negative characterization Plantinga gives to creative antirealism in general.

It might be well to note here that realism's epistemological claim, that knowledge conforms to its objects, presupposes a metaphysical claim, that this is in principle possible. It is not easy to state the latter, for it goes beyond the notion that there is a world independent of our apprehension of it. It is also the claim that the world is a certain way and that that way can in principle be expressed in the sorts of things usually associated with knowledge — judgments and propositions, for example. In other words, by denying the radical doctrine of flux to be found in Buddhism or the hyper-Heracliteanism of Cratylus, realism denies the claim that all judgments or propositions are necessarily false, that regardless of their content they distort the real by treating its flow as if it had stopped. Gorgias of Leontini seems to have set forth such a view in *On Not Being or Nature*. According to Eduard Zeller, "He established three propositions (1) that nothing exists (2) that if anything existed it could not be known and (3) that if it would be known it could not be communicated to others."[2] Realists hold the world to be such that it can in principle constrain our judgments and beliefs positively, not just negatively as a call to silence.

Because this assumption is often taken for granted, it is often not argued (a notoriously difficult task) or even expressed. Christian theists typically make this assumption; in fact, it would probably be seriously misleading to call any metaphysics theistic that permits only a *via negativa*, epistemologically speaking. I mention this only to note that I find nothing in Kantian idealism that challenges this assumption, even implicitly. Kant should not be confused with Cratylus or Gorgias.

The epistemological claim of realists, correspondingly, is that "knowledge must conform to objects" because such conformity (however difficult it may be to state wherein it consists) is both possible in principle and just what it takes to make our judgments or beliefs into knowledge. Thus "knowledge must conform to objects" is really shorthand for "our beliefs and judgments must conform to their objects if they want to deserve the name of knowledge." It is this claim that Kant seeks to qualify substantially. Much of what he counts as human knowledge is not our conforming to the way things are but their conforming to the way we apprehend them.

My experience in trying to teach Kant is that students are so deeply wedded to some sort of commonsense realism that they have a difficult time, not so much in accepting Kant's claim as in first understanding what he is saying. So when I teach the First Critique I resort to homely examples. I ask how it is possible for me to know a priori, that is, before turning on the TV to watch the evening news, that Dan Rather's tie

---

2. Eduard Zeller, *Outlines of the History of Greek Philosophy*, trans. L. R. Palmer, 13th ed., revised (New York: Dover, 1980), pp. 86-87. Cf. *Sextus Empiricus*, Loeb Classical Library, trans. R. G. Bury (London: Heinemann, 1935), 2:65. Jean-François Lyotard compares this triple negation to the defense cited by Freud in *Jokes and Their Relation to the Unconscious*. A man accused of returning a borrowed kettle with a hole in it replied (1) that he had not borrowed the kettle, (2) that the kettle had a hole in it when he borrowed it, and (3) that there was no hole in it when he returned it. Lyotard, *The Differend: Phrases in Dispute*, trans. Georges Van Den Abbeele (Minneapolis: University of Minnesota Press, 1988), p. 15.

will be various shades of gray. A typical answer will have an inductive character quite contrary to Kant's meaning. Dan Rather has been wearing gray ties all week, so I infer that he will do so again tonight.

I insist that I have not been watching the news lately and have no observational basis for such an inference, but nevertheless I know for sure that the tie will be gray tonight. Silence. Then suddenly a light goes on and some student solves the puzzle. "You're watching on a black-and-white TV set." From there it is fairly easy to show that Kant thinks of the human mind as a kind of receiving apparatus whose "spontaneity" permits things, regardless of what they are actually like, to appear only in certain ways.

Crude as this model is, it illustrates several key elements in Kant's account. First, it attributes some but not all of the features I perceive the object to have to my receiving apparatus. I can know the tie's color a priori, for example, but not whether it will be polka dot or striped. For Kant, the features due to the "spontaneity" of the human mind are formal, the forms of intuition and the categories of understanding. Hence the appropriateness of describing the Copernican Revolution as attributing the "basic structure" of things in the world to "the noetic activity of our minds."

Second, this model helps us resolve the question of whether things in the world owe "their very existence" to that same activity. Plantinga's answer (above) to the question of whether Kant makes such a claim is "perhaps."[3] It might be better to say, "It depends." One way of talking about Dan Rather's tie is to say that there are two of them, the red and blue one I would see if I were in the studio and could see it without dependence on my black-and-white receiving apparatus, and the gray one I see while watching TV. On the other hand, since I more naturally say that I am watching Dan Rather than that I am watching his image on the screen (unless I am comparing two sets with higher and lower resolution), it might be better to speak of only one tie and of two ways of seeing it. In both cases I look at his red and blue tie, but in the studio I see it as it truly is, while at home watching TV I see it as it has been systematically distorted by a receiving apparatus that simultaneously makes it possible for me to see the tie at all (since I'm not in the studio) and makes it impossible for me to see it as it truly is.

3. In his discussion of creative antirealism in his 1982 Presidential Address to the Central Division of the APA, Plantinga exhibits the same uncertainty. See "How to Be an Anti-Realist," *Proceedings and Addresses of the American Philosophical Association* (1983): 48 and 50.

Now Kant often talks in the first way, as if there were two worlds, a noumenal world of things in themselves and a phenomenal world of appearances. But a careful reading makes it clear that this is just a *façon de parler*, a convenient, all but inevitable way of speaking about two ways of apprehending one set of objects (about which, more below).

Both ways of speaking have their point, but as with the distinction between use and mention or between the material and formal modes, it is important to be clear which one is operative in any given context. If we are speaking the language of two worlds, then it makes sense to say that "the things in the [phenomenal] world owe their . . . existence to the noetic activity of our minds." For without that activity there would be no such world and no such things.

If, on the other hand, we are speaking of one object and two modes of apprehension, it would be misleading to attribute the existence of things to our noetic activity for just the same reason that it would be silly to attribute the existence of Dan Rather's red and blue tie to the "spontaneity" of my black-and-white TV set. Without leaving this mode of thought, however, we could say that the thing (the only tie there is, the red and blue one) *as known by us* (and thus seeming to be gray) owes its existence to the receiving apparatus, though the thing as it is in itself does not. This way of speaking brings us so close to the language of two objects and two worlds that the virtual inevitability of this mode of speaking becomes clear.

A third advantage of our crude model is that it illuminates Kant's theory of the thing in itself and in so doing reveals the realism at the base of his idealism. Two important points about Kant's theory of the thing in itself are suggested by our model. In the first place, by refusing to jettison the thing in itself, as later idealists from Fichte and Hegel to Husserl and Rorty have wanted to do, he makes it clear that the world whose existence is dependent on our apprehension is not *the* world. It is only *our* world, the world of appearances, the world as known by us; and the dependence of that world on our apprehension is tautological.

In the second place, our model illustrates the fact that for Kant the thing in itself, which is what it is independently of our noetic acts, is not best identified merely by that independence. It is true that the real tie, the red and blue one, is what it is without reference to the black-and-white TV sets through which it may appear. If all those sets were destroyed, it would still be there. But it is not necessary to identify the tie without any reference to its being observed. On the contrary, it is most easily identified as the tie as seen by those in the studio.[4]

For Kant, to be in the studio means, quite simply, to be God. Thus, for Kant, the thing in itself is the thing as apprehended by God.[5] In the aftermath of Kant there has often been debate over whether it makes any sense to speak of a world, of objects and properties, of facts and truths, independent of any and all apprehension of them. It is an interesting debate; but in view of the tight link Kant makes between the thing in itself and God's knowledge, it is a debate rendered not in the least necessary by the First Critique.

In that context, of course, Kant cannot simply help himself to God's existence, so the point must have a hypothetical character. The thing in itself is the thing as apprehended by the God of classical theism if there is such a God. But even in this hypothetical mode, Kant does not know how to identify *the* world, except by reference to God's knowledge. Kant is, we might say, a perspectivist, and unless God (or some viable surrogate) represents *the* perspective on the world, it is not clear that there is anything that deserves to be called *the* world.

Now it becomes clear how the Kantian version of creative antirealism, so far from being one of the major modern threats to Christian theism, is itself an essentially theistic theory.[6] The whole point of the

4. If there are color-blind people in the studio we need only apply our analysis of the TV set as a distorting apparatus to their biological sensing equipment. The tie in itself is the tie as apprehended by viewers whose cognitive equipment is properly functioning. But if I am watching a black-and-white TV set instead of being present in the studio, the proper functioning of my cognitive equipment will avail nothing so far as seeing the thing as it is in itself is concerned.

5. For a more detailed textual presentation of this thesis and its implications, see my essay "In Defense of the Thing in Itself," *Kant-Studien* 59, 1 (1968): 118-41.

6. Thomas Aquinas writes, "Even if there were no human intellects, there could be truths because of their relation to the divine intellect. But if, *per impossibile,* there were no intellects at all, but things continued to exist, then there would be no such reality as truth." Plantinga quotes this passage from *De Veritate* q.1, a.6, in "How to Be an Anti-Realist" (p. 68) as part of his argument that the best way to be an antirealist is to be a theist. He affirms the antirealist intuition that truth is not independent of minds or persons (pp. 67-70), and summarizing Aquinas, whom he takes to speak here for the theistic tradition, he affirms "that truth is independent of our intellectual activity but not of God's. . . . Creative anti-realism, I said, is the claim that truth is not independent of mind: and divine creative anti-realism is the view that truth is not independent of God's noetic activity" (pp. 68-69). As we have seen, this is Kant's view of Truth, although he also recognizes a second-order truth dependent on the properly

distinction between appearances and things in themselves is to distinguish between human and divine knowledge, between the way the world appears to God's infinite and eternal mind and the way it appears to our finite and temporal minds, *precisely when our cognitive equipment is properly functioning.* This distinction, in some form, would seem to me to be essential to any kind of Christian theism.

It is misleading, then, for Plantinga to treat 'creative antirealism' as essentially interchangeable with 'Enlightenment humanism' (*TP* 10, 14). There are indeed humanist versions, and I shall shortly discuss two of them, but at its locus classicus creative antirealism is a theistic theory undeserving of the blanket dismissal that identifies it as an enemy of theism. Plantinga sees creative antirealism as a theory that "vastly overestimates" the place of human beings in the universe because "we human beings, insofar as we confer its basic structure upon the world, really take the place of God" (*TP* 17). But according to Kant it is just where human cognition becomes creative or constitutive of the world (as apprehended) that we are cut off from Truth. For Kant, to paraphrase Protagoras, man *(sic)* is the measure of human truth, but not of Truth, whose only measure is God.

The matter is somewhat more complicated with another phrase Plantinga uses that is virtually synonymous with 'creative antirealism,' namely 'Enlightenment subjectivism' (*TP* 10, 14). On Kant's view, human cognition of the world, even when our epistemic equipment is properly functioning, is essentially different in certain important respects from God's. Since God's view is the standard of truth, reality, and hence objectivity, human understanding is necessarily subjective.

But to the transcendental idealism that affirms this subjectivity Kant unites an empirical realism that confers upon it a certain objectivity and permits him to call it (human) knowledge.[7] For Kant distinguishes the way the world appears to a human mind that is properly functioning from the way it appears to a human mind that is not and that is thus, as we would normally say, in error.

---

functioning human mind. Unfortunately, Plantinga nevertheless associates Kant with the humanistic forms of creative antirealism he rejects.

7. The First Critique opens with the words "Human reason." Humanists (where humanism designates an alternative to theism) assume that the human point of view is *the* point of view; consequently, they have little reason to speak of human reason as distinct from simply reason. Theists, however, have good reason to distinguish human reason from divine reason. The theistic character of Kant's critical antirealism thus appears in these first two words.

There is, we might say, the thing as it is for God, the thing as it is for us, and the thing as it is for me; the distinction between us and me is obviously intended to express the distinction between properly and improperly functioning human minds. Now what Kant calls the phenomenal world is the world for us. Relative to the world for God it is subjective, but relative to the world for me it is objective. So there is no contradiction in calling the cognitive correlative of the phenomenal world (human) knowledge, speaking in an empirically realistic tone of voice, while denying it the status of knowledge ("I have therefore found it necessary to deny *knowledge* . . ." [B xxx]), speaking in a transcendentally idealistic tone of voice. Under such circumstances the term 'creative antirealism' is less likely to be misunderstood than 'Enlightenment subjectivism'.[8] There are two kinds of truth that Kant does not allow to be dissolved by subjectivistic skepticism: the Truth represented by the knowledge of God, and the truth represented by the human mind, properly functioning.

Now many commentators on Kant are not especially interested in theism, and some, I suppose, are positively allergic to it. The result is that the theistic character of Kantian idealism is often overlooked entirely and almost never emphasized. Humanists often treat Kant as if he were a humanist. While this helps to explain the negative reaction Christian philosophers often have toward Kant, it does not justify it. For the humanist reading of Kant does great violence to the text, while a textually responsible reading develops an important theistic theme.

It is the general structure of the Copernican Revolution that I wish to commend to Christian philosophers, not necessarily its details. In other words, I am not interested in defending the specifics of Kant's account of how human knowledge differs from divine knowledge. But I do want to look at a couple of "details" that play a significant role in Plantinga's critique to try to clear away what I see to be misunderstanding. Still speaking about Kant, he writes:

8. The phrase 'creative antirealism' is itself not entirely free of misleading implications. The Copernican Revolution says that we are "responsible for the structure and nature of the [phenomenal] world." But on Kant's view we are responsible in the way a virus is responsible for an illness and not in the way an artisan is responsible for an artifact. So it could easily be misleading to refer to us as "architects of the [phenomenal] universe" (*TP* 14). Plantinga concludes his brief account of Kantian idealism by asking, "And if the way things are is thus up to us and our structuring activity, why don't we improve things a bit?" (*TP* 16). One hopes that he has not taken the architect metaphor too literally, but rather is speaking in jest.

Such fundamental structures of the world as those of space and time, object and property, number, truth and falsehood, possibility and necessity — these are not to be found in the world as such, but are somehow constituted by our own mental or conceptual activity . . . they are not to be found in the things themselves. . . . Were there no persons like ourselves engaging in noetic activities, there would be nothing in space and time, nothing displaying object-property structure, nothing that is true or false, possible or impossible, no kind of things coming in a certain number — nothing like this at all. (*TP* 14-15)[9]

The reference to truth and falsity makes it look as if Kant identifies truth with human truth after all, qualifying for the humanist designation and the opposition of theists. But what does Kant mean by saying that these characteristics are not to be found "in the world as such," that is, in the world as it really is? Nothing more than that the "world as such," which is to say, the world as God sees it, does not have the temporal characteristics of human experience. For all of the a priori features that define the phenomenal world and that would be lacking in the absence of human knowers are essentially tied to the human experience of time. (1) Time, for Kant, is the sequential flow of inner and outer sense, without which there is no human experience at all. (2) Space is essentially temporal for Kant as well, since, to put it crudely, it takes time for perception to move from here to there. (3) Finally, all twelve categories, insofar as they constitute the world of human experience and are not merely formal features of judgment, are schematized with an essential reference to time. Thus the object and property that would disappear from the world in the absence of human knowers are not object and property per se, but substance and accident *as defined by human temporality*. Similarly, the truth and falsity that would disappear derive from the categories of reality and negation *as essentially linked to our experience of time*. Thus we are back to the tautology that in the absence of human cognition the world as apprehended by human minds would disappear.

All of this leaves God free to apprehend objects and their properties

9. Although such terms as 'truth' and 'falsity', 'object' and 'property' do not appear in Kant's table of categories, it is not difficult to identify the categories Plantinga expresses with these terms, 'reality' and 'negation', 'inherence' and 'subsistence' respectively (A 80 = B 106).

and to distinguish truth from falsity in the manner proper to divine knowledge. On Kant's view (and Plantinga's, according to his essay in this volume), what we know about the nature of divine knowledge is somewhat overwhelmingly exceeded by what we don't know. But surely, on the basis of what Kant has said, we are not entitled to say with regard to such features of our world as object and property or truth and falsity that without us there would be "nothing like this at all."

My teacher, Wilfrid Sellars, used to talk about the thing in itself as being in "sprace" and "trime." Though no theist, and wishing to put Kant to essentially humanist uses, he recognized that Kant assumes some kind of correlation between the phenomenal and noumenal worlds. Of course, he is not in a position to prove this or to specify the nature of what we might call the analogy between the two by translating the metaphors of "sprace" and "trime" (Sellars's metaphors, not Kant's) into the prose of the phenomenal world. The point is simply that nothing Kant says prohibits the assumption of such an analogy. Kant's doctrine only prohibits the claim that our knowledge and God's are univocal.

Objection: Kant's theism makes too sharp a distinction, more Platonic than biblical, between time and eternity. Today some theists want to move away from the *totum simul* tradition and to say that God is in some sense in time. That would seem to make Kant's move unnecessary.

Reply: (1) Even if God is in some sense in time, there might well be such a significant difference between divine and human temporality that the distinction between the world for God and the world for us remains necessary for the theist. (2) To say, on the other hand, that God's temporality is so nearly univocal to ours that the distinction is otiose is to stretch theism to its limits or beyond; but in any case, the Kantian attempt to preserve the distinction would be an intra-theistic debate rather than the onslaught of the *Civitas Mundi* on the *Civitas Dei*.

Objection: But Kant's theory is not just about our knowledge of the world. It is also about our knowledge of God, and it entails that we cannot prove the existence of God, thereby depriving faith of its rational foundation.

Reply: (1) Kant's rejection of the ontological argument does not derive from the Copernican Revolution but from the quite different doctrine that existence is not a predicate. If he is mistaken about that, the ontological argument might work. (2) Kant's theory does nothing to preclude the moral argument for the existence of God and might be seen as paving the way for it. (3) Theistic proofs are not in any case an integral part of theism, only of certain theistic systems. Many theists reject some or all of the traditional proofs, and some go so far as to argue that the very project of trying to prove the existence of God is dangerous, if not to theism, then to the faith theism means to express. In short, the debate over theistic proofs is not the confrontation between the *Civitas Mundi* and the *Civitas Dei* either.

Objection: The previous objection raised the right issue but in the wrong way. It is our knowledge of God that is primarily at issue; but the issue concerns revealed rather than natural theology. Scriptural revelation, received in faith, gives us a knowledge of God fully on a par with God's own self-knowledge. But Kant's distinction between human and divine knowledge denies this possibility.

Reply: There is a considerable difference between the claim that biblical revelation teaches us things we need to know and, given our finitude and sinfulness, cannot discover on our own and the claim made for revelation by the objector, whose theism might well be described as hubristic theism. My teacher, Kenneth Kantzer (well known, like the objector, for his "high" view of Scripture), used to say that the Bible gives us the divinely revealed misinformation about God. That was his way of saying that revelation is incarnational, that it comes to us as we are rather than lifting us quite completely out of the human condition. Kant is no threat to this kind of theism; and if he is a threat to the hubristic theism of the objector, he is in good company. Was it not St. Paul who said that "we know only in part" and see even that part "in a mirror dimly" (1 Cor. 13:9, 12)? Once again, the Copernican Revolution is not a Trojan horse that the *Civitas Mundi* is trying to sneak into the *Civitas Dei*. It rather serves as a reminder to the citizens of the latter that the city of their love was not named after them.

Having promised to discuss four kinds of "Kantian" idealism, I turn briefly to three versions that differ in important ways from Kant's own. All of them reflect the fact that the history of the Copernican Revolution, in spite of the universalist character Kant gave to it, has been, from at least the time of Hegel on, particularist and pluralist. For Kant, the forms and categories that constitute the phenomenal world are at work in all human cognition, at all times, and in all places. But almost immediately people began to notice the operation of historically specific a priories constituting a variety of human worlds.

Thus Plantinga writes, "You may then note that human beings apparently do not all construct the *same* worlds," and he points to the ambiguity in the Protagorean dictum, "Man *(sic)* is the measure of all things." We can take 'man' to refer to "all human beings . . . or we can take it as the idea that each of some more limited group of persons — perhaps even each individual person — is the measure of all things" (*TP* 18-19).

I like to illustrate this variation on the Kantian theme with another homely example. Suppose I am a racist and I meet a member of a racial group I despise. I "know" a priori that this person will have a number of undesirable characteristics and will be inferior to me intellectually and morally. For my racism has turned my mind into a receiving apparatus that will only allow people of that race to appear in that way, just as the black-and-white TV only allows red and blue ties to appear as gray. This racism is no doubt shared by others with whom I live together in a world constituted by our shared racist a priori. In that world persons of the race(s) in question appear of necessity to be quite different from what they are in themselves — that is, different from the way God, and for that matter humans whose cognitive apparatus is functioning properly, see them. It is quite easy to apply a Kantian analysis to the many different worlds (good, bad, and indifferent) that make up human history. We usually call them cultures (or subcultures).

It is at this point that humanist-relativist creative antirealism enters the scene. Lacking any possible reference to God's perspective as the criterion of *the* world, and faced with the overwhelming variety of human worlds (even in the natural sciences, in the aftermath of Kuhn, et al.), it is easy for the humanist to conclude "that there simply isn't any such thing as objective truth. . . . The whole idea of an objective truth, the same for all of us, on this view, is an illusion, or a bourgeois plot, or a silly mistake. Thus does anti-realism breed relativism and nihilism" (*TP* 18).

In his Stob Lectures Plantinga calls this view "deeply antagonistic to a Christian way of looking at the world" (*TP* 19; cf. 20). In his 1982 Presidential Address to the Central Division of the American Philosophical Association, he attributes this view to Richard Rorty and suggests that it represents an illegitimate inference from the true premise that there is "no methodical way to settle all important disagreements."[10] It is, we might say, like concluding from the fact that the jury is hung that the defendant was neither guilty nor innocent.

10. Plantinga, "How to Be an Anti-Realist," pp. 62-64.

I agree with both of these assessments of this particularist Protagoreanism. I also find it both logically and theologically problematic. But I demur to the tag line, "Thus does anti-realism breed relativism and nihilism." For what drives this relativism is its humanism, not its antirealism. The two together can give rise to views like Rorty's. But theism, combined with a bizarre reading of Genesis 11, has generated a theological rationale for apartheid in South Africa. Yet it would be strange to say, "Thus does theism give rise to racism." Plantinga's dire warnings should have been directed at this particular species of creative antirealism, not at the entire genus. Only some mushrooms are poisonous.

There is another humanist variation on the Kantian theme. Let us call it humanist-objectivist creative antirealism. It recognizes the plurality of human worlds (cultures, paradigms, language games) and even the absence of any neutral algorithm for resolving our deepest disputes about how the world is or ought to be. At the descriptive level it is as pluralist as the previous view. But it does not find it necessary to abandon the notion of objective truth.

Lacking God, it needs what was previously referred to as a viable surrogate for the divine perspective that would signify *the* world. It designates the consensus of the ideal (counterfactual) human community of investigators as the criterion of Truth. A classic expression of this view is Peirce's definition of truth: "The opinion which is fated to be ultimately agreed to by all who investigate, is what we mean by the truth, and the object represented in this opinion is the real."[11]

According to this view, the distinction between appearances and the thing in itself returns. The thing in itself is the object of that ultimate consensus. Anything else is appearance. Thus we may (think we) have good reason to think that Newtonian physics is closer to the truth than Aristotelian, and relativity and quantum physics closer than Newtonian. But none of these can claim to be more than our best approximation to the Truth, our current truth. Since the idea of Truth functions as a regulative ideal, any current truth is phenomenal and not noumenal truth.

Habermas's notion of a consensus reached by an ideal speech community or in accordance with the counterfactual norms implicit in ordinary discourse is an extension of this idea to normative as well as

---

11. *Collected Papers of Charles Sanders Peirce*, ed. Charles Hartshorne and Paul Weiss (Cambridge: Harvard University Press, 1931-35), 5:407.

factual truth. Its explicit purpose is to retain, in the face of various forms of ethical relativism, an objective truth for ethics analogous to what is available for science.[12] Here, too, the clear implication is that, while all our judgments, whether of fact or of right, are open to challenge and revision, these truths are answerable to the Truth.[13]

In his Presidential Address, Plantinga discusses the antirealism of Hilary Putnam in much greater detail than that of Richard Rorty. If I understand him correctly, Putnam is as good an example of the humanist-objectivist (Peircean-Habermasian) variation on Kant as Rorty is of the humanist-relativist version. What leads Putnam to an antirealist position is not the intractable plurality of human language games but the deep intuition best expressed as the question: "How could it be that what is certified, even ideally certified, by our best methods — is nonetheless false? Isn't that just unthinkable?"[14]

Of course, for a theist that is not at all unthinkable. On the contrary, it is entirely natural for a theist (like Kant) to think that an "ideally certified" human theory would fail in significant ways to conform to the Real, the world as known by God, though it would conform to the real, the world as it would appear to an ideal human observer. And so Plantinga is surely right in suggesting that there is an important disagreement between the theist and humanist-objectivist creative antirealism.

But once again it is important to locate the disagreement correctly. Plantinga's proper complaint against Putnam is that he is a humanist, not that he is an antirealist. It is the former and not the latter that makes him a partisan of the *Civitas Mundi*.

12. Habermas does not treat all value judgments as objective. Some remain matters of taste, so he distinguishes the right from the good. Drawing the line is a difficult and hotly disputed task. But the point is that Habermas is an ethical as well as a factual objectivist. In the midst of de facto moral pluralism, he holds that our judgments about what is right are responsible to a norm independent of what we or anyone else at any given moment may happen to think. See especially Habermas's "Discourse Ethics: Notes on a Program of Philosophical Justification," in *Moral Consciousness and Communicative Action,* trans. Christian Lenhardt and Shierry Weber Nicholsen (Cambridge: MIT Press, 1990).

13. Habermas is more explicit than Peirce about the humanist character of his view. This comes most fully to expression in his theory of the linguistification of the sacred, the substitution of human language for God. See Habermas's *Theory of Communicative Action,* trans. Thomas McCarthy (Boston: Beacon Press, 1984, 1987), 2:77ff.

14. Plantinga, "How to Be an Anti-Realist," p. 62. Cf. pp. 50-51 and 55 for further indications that Plantinga takes Putnam to be defending, not our best theory to date, but an "*ideal* theory."

At the same time, the theist has reason to appreciate several features of this view in spite of its humanism. First, the PHP (Peirce-Habermas-Putnam) version of creative antirealism can recognize at the descriptive level the unsurpassable plurality of human perspectives without abandoning the notion of objective truth. Unlike relativistic antirealism, it doesn't conclude from a hung jury that the defendant neither did nor did not commit the crime. Thus it can avoid the temptation, to which the Enlightenment succumbed, of having to make excessive claims for human reason's actual ability in order to preserve the notion of objectivity.

Second, it can nevertheless reflect critically about the criteria and the methodologies by which our efforts to know the real are shaped. The goal, ideal human consensus (which the humanist will call Truth, the theist truth), may well enable us to specify norms with whose help our progress is more likely to be in the right direction than without them. For the humanist this will primarily concern science (the realm of objective fact) and ethics/politics (the realm of objective value). For the theist it will also include theology, and the theologian (whose proper goal is also an ideal human consensus) might well learn from the philosophy of science and from critical social theory lessons that will help to develop a sounder hermeneutics for interpreting the data of experience and biblical revelation. The task of finding a middle ground between arrogant objectivism and cynical relativism is just as difficult for theology as for science and ethics.

Finally, the theist can appreciate and appropriate from the PHP version of Kantianism its strong sense of the penultimate (at best) character of our current theories and of the de facto pluralism of perspectives from which we find ourselves unable to extricate ourselves other than by fiat. The reminder that our best theories to date, including our theologies, are in their very structure and not just in their details fallible, open to critique, and revisable can be welcomed by the theist, who is committed to taking both human finitude and human sinfulness seriously.

This reference to sinfulness brings us to our fourth and final version of Kantianism. It is a theistic view that equates the thing in itself with the thing as known by God. Thus it holds to an objectivist notion of truth. Its idealistic interpretation of human understanding differs from Kant's and agrees with the two humanist variations we have examined by giving a pluralist account of the phenomenal world. The a prioris that define human cultures, paradigms, language games, and so forth are legion. We can call this view theist-pluralist creative antirealism to distinguish it from Kant's own theist-universalist version. It also differs from Kant's view by making sin rather than finitude the primary barrier between human and divine knowledge. For my money Kierkegaard is the best proponent of this view.

Our racism example is helpful here. There we encounter a human world that has two important characteristics: (1) It is one of many different worlds constituted by human patterns of apprehension. Thus the worlds of white racism, black racism, anti-Semitism, nationalism, sexism, and so forth represent distinctively different ways in which the human receiving apparatus requires others to appear. (2) It is a result of human sinfulness. If for Kant the primary barrier between God's view of the world and ours is our finitude — more particularly, our temporality — for Kierkegaard it is our sinfulness. While Kant points to differences that obtain when our cognitive equipment is properly functioning, Kierkegaard, in the tradition of Paul, Augustine, Luther, and Calvin, points to the fact that our cognitive equipment never is properly functioning, that with respect to at least some kinds of truth, including above all else the truth about God, we are disposed to "suppress the truth" and thereby to become those whose "senseless minds [are] darkened" (Rom. 1:18, 21). Paul, whose words these are, immediately connects them to idolatry (v. 23), to the gods who are created in the human image, that is, constituted by the human mode of apprehending them.

Plantinga notices that creative antirealism can talk this way about the divine. In contrast to simple atheism, it takes the essentially Feuerbachian view "that there is such a person as God, all right, but he owes his existence to our noetic activity — [a view that] seems at best a bit strained" or "seems at best a piece of laughable bravado."[15] Would that it were only laughable bravado that we have to do with here, and not the inveterate human tendency toward idolatry!

In spite of his professed Calvinism, Plantinga fails to recognize in what he aptly calls creative theological antirealism a cogent and powerful account of the noetic effects of sin. We might say that he is so devoted to giving an account of human knowledge in terms of the proper functioning of our cognitive equipment that he tends to ignore its persistent propensity toward malfunctioning.

15. Plantinga, "How to Be an Anti-Realist," pp. 49 and 54.

Or we might say that he has failed to make the kind of distinctions among various forms of antirealism to which this essay is devoted. In a humanist context, the view that we create God in our own image is the whole story about God and is but a sophisticated version of atheism. But in a theist context, it is the recognition that, in spite of what God truly is, our sinfully corrupted receiving apparatuses generate gods conveniently suited to our demands.

We may be looking at the red and blue God present in nature or in Scripture, but we see one of the many gray gods that make up the story of human religion. This is not to say that we create these gods out of whole cloth. Kantianism never confuses the phenomenal world with fiction. Thus idolatry is perhaps better thought of in terms of edited gods than of fabricated gods, just as propaganda is most effective when liberally laced with truth.

This means that the God we actually worship, the phenomenal God constituted by the sinful "spontaneity" of our receiving apparatus, may be (1) all comfort and no demand (Freud), (2) the justifier of our position of social privilege and power (Marx), or (3) the justifier of our resentment and revenge against our enemies (Nietzsche).[16]

In short, where the humanist finds a sophisticated version of atheism, the theist *can and should* find a powerful expression of prophetic monotheism and its protest against the human tendency, even among God's covenant people, to idolatry. Such a warning, it seems to me, should be part of every epistemology that purports to be guided by Christian theism, and this is the most important reason why Christian philosophers should take the Copernican Revolution seriously.

In other words, Kierkegaardian Kantianism is more important than Kantian Kantianism. Why? Kant's version helps the theist to express the limitations of human knowledge due to finitude, while Kierkegaard's helps to express those due to sin. Both are important, but epistemic finitude seems to get itself expressed more easily without help from the Copernican Revolution than does epistemic fallenness.

Take the cases of Aquinas and Plantinga (who may be more a Thomist than a Calvinist). Both give antirealist accounts of Truth,

16. For a detailed study of these three masters of the hermeneutics of suspicion as presenting an essentially prophetic critique of religion from a secular perspective, see my *Suspicion and Faith: The Religious Uses of Modern Atheism* (Grand Rapids: Eerdmans, 1993).

making Truth and God's knowledge necessarily coextensive.[17] But when it comes to human knowledge, the matter is different. Aquinas gives a classically realist account, and Plantinga treats all forms of creative antirealism as assaults on the Kingdom of God. Neither has trouble expressing the finitude of human knowledge vis-à-vis the divine,[18] though neither of them notices the "Kantian" implications of the distinctions they draw. Finally, neither of them is very sensitive to the noetic effects of sin. Compared to Augustine, Luther, and Calvin, for example, Aquinas does epistemology as if in the garden of Eden. And Plantinga, as already noted, has an epistemology all but entirely oriented toward the proper functioning of the human mind. He is unable to see in creative theological antirealism anything more than what it is in the hands of humanists.

Could it be that realism/hostility toward antirealism in our account of human knowledge tends to blind us to the noetic effects of sin and encourages us to treat as episodic (empirical) error what needs to be seen as systematic (a priori) suppression of the truth? If so, then Christian philosophers would do well to start out by making friends with the Copernican Revolution.

---

17. See the passage from Aquinas quoted by Plantinga in note 6 above. His own view comes down to the claim that "the fundamental anti-realist intuition — that truth is not independent of mind — is correct. This intuition is best accommodated by the theistic claim that necessarily, propositions have two properties essentially: *being conceived by God* and *being truth if and only if believed by God.* So how can we sensibly be anti-realists? Easily enough: by being theists" ("How to Be an Anti-Realist," p. 70).

18. In Plantinga's case, his essay in this volume is eloquent testimony to this fact.

Zarathustra's Songs:
Faith after Nietzsche

Galen A. Johnson

It is perverse, no doubt, to speak of the faith of Nietzsche, perhaps even of faith after Nietzsche. Yet it is well enough established that Nietzsche's critique of Christian metaphysics remained metaphysical and his critique of Christian religion remained religious. Heidegger's text on this point is clear: "That Nietzsche experienced and expounded his most abysmal thought [the thought of eternal return] from the Dionysian standpoint only suggests that he was still compelled to think it metaphysically, and only metaphysically."[1] Part III of *Thus Spoke Zarathustra* closes with a song in seven parts to eternity called The Amen Song, and each part ends with the refrain, "For I love you, O Eternity." At the beginning of that work, Zarathustra taught the fallen and dying tightrope walker that there is no heaven and no hell, but at the closing of the work he faced and accepted a metaphysical concept of eternity taught him by his animals and a faith in eternal life that embraced the value of love.

Though Nietzsche's criticism of Christianity remains *the* criticism of our age, in my judgment, it still today remains difficult to know exactly what the criticism amounts to and just as difficult to take seriously as a *philosophical* position when it is initially stated. If it is simply Nietzsche's view that religions and moralities grow from a hidden resentment *(ressentiment)* against life, then to the extent that his own words regarding the "death of God," overman, eternal return, the natural

---

1. Martin Heidegger, "Who is Nietzsche's Zarathustra?" in *The New Nietzsche*, ed. David B. Allison (Cambridge: MIT Press, 1985), pp. 76, 79.

order of rank, and love of fate remain metaphysical, they can easily be dismissed as also growing from such a resentment. Nietzsche's criticism seems self-referentially defeating in a way that is parallel to the self-referential paradox involved in Freud's suspicions of religion based on unconscious motivation or Marx's based on economic class oppression. Freud's or Marx's own theories of religious life would necessarily seem to be based in the same unconscious motivation or economic class status that they claim undermines religious belief. Yet I remain uneasy with this formalist dismissal of Nietzsche, as of Marx or Freud. The self-referential difficulty seems like winning on paper, and it seems not to touch the power of the criticisms. Of the three critics of religion, Marx, Nietzsche, and Freud, I believe that Nietzsche is best equipped to show us why.

In this essay, I will argue that Nietzsche offers at least two separate arguments against the truth of Christianity. The first has to do with what he calls the "metaphysics of language," and it shows us why the theoretical case for or against Christian faith should be abandoned in favor of a practical case. This is essentially a Kantian turn toward practical rationality. The second has to do with a set of "accusations" against the practical value of Christianity founded on his genealogy of morals and psychology of *ressentiment*. Christian love, he claims, is a disguised form of revenge that makes us sick. In this regard, it was important for Nietzsche to convince us that Christianity is not merely false, it is a lie. The accusatory force of the word "lie" carried Nietzsche far beyond a theoretical case against Christianity toward a style of writing that he himself characterized as open warfare with Christianity as a dangerous enemy of life.

These two arguments outline the first two sections of this essay. Our focus will be upon Nietzsche's two late texts *The Genealogy of Morals* and *Twilight of the Idols*. In a third section, we should make some assessment of Nietzsche's critique, and this will involve us in reflections on the relation between religious and aesthetic experience. Ultimately, it seems to me, what is at stake in Nietzsche's attack on Christianity is the view that there is a disingenuous religious life that needs to be corrected by the tragic faith shown us in aesthetic life. Here we shall need to reflect upon what Nietzsche calls the "innocence of becoming" and some texts from *The Birth of Tragedy* in order to think for ourselves about the meaning of religious faith and love after Nietzsche.

The Metaphysics of Language

Friedrich Nietzsche was keenly aware of the problem of language in religious knowledge and faith. There is a key passage in the third chapter of *Twilight of the Idols*, titled "Reason in Philosophy":

> Precisely insofar as the prejudice of reason forces us to posit unity, identity, permanence, substance, cause, thinghood, being, we see ourselves somehow caught in error, compelled to error. . . . In its origin language belongs in the age of the most rudimentary psychology. We enter a realm of crude fetishism when we summon before consciousness the basic presuppositions of the metaphysics of language, in plain talk, the presuppositions of reason. . . . I am afraid we are not rid of God because we still have faith in grammar.[2]

Nietzsche undertook a linguistic turn in metaphysics, not toward a logical analysis and elimination of metaphysical terms as meaningless, but toward a genealogy of language that casts suspicion on the truth of metaphysical propositions such as "God exists."

A clear example of the close conjunction between knowing and saying in metaphysics is found in the opening chapter of Hegel's *Phenomenology of Spirit*. In the chapter on "Consciousness" called "Sense-Certainty," Hegel relied upon the "divine nature of language" in order to set in motion the growth toward Self-Consciousness and Spirit. His argument had run like this. The commonsense or naive realist who claims to *know* that the world consists in individual things separate from knowers is unable to *say* what these individuals are. He or she is

2. Friedrich Nietzsche, *Twilight of the Idols*, in *The Portable Nietzsche*, ed. and trans. Walter Kaufmann (New York: Viking Penguin, 1982), III.5.482-83. Hereafter, citations of Nietzsche's writings will be given parenthetically in the text (referring to part, section, and page numbers) using the following abbreviations:

GM   *The Genealogy of Morals*, in *The Birth of Tragedy* and *The Genealogy of Morals*, trans. Francis Golffing (New York: Doubleday Anchor, 1956), pp. 149-299.

OTL   *On Truth and Lie in an Extra-Moral Sense*, trans. Walter Kaufmann, in *The Portable Nietzsche*, pp. 42-47.

TI   *Twilight of the Idols*, trans. Walter Kaufmann, in *The Portable Nietzsche*, pp. 463-563.

Z   *Thus Spoke Zarathustra*, trans. Walter Kaufmann, in *The Portable Nietzsche*, pp. 103-439.

reduced to saying the most general and universal things, "that" or "this" combined with indexicals like "here" and "now." When the common-sense realist speaks of the existence of external objects, he or she wants the absolutely singular individual but is only able to get the universal. "The sensuous This that is meant *cannot be reached* by language," Hegel concluded.[3] Experience teaches us that this bit of paper is a "Here," a "Here and not-There"; it is a universal that applies to all bits of paper. At this point, two paths would be open to sense-certainty. The first would be to refuse to speak, to refuse the requirement of saying and remain silent. Such a move toward silence, however, blocks the move toward knowledge. The second would be to follow the path of language toward the self and the Absolute Self in the quest for knowledge of the world. Language, Hegel said, "has the divine nature of directly reversing the meaning of what is said, of making it into something else, and thus not letting what is meant *get into words* at all."[4]

Hegel's opening argument revealed that his phenomenology of knowledge would trace the metaphysics of language. In much the same way that Aristotle's *Categories* proceeded from "things that are said" to the kinds of "things that are," grammar outlines the categories of being. As in Aristotle and Hegel, Nietzsche enters into metaphysical thinking with an explicit awareness of how much work language does in attempting to penetrate the opacity of the gap between the subject and the world that we call knowledge. Language and its implicit logic are powers, ways of taking symbolic possession of the world. Nietzsche writes in *The Genealogy of Morals:*

> The lordly right of bestowing names is such that one would almost be justified in seeing the origin of language itself as an expression of the rulers' power. They say, "This *is* that or that;" they seal off each thing and action with a sound and thereby take symbolic possession of it. (*GM* I.2.160)

If language is a power, its logic a way of winning the argument and silencing the doubter, it remains an open question if the categories are correct or if the conclusions are true that emerge from the "metaphysics

---

3. G. W. F. Hegel, *Phenomenology of Spirit*, trans. A. V. Miller (Oxford: Oxford University Press, 1977), par. 110, p. 66.

4. Hegel, *Phenomenology of Spirit*, par. 110, p. 66.

of language." It remains an open question if language is able to heal the wound in being and knowing between subject and object. The philosophers, from Aristotle to Hegel, put their faith in the healing balm of the word. Nietzsche did not. The Greeks hit upon rationality as their "saviour" and upon Socrates as "physician." There was but one choice for the Hellenic philosophers living in an age of decline and danger, Nietzsche says, "either to perish or — to be *absurdly rational*" (*TI* II.10.478).

Here are the categories, according to *Twilight of the Idols,* to which the metaphysics of language leads. Language distinguishes the doer from the doing; it posits the doer as the cause of the doing; it thereby leads to belief in the ego and in the ego as substance, unified, permanent, and self-identical; finally, it posits the thing that is the object of the doing. Language "doubles the doing" into a thing and an action when we say that "lightning flashes" or "energy causes" (*GM* I.13.179). The prominent categories of the metaphysics of language begin to emerge: subject, cause, thing, substance, and permanence (being). Together with these, the prominent laws of logic also appear: unity, identity, and self-identity. Finally, the ultimate reality necessarily comes into view, the cause of the whole world, the *causa sui*, the *ens realissimum*, God. Therefore, not only would Nietzsche consider the ontological proof as a grammatical argument; he would consider the cosmological proofs that rest upon the concept of "cause" and the teleological proof that rests upon the concept of the universe as a "thing" designed by the Creator as grammatical arguments as well. "I am afraid we are not rid of God because we still have faith in grammar" (*TI* III.5.483).

Based on his skeptical withdrawal from the "metaphysics of language," I hope that we are now able to see why Nietzsche believed that the theoretical proofs for God's existence had to be replaced with a consideration of the practical values and disvalues of religion. I hope that we can also see that Nietzsche himself is now faced with a profound problem of expression. His own philosophical outlook must emerge from that space in-between complete silence and total rationality, a space Aristotle and Hegel did not believe to exist. If there is to be anything like a "new metaphysics" from Nietzsche, it must be an ontology of the most indirect form that relies upon all the linguistic devices with which Nietzsche experimented: humor, hyperbole, aphorism, parable, and story. Nevertheless, I hope we can also see that at least Nietzsche would not be moved by a formalist accusation of self-referential paradox; the demand for total rationality is the assertion of a power, a value that itself must be defended. Is the *life* and *faith* in total rationality the best life?

On Truth and Lie

Nietzsche's progress from theoretical atheism to practical atheism is concentrated in the famous phrase "God is dead." This pronouncement by the madman of *The Gay Science*, taken up by the prophet Zarathustra, is by no means the simple assertion that "God does not exist." In fact, in a curious way, the message that God has died remains strangely ambiguous with respect to God's nonexistence. For God to have died, it seems that he must have once existed; yet the kind of being who is capable of death could never have been the eternal God of Hebrew-Christian theology, and moreover if we reflect on the meaning of eternal return we immediately see that if God once existed but now is dead, and if all that once was will come again, this God awaits a rebirth. After all, as Hegel pointed out, it was Christian faith itself that spoke the message that God — in this case meaning Christ — is dead, Christ is risen, Christ will come again. It is well known that Nietzsche regarded Jesus as overman, every bit as much as Dionysus, and the whole expression of the death of God remains overlain with a mythology that has even tempted some scholars into developing a Nietzschean "Christian" theology.

In spite of these hermeneutical ambiguities, Nietzsche did mean in these words to attack the truth of Christianity and to denounce the illusion of God. Which God is dead? What does it mean for a *philosopher* to hear these words? It means nothing else than the proclamation of the absence of first cause, of prime mover, of self-caused cause *(causa sui)*, of the eternal God of Hebrew-Christian theology and the metaphysics of Augustine, Aquinas, Descartes, and above all, Kant. In Kant we find the immediate antagonist of Zarathustra, for in Kant's practical philosophy the foundation for morality had been reduced to the intimacy between religion and ethics. The universal morality of reason, duty, law, and obedience had no other basis than a divine authority who would oversee the just distribution of rewards and punishments in the afterlife. In Kant, Nietzsche believed he saw revealed the heart of religion as this desire for judgment, condemnation, and punishment of the wicked of this world, coupled with the internal punishment of ourselves when tempted by similar worldly wickedness. The essence of a religious life founded upon faith in the authority of the God of onto-theology, according to Nietzsche's analysis, is the cycle of a vicious movement that originates in accusation and ends in consolation.[5] It is one and the same religion that first accuses and then offers protection. Without the accusation there would be no need for the consolation.

We stand accused before the Law, and this accusation of guilt produces fear of punishment. It also produces a spirit of judgment and resentment against those who ignore or willingly and openly transgress the Law, and we secretly or openly desire revenge against the transgressors. Consolation and forgiveness for transgression of the Law are then proffered us by the very originator of the accusation on conditions of confession, humility, meekness, and obedience. Yet the whole cycle from accusation to consolation is a house of cards, for without the accusation, no consolation is required. Without the accusation, fear, guilt, and resentment dissipate. Exactly because the accusation of Law founded on the Lawgiver produces this life of fear, guilt, rancor, and the desire for vengeance, Nietzsche contends, the God of Hebrew and Christian onto-theology must be repudiated. The religious life founded on faith in such a God renders us emotionally and physiologically sick.

We might inquire whether New Testament religion was not the summary and transformation of Law in a gospel of love. Perhaps here, with respect to emotional life and especially to love, Nietzsche's critique crescendoes to its high point. For example, in passages of *The Genealogy of Morals*, Nietzsche speaks of the "emotional slackness" that characterizes the religious. "Their happiness is purely passive and takes the form of drugged tranquillity, stretching and yawning peace, 'sabbath'" (*GM* I.10.172). Natural life experiences and expresses love as a passionate attachment to a particular, fragile, and irreplaceable individual, whose well-being and safety from danger one protects as dearly as one's own. Now a new form of "Christian love for the whole world" is born, sweeter than honey, sugary and soft. This love amounts to a kind of stoic detachment that results in an impotence that cannot retaliate, submission before those one hates, in short, "loving one's enemy — accom-

5. Cf. Paul Ricoeur, "Religion, Atheism, Faith," trans. Charles Freilich, in *The Conflict of Interpretations: Essays in Hermeneutics*, ed. Don Ihde (Evanston: Northwestern University Press, 1974), p. 441.

panied by much sweat" (*GM* I.14.180-81). Love of the world, even of the enemy, is a peculiar and anti-natural form of self-hatred, Nietzsche argues, hatred of one's own weakness and misery, posing as its opposite, charity to neighbor. This kind of love chooses to think only about the other person's feelings, the other person's misery and suffering — even the enemy's — rather than about his or her own feelings and suffering and that of those to whom he or she is genuinely attached. In his classic essay on Nietzsche's analysis of "ressentiment," Max Scheler has claimed that modern philosophy found a revealing term for this false love: "altruism." Scheler writes: "Thus, the altruistic urge is really a form of hatred, of self-hatred, *posing* as its opposite. . . . [L]ove for the small, the poor, the weak, and oppressed is really disguised hatred, repressed envy, an impulse to detract, etc., directed against the opposite phenomena: wealth, stength, power, largesse."[6]

Let us return for a moment to the phrase "loving one's enemy — accompanied by much sweat." The conjunction of Christian love with "sweat" reflects Nietzsche's reductive naturalism in which the passions, bodily life, and will are the basis for abstraction and conceptualization. In *Twilight of the Idols*, Nietzsche writes:

> The other idiosyncrasy of the philosophers is no less dangerous; it consists in confusing the last and the first. They place that which comes at the end — unfortunately! for it ought not to come at all! — namely, the "highest concepts," which means the most general, the emptiest concepts, the last smoke of evaporating reality, in the beginning, *as* the beginning. (*TI* III.4.481)

In the attachment to reason and concepts, the philosopher and the priest have joined forces to create a "Platonism for the people" in which the best life seeks detachment from emotions, passion, and bodies. Whereas every "healthy morality" is dominated by an instinct for life, Nietzsche says that religious life stresses the discipline, the extirpation of strong emotions. "But an attack on the roots of passion means an attack on the roots of life: the practice of the church is *hostile to life*" (*TI* III.1.487).

Nietzsche's remarks on the relation between passion and physiology

6. Max Scheler, "Ressentiment," trans. William Holdheim, in *Nietzsche: A Collection of Critical Essays*, ed. Robert Solomon (New York: Doubleday Anchor, 1973), p. 251.

clearly anticipate Freud's insights regarding repression and psychosomatic illnesses. Smoldering, unexpressed, and internalized emotions such as desire for vengeance inevitably find their way into our physiology, producing insomnia, bad digestion, and ulcers, "the noise and agitation with which our lower organs work for or against one another" (*GM* II.1.189). "Blessed are the sleepy ones: for they shall soon drop off. Thus spoke Zarathustra" (*Z* I.2.142).

Within such a disingenuous life, what could claims about truth amount to? In a sense, here we come to the heart of the matter regarding the truth of onto-theological religion from the Nietzschean perspective. From a life built upon fear, guilt, and the desire for revenge, combined with the bad physiology, emotional slackness, and detachment endemic to "loving" the whole world, how could we expect to hear a forthright and honest word? Rather, we find a range of dissimulations, a mind that loves "hide-outs, secret paths, and back doors," a person of long memory, of course capable of forgiving, but only because he or she is never able to forget an insult or meanness suffered (*GM* I.10.172-73).

In 1873, only a few months after *The Birth of Tragedy*, Nietzsche wrote a remarkable essay on truth that was published only posthumously and titled *On Truth and Lie in an Extra-Moral Sense*. Here Nietzsche regards the intellect as the chief means that humans have in the struggle for survival and self-preservation. Denied horns or fangs in the struggle for existence, intelligence is the means by which weaker, less robust, human animals preserve themselves in the "war of all against all." For the weak individuals within the already weak class of human beings, the "art of simulation" must necessarily reach its peak; deception, flattery, talking behind the back, posing, being masked, and acting a role before others become the rule of life. "In short," Nietzsche writes, "the constant fluttering around the single flame of vanity is so much the rule and the law that almost nothing is more incomprehensible than how an honest and pure urge for truth could make its appearance among men" (*OTL* 43). What, then, Nietzsche asks, is truth? The answer he gives is well known but still bears citing at length:

> What, then, is truth? A mobile army of metaphors, metonyms, and anthropomorphisms — in short, a sum of human relations, which have been enhanced, transposed, and embellished poetically and rhetorically, and which after long use seem firm, canonical, and obligatory to a people: truths are illusions about which one has

forgotten that this is what they are; metaphors which are worn out and without sensuous power; coins which have lost their pictures and now matter only as metal, no longer as coins. (*OTL* 46-47)

The following paragraph adds, "to be truthful means using the customary metaphors — in moral terms: the obligation to lie according to a fixed convention, to lie herd-like in a style obligatory for all" (*OTL* 47).

Nietzsche's view on metaphorical language here is quite unusual, perhaps unique: he thinks all human beings have a natural, biological "instinct" to create metaphors. It is our chief weapon in the struggle for existence and the chief expression of our power. Yet there is in us a tendency to forget that our metaphors are not literal, univocal descriptions of the world, and the metaphors come to be taken realistically; they harden into obligatory rules for life that lack "sensuous power" and no longer electrify the spirit. Thus they are false, weakening life rather than strengthening it. It is the weak ones who need "truths," who need the dissimulations of the intellect to protect themselves against the strong. The onto-theological God as Lawgiver is just such a metaphor that lacks "sensuous power," an illusion that offers protection to those who fear passions and bodily life.

Now we might say that the position taken on truth in this essay introduces something like a personal precondition for truth, much as Heidegger introduced "openness" or "freedom" as the precondition for responding to things and expressing the correspondence between signs and things in his essay "On the Essence of Truth."[7] The way in which we search for something establishes the frame for what we will find. This "epistemology of the personal," if we may call it such — it is as easily viewed as an anti-epistemology pure and simple — certainly creates as many problems for Nietzsche's own accusations against Christianity as for the vicious cycle of accusation and consolation he finds in religion. His own writing is some of the richest in metaphor, and no philosophical writing, with the possible exception of Marx's, is so filled with accusation and the struggle against firm, canonical, and obligatory metaphors and human relations as his. Filled as he is with the spirit of

---

7. Martin Heidegger, "On the Essence of Truth," trans. John Sallis, in *Martin Heidegger: Basic Writings*, ed. David Krell (New York: Harper & Row, 1977), pp. 122-25. See also Henry Pietersma, "Heidegger's Theory of Truth," in *Heidegger's Existential Analysis*, ed. Frederick Elliston (The Hague: Mouton, 1978), pp. 219-29.

vengeance, how could we expect to have an honest word regarding religion from Nietzsche? The problem of Nietzsche is this problem of vengeance. It is the problem against which Zarathustra struggled in the long, winding course of his philosophical story, from the three early speeches of the prologue on abyss, overman, and condemnation of the "last man" who blinks at what should be a startling message, to the climactic dance, joy, and songs to eternity at the conclusion of Part III.[8] But what was Nietzsche's problem and Zarathustra's problem is now a problem they have bequeathed to us. In what does the authority of Nietzsche's message consist? Is there a faith beyond vengeance?

Tragic Faith and the Innocence of Becoming

Why should anyone listen to Nietzsche's accusation against religious accusation? For it is that, an antireligious accusation that remains very much within the spirit of vengeance it denounces. Since we have noted Nietzsche's view of the uncertainty of the relation of signs to things and the assumptions of the "metaphysics of language," the authority of Nietzsche's accusation can really reside only in the power of the message that persuades a reader to listen. The message is a personal one that will persuade some and that will be simply dismissed by others. Yet we are not preachers; we are philosophers and thinkers, and so we are obliged to enter into this troublesome space between the power of the preacher's message and the reflection on its meaning.[9] Other than this power of personal persuasion, is there nothing else? After Nietzsche, how should we reflect as thinkers on his repudiation of this ontological-theological God who is the guarantor of ethical law and duty?

Nietzsche built his practical case against Hebrew and Christian religion on the basis of a genealogical analysis of the origin and value of the life built on such a faith. What is at stake here is what Nietzsche means by a "genealogy" of value, and whether his genealogy, which traces the essence of religious life to the cycle of accusation and con-

8. The view that Zarathustra's development from vengeance to acceptance of eternal recurrence is the central problem of *Thus Spoke Zarathustra* is defended by Laurence Lampert in his *Nietzsche's Teaching: An Interpretation of "Thus Spoke Zarathustra"* (New Haven: Yale University Press, 1986), pp. 1-11.

9. Again, this is Paul Ricoeur's way of posing the problem in "Religion, Atheism, Faith," pp. 447-48.

solation, is the heart of Christian faith. We need to remember that Nietzsche did not come to philosophy and the question of religious truth from a background in logic, nor even history, but from a background in classical philology. This means that he was schooled in the ancient classical languages and literature and was especially well versed in the Greek tragedies. This background controls what he meant by genealogy: a form of criticism based on the study of the origin and development of words, quite akin to Heideggerian hermeneutics, though with a harsher, more reductive and critical intent. On this basis, Nietzsche had observed a crucial transition in the meaning of the term "good" in its development from the period of the great Greek tragedians, especially Aeschylus and Sophocles, to the way the term "good" functioned as a moral term in the philosophical thinking of Socrates and Plato and in the religious teachings of the New Testament.

Nietzsche observed that in the Greek tragedies it was the strong, noble, and privileged aristocrats, such as King Agamemnon and King Creon, who called themselves "good" *(agathoi)*, with reference to their noble birth, in contrast to those of inferior, ignoble, plebeian, or "bad" birth *(kakoi* or *deiloi)*, such as beggars or slaves *(GM* I.5.163). In Homer, the term "bad" *(deilos)* even had a compassionate sense — for example, "poor wretches" *(a deiloi)* — though it also conveyed cowardice or worthlessness. By the time of Socrates, Plato, the Stoics, and then the New Testament, the term "good" had become a moral term used by common people for their own way of life founded on humility and obedience, while the contrasting term "bad" *(kakos)* now took on the moral sense of the word "evil" and was used by common folk to condemn their aristocratic enemies. The difference in meaning is still available to us linguistically, Nietzsche argued, in the form of the two negative German terms *schlecht* (bad) and *bose* (evil), as well as in similar pairs of terms in languages such as Latin and Gaelic *(GM* I.5.164). This transition in the meaning of the term "good" from a genealogical, physiological, and political term to a moral term infected the Platonic dialogues, which regularly employed doctors, physical trainers, and medical health in general as analogies in forming moral arguments regarding not the body but the inner soul or character. The strange and remarkable Platonic inversion that occurs in many of the dialogues, such as in *Phaedo*, is that strength of soul *(psyche)* is analogized to physical health, while caring for bodily life itself is steadily denigrated. In philosophic terms, what we see in this transition of meaning is a reversal of values in which the characteristic negative traits of natural inferiority and weakness, such as humility, obedience, and "love of enemies," assumed the positive value of moral goodness.[10] It was this anti-natural reversal of values that Nietzsche sought to reverse once again in his famous "transvaluation" and accompanying naturalistic return to bodily life and health.

It is worth going into this context in order to establish more clearly that Nietzsche's accusation against Christian faith is not an accusation against faith per se, nor even, perhaps, an accusation against all that Christian faith is. Nietzsche's writings seek to return us to a more tragic faith,[11] expressed in Greek tragedy, which may or may not be Christian. A philosopher such as Nietzsche could scarcely deny the validity and value of faith, given what he has told us about the wound between language and being and the biological necessity of metaphor. Here we will do well to remind ourselves of Nietzsche's own Lutheran heritage; it will not be far wrong to see in Nietzsche a naturalistic inversion of Luther analogous to Marx's naturalistic inversion of Hegel.[12] Nietzsche no more denies the "logic" and life of faith than Marx denied the dialectic. Just as Marx could not rid himself of thoroughly idealist concepts, such as alienation and universal class, but naturalized them, so Nietzsche retains the fundamental outline of Lutheran thinking regarding a chosen people, predestination, eternity, and love. Yet these had to be naturalized from the perspective of Greek notions of fate and tragedy.

What is required for a life beyond vengeance? To formulate any complete reply to this question is something we still await, and no doubt any reply will force us beyond Nietzsche. Yet Nietzsche grasped several essential features of a reply, which he built into his teaching of the

10. The transvaluation of values has been very succinctly and clearly presented by Philippa Foot, "Nietzsche: The Revaluation of Values," in *Nietzsche: A Collection of Critical Essays*, pp. 157-58.

11. The phrase "tragic faith" is provoked by Peter Bertocci's phrase "the tragic goodness of God," used throughout his book *The Goodness of God* (Washington, D.C.: University Press of America, 1981).

12. The Marx-Hegel analogy for Nietzsche's inversion of Luther may be referred to the well-known preface by Marx to the first German edition of *Capital* written in 1867: "With him [Hegel] the dialectic is standing on its head. It must be turned right side up again, if you would discover the rational kernel within the mystical shell." Cf. Robert C. Tucker, ed., *The Marx-Engels Reader* (New York: W. W. Norton, 1978), p. 303.

eternal recurrence. Nietzsche meant this troublesome teaching as his response to the question of nihilism, which framed the narrative of *Thus Spoke Zarathustra*. Eternal return demanded of Zarathustra a kind of heroic acceptance of life, including the very weaknesses and weak individuals he despised, without explanation, justification, appeal, or remorse. This is a positive nihilism born of strength, not weakness; born of abundance, not deprivation; born of will, not pessimism. It should be referenced to the conclusion of Camus's myth of Sisyphus, that mortal who was condemned to his rock as eternal recurrence of the same but who refused to succumb to sorrow or despair. "If the descent [of Sisyphus] is sometimes performed in sorrow," Camus wrote, "it can also take place in joy. . . . The struggle itself toward the heights is enough to fill a man's heart. One must imagine Sisyphus happy."[13]

It was this "most abysmal thought" that first presented itself to Zarathustra as the vision and riddle of a black snake hanging from the mouth of a shepherd, causing him to writhe and gag (Z III.2.271). Zarathustra's convalescence and redemption from vengeance began when he was at last able to swallow this monster: "Alas, man recurs eternally! The small man recurs eternally" (Z III.13.331). Then Zarathustra began to sing new songs to eternal life: "Behold, Zarathustra, new lyres are needed for your new songs. Sing and overflow, O Zarathustra; cure your soul with new songs" (Z III.13.332). This moment, this Now, is your life — your eternal life.

Zarathustra's heroic resignation of vengeance has an epistemological aspect, the resignation of what Nietzsche himself called the "telescopic eye." We return to *On Truth and Lie* for this text: "just as every porter wants an admirer, the proudest human being, the philosopher, thinks that he sees the eyes of the universe telescopically focussed on all sides on his actions and thoughts" (*OTL* 42-43). Here Nietzsche anthropomorphized the universe as eyes — perhaps as God's pair of eyes — seeing us from all sides, knowing all there is to know about us instantaneously in an objectifying glance. The image might equally suggest the pride of an actor in an opera, perhaps a Wagnerian opera, with the eyes of all the audience riveted upon himself or herself. The audacious pride of the philosopher is not only the belief that the eyes of the universe are focused upon him or her as the center; the audacity is also

---

13. Albert Camus, *The Myth of Sisyphus and Other Essays,* trans. Justin O'Brien (New York: Random House, 1954), pp. 90-91.

that the onto-theological philosopher "thinks that he sees" these eyes that see all. But to see the "eyes that see all sides" is an obvious contradiction in terms, for there would have to be one perspective, one side, omitted from which the cosmic eyes themselves were seen. This is the absurd "transcendental pretence" of a philosopher such as Kant,[14] but in general the absurd epistemological pretence of onto-theology is that it believes in its own epistemic privilege as "thought situated nowhere" and produces the vicious harshness of the cycle of accusation and consolation.

Life beyond vengeance begins with renunciation of what Nietzsche called the "telescopic eye" and what Merleau-Ponty called *la pensée survol*, a phrase that is difficult to translate but that is meant to describe the pretence of a kind of thought which claims to be undertaken from a godlike position of overview, survey, or flight above the earth, not rooted in a position or situation on the earth. In the working notes for his work in progress at the time of his death, which was published posthumously as *The Visible and the Invisible*, Merleau-Ponty spoke of the "blind spot" in the eye. The eye does not see itself for reasons of principle, for the eye contains a blind spot. What the eye does not see is the very thing in it that prepares and makes possible the vision of everything else, for the retina is blind at the point where the fibers that permit vision spread out into it.[15] Consciousness, too, has its blind spot in seeking to know itself and its own source.

If the eye of sight and the eye of philosophic insight are weakened or blinded, this marks a shift away from the privilege of the eye as the controlling sense and of visual perception as the central philosophic problem of modern thought in favor of a less cognitive and more affective philosophic concern — perhaps we could say moral concern, if the Nietzschean context did not prevent it. Nietzsche's philosophic project remains conceptually disunified in many respects, but a continuous sensual thread links the works, from the *Birth of Tragedy*'s praise of music to Zarathustra's songs to the tuning fork that is the hammer which sounds out idols in *Twilight of the Idols*. That thread is the critique of the eye and attention to the ear. *The Birth of Tragedy from the Spirit*

14. The phrase "transcendental pretence" is Robert Solomon's in his *Continental Philosophy Since 1750: The Rise and Fall of the Self* (Oxford: Oxford University Press, 1988), pp. 3-7.

15. Maurice Merleau-Ponty, *The Visible and the Invisible*, trans. Alphonso Lingis (Evanston: Northwestern University Press, 1968), p. 248.

of Music argues that the era of the great Greek tragedians ended in Euripides' reduction of the chorus from the music of dithyramb to hyper-rationalized speech.[16] Then, in a telling passage from the section of *Thus Spoke Zarathustra* entitled "On Redemption," Nietzsche writes of what he calls "inverse cripples," "human beings who lack everything, except one thing of which they have too much — human beings who are nothing but a big eye or a big mouth or a big belly" (*Z* II.20.250). The passage goes on to speak of an inverse cripple — probably Nietzsche himself — who has "an ear as big as a man." In the Preface to *Twilight of the Idols,* Nietzsche describes himself as one who seeks to "sound out idols" with his "evil ear" — "what a delight for one who has ears even behind his ears" (*TI* Preface, 465).

For Nietzschean heroic renunciation, the suffering of weakened eyesight makes room for a listening and response beyond vengeance. The eyes of the blind, though they do not see, are capable of tears.[17] Here we find a quite direct convergence between Nietzschean tragic faith and Hebrew and Christian faith, for the wisdom of the blind is a thought that comes down to us from both ancient sources, Greek tragedy as well as the Old and New Testament biblical literature. In Sophocles' play *Antigone,* the blind character Teiresias is portrayed as having the power of prophecy based on knowing the future. Antigone, daughter of Oedipus — who had blinded himself before his death — persisted in the burial of the body of her brother against the command of King Creon, and Teiresias foretold the ruin that would come to Thebes.

Among the patriarchs of Judaism, we remember the blindness of Isaac, which provided the possibility of deception and theft by his son Jacob (Genesis 27). There is also a less well known biblical tradition recorded in the Apocrypha about a different blind father, whose suffering was hearkened to and healed by his son. The father's name was Tobit, and he lived in exile in the land of Nineveh with his wife Anna and his son Tobias. Tobit was a righteous man who went about Nineveh

16. For discussion and analysis of the conflicting views on music defended in *The Birth of Tragedy,* see Peter Heckman, "The Role of Music in Nietzsche's *Birth of Tragedy,*" *British Journal of Aesthetics* 30, 4 (Oct. 1990): 351-61.

17. Cf. Jacques Derrida, *Memoires d'aveugle: L'autoportrait et autres ruines* (Paris: Editions de la Reunion des musées nationaux, 1990), pp. 124-30, for his moving discussion of blindness and crying in the life of Nietzsche and in his key works such as *The Birth of Tragedy.*

giving bread to the hungry and clothing to the poor, and burying privately the bodies of his fellow Jews which had been left on the city wall at the command of the king. When Tobit became blind in his old age, he was healed by his son Tobias, who applied the gall of a large fish to Tobit's eyes under the instruction of the angel Raphael. Before he was healed, Tobit had grieved and wept. He prayed to the Lord: "Remember me, and look on me; take not vengeance on me for my sins and mine ignorances, and the sins of my fathers, which sinned before thee."[18] Tobit was blind. He thought he was being punished and expected the Lord's vengeance. What he received was the angel's healing mercy administered by his son.

Nietzsche's steady praise for the tragic artist seems to me to be founded on his recognition of the necessity of creative affirmation of life in the face of such suffering. The Nietzschean image was that of "going under" — as in the movement of the sun from twilight to dawn, of Dionysus from life to death, of overman from suffering to love. This is the eternal return. Can we agree with Nietzsche that our philosophic pride and desire for vengeance are forms of life that are incompatible with tragic faith? Can we also agree that the onto-theological God of vengeance is unworthy of our songs? Would not worship of such a God be the most "cruel worship?"[19] For myself, I will also ask what Nietzsche did not, by way of mention of Job.

Job was not blind, yet he was afflicted with sudden and incomprehensible suffering by a "gaming God" who bargained with the devil. Job said his vision (understanding) was darkened. All around him were friends and counselors who were convinced that he was being punished and that God was being avenged. Job was one of those strong ones of tragic faith who refused to listen to the counsel of their paltry theodicies; instead, he hearkened to a voice in a whirlwind that did not explain but healed — a voice beyond the cycle of accusation and consolation, of good and evil. Can we affirm that Christian faith is also a tragic faith of heroic renunciation of vengeance and affirmation of life in the face of suffering? Is it also a form of listening to the whirlwind that ignites an excess of exuberance, song, praise, and creation?

18. *Tobit*, in *Biblical Idylls*, ed. Richard G. Moulton (New York: Macmillan, 1896), pp. 92-93.

19. Cf. Bertrand Russell, "A Free Man's Worship," in *Mysticism and Logic and Other Essays* (London: George Allen and Unwin, 1910, 1951), p. 46.

To keep me from whirling, my friends, tie me tight to this column. Rather would I be a stylite even, than a whirl of revenge.

Verily, Zarathustra is no cyclone or whirlwind; and if he is a dancer, he will never dance the tarantella.

Thus spoke Zarathustra. (Z II.7.214)

Persons of Flesh

Donn Welton

I should like that those not versed in anatomy should take the trouble, before reading this, of having cut up before their eyes the heart of some large animal which has lungs. . . .

René Descartes, *Discourse on the Method*

It may be that the key to Descartes's and thereby the modern understanding of the relationship between mind and body is found, not in his modification of a medieval problematic, not in a rationalist enterprise requiring a single principle grounding the postulates and axioms of the edifice of knowledge, not in the immediacy of our own reflective awareness of the stream of consciousness, but rather in his theory of the body — or, more accurately, in the simultaneous demands placed upon his method by the need to develop a scientific account of the body and upon his description of the body by a new method that transformed the space of its disclosure.

Some twelve years before the *Meditations on First Philosophy* (1641),[1] Descartes drafted a work that he never published, what we now know as

---

1. The first edition of Descartes's *Meditations on First Philosophy* was published in Paris in 1641, the second expanded edition in Amsterdam in 1642. The latter is the basis for the English translation in *The Philosophical Works of Descartes*, trans. and ed. Elizabeth Haldane and G. R. T. Ross (Cambridge: Cambridge University Press, 1968), vol. 1, pp. 131-99, and in all of vol. 2. (Hereafter cited as *Works*.)

Rules for the Direction of the Mind (1628).[2] It was surprisingly free of the metaphysical formulations of the *Meditations* as it attempted to integrate the recent discovery of algebra into a larger account of proper philosophical method. Only in Rule 12 does he distinguish the faculty of the mind from "every part of the body" (*Works*, I:38), but then he defines it largely in terms of its unique functions and operations. When the notion of extension is elaborated in Rule 14, Descartes does not use it to drive a wedge between mind and body but only to define the nature of physical reality. This changes by the time his *Discourse on the Method* appears (1637),[3] in which we find Descartes formulating ideas that figure prominently in his *Meditations*. No doubt both the *Rules* and the *Discourse* deal with the method of true philosophy or "rightly conducting the reason" and the method for "seeking for truth in the sciences," as the full title of the *Discourse* tells us. And both attempt to place mathematics in relation to its account of method. But in the *Discourse* the treatment of mind in terms of the notion of extension, the constitutive roles of skeptical reflection, and the use of an ontological proof for God's existence move to the center of his account. If we read this development backward from the *Meditations*, it is all too easy to interpret his project as controlled by the need to secure the legitimacy of immediate access to the mind and thereby preserve it from the destruction of metaphysics unleashed by his own account of nature. Descartes's dualism, we are inclined to say, is the result of his description of mental life. Alter that description and perhaps we can discover a dualist theory that is cogent.

We are somewhat surprised to discover Descartes, the year after drafting his *Rules*, visiting a butcher's shop "almost daily" to witness the slaughter of animals, and even selecting certain parts to be taken home for further dissection.[4] It seems that the entire winter of 1629 in Amsterdam was spent on animal anatomy and that these studies continued for some time afterward. His labors culminated in a little-known work entitled *The Treatise on Man*, an extensive physiological account of the human body, which was probably finished in 1632, four years after his *Rules* and five years before the *Discourse*.[5] Originally this was

2. In *Works*, I:1-77. Subsequent citations will be given parenthetically in the text.
3. In *Works*, I:81-130.
4. See the Foreword to René Descartes, *Treatise on Man*, trans. and with a commentary by Thomas Steele Hall (Cambridge, MA: Harvard University Press, 1972), p. xiii. (Hereafter cited as *Treatise*.)
5. See Hall's Introduction, *Treatise*, p. xxiii.

to be the second part of a larger work for which he had selected the title *The World*,[6] but "certain considerations," as he understated it, prevented him from publishing it (*Works*, I:107).

That Descartes had a fully elaborated physiological theory before he began to spell out his ontology of the mind should give us pause. Perhaps the mind-body problem is generated not by his description of the mind but by his theory of the body. And perhaps any theory of the mind that treats the body as the unproblematic term will inevitably fall into the antinomies of a Cartesian account.

We will begin in section I of this essay by tracing Descartes's account of the body, looking for those aspects of it that will then enable us to understand his method (section II). The essay is largely concerned with an alternative approach to the body and its place in a theory of the person; section III will offer some suggestions along these lines. In the last section I will attempt to find an internal link between the body and the question of religious knowledge as it emerges in the Gospel of John.

I

Descartes's account of the body is itself fascinating; we are surprised at the extent of its break with the tradition.

(1) Descartes suggests an imaginative variation in which the body might be understood as an "earthen machine" whose functioning depends upon "mere matter" and the "arrangements of our organs" (*Treatise*, 1). At first it seems that Descartes employs something like the qualitative distinction between various kinds of matter found in the medievals, for his matter consists of three elements: fire, air, and earth. But we find that they differ only in size and shape and thus are based on a single substance: fire is an element in perpetual movement with changing shape and size such that "there is never a passage so narrow or angle so acute betwixt the parts of other bodies but that the parts of this element enter easily and fill these spaces exactly";[7] air consists of

---

6. The first part is his *Treatise of Light*, a work concerned with the physics of earthly and heavenly bodies; the third part, *Of the Soul*, would have been his psychology. The complete text of the *Treatise of Light* is found in *The Philosophical Writings of Descartes*, trans. J. Cottingham, R. Stoothoff, and D. Murdoch (Cambridge: Cambridge University Press, 1984), vol. 1, pp. 81-98, but under the title "The World."

7. *The Treatise of Light*, as cited by Hall in *Treatise*, p. 3 n. 4. See this entire note for Descartes's theory of matter.

particles that are round and responsive to force; earth has the largest particles and is resistant to force. While the body is composed of the third element, its dynamics are explained by the movement of these three elements through its internal parts. It is their *mechanical* interaction that will cause various bodily functions.

(2) Food in the stomach is digested through a process in which liquids, brought steaming hot from the heart to the stomach, "separate, shake and heat" the food particles. The coarser ones "descend" and are eliminated; the smaller are absorbed by "an infinity of little holes" that convey them to the large vein going to the liver and elsewhere (*Treatise*, 7-8).

(3) The blood in the veins moves toward the right cavity of the heart, which "contains in its pores one of those fires without light." Thus when blood enters, it is "promptly inflated and dilated" and thus propelled toward the lungs, where it is "thickened" and reconverted into blood. From there it "falls drop by drop" into the left cavity of the heart where it both "nourishes the fire that is there" and "is distributed through the body" (*Treatise*, 9-11).

The idea that only the blood returning to the heart in liquid form can nourish the fire shows the extent to which Descartes is utilizing a mechanical explanation. Fire involves the direct action of first element particles (fire) on third element particles (earth). Second element particles (air) must be driven out; otherwise there will be evaporation rather than combustion. The "blood vapors," then, created on the right side of the heart, cannot burn since they are of the wrong form. Thus in Descartes's curious confusion of states of an element with a difference between elements, it is only as a liquid that blood can fuel the fire.[8]

Hall argues effectively that this piece of obsolete cardiology shows us the extent to which Descartes is pressing for a physical description of the body, rooting out all vestiges of animism. Descartes follows Galen's idea that the motion of the blood can be explained through heat, but he clearly rejects Galen's thesis that it is the part of the soul residing in the heart that causes the heat.[9] And while Descartes mistakenly disregards Harvey's idea (published in 1628) that the heart is a pump, his analysis is much more consistently physicalistic. Harvey had argued that in addition to being a pump the heart is also the place where blood is heated, reliquified, and "impregnated with spirits."[10] Descartes rejects the latter.

8. Following Hall's account in *Treatise*, p. 9.
9. See *Treatise*, p. 10 n. 10.
10. Quoted in *Treatise*, p. 10.

This first round of descriptions (1) through (3) giving us the rudiments of Descartes's cardiology is augmented by a second round, (4) through (6), which accounts for the functions of the brain and nervous system.

(4) In Descartes's map of the circulatory system there is a narrow but direct tube going from the heart to the brain. It is not hard to guess what he will do with this idea:

> all the liveliest, strongest and subtlest parts of this blood proceed to the cavities of the brain, inasmuch as the arteries that bring them there are the ones that come in the straightest line from the heart; and, as you know, all bodies in motion tend insofar as possible to continue moving in a straight line. (*Treatise*, 17)

As the blood is expelled from the heart it tends to move toward the brain. Because the passage is narrow "the strongest and liveliest particles" repel the weaker and coarser. By this Descartes must mean that only the more rarified or "subtlest parts" of the blood pass into the network of small capillaries. As these approach the center of the brain, which for Descartes is the pineal gland, the blood is further rarified. This progressive refinement must effect another transformation of the blood. Though Descartes does not explicitly say so, the decreasing size of the vessels acts to sift the blood, which must have the effect of further eliminating the presence of third element particles (earth) and raising the proportion of the first element (fire). The arteries and capillaries act like a sieve, and it is because of this *physical* action that the blood becomes "a very lively and very pure flame" (*Treatise*, 19). Descartes puts it this way:

> And thus, without any preparation or alteration except that they are separated from the coarser ones and still retain the extreme rapidity that the heat of the heart has given them, they cease to have the form of blood and are designated animal spirits. (*Treatise*, 21)

The notion of animal spirits, then, is anything but the introduction of the soul into his theory. Indeed, the notion was designed to displace the soul in accounting for the actions of the body. Animal spirits are the most refined of third element particles combined with a large proportion of the first element. Only in this state do they gain access to the pineal gland.

(5) The nervous system actually consists of two systems that tie the brain to the body. In the first, nerves are understood as "little tubes" sheathing "fine fibrils" but with enough room for animal spirits to flow through them into the muscles. By a complex system of tubes, and by changing quantities of animal spirits entering and leaving these tubes, all the movements of the body are explained (*Treatise*, 24, 32). The second system accounts for sensory detection. The marrow of the nerves has filaments; objects impinging on the body "move" them much like the hand pulls a cord. The filaments, in turn, "pull the parts of the brain from which they come" — an immediate mechanical transmission — and thereby "open the entrances to certain pores in the internal surface of the brain" (*Treatise*, 34). The constancy hypothesis finds its origins in this account:

> Although the threads I speak of are very thin, yet they extend safely all the way from the brain to parts that are farthest therefrom, nor is there anything in between that breaks them or that prevents their activity through pressure, even though the parts are bent in myriad ways. (*Treatise*, 36)

Objects contacting the body cause a registration inside the brain "just as, pulling one end of a cord, one simultaneously rings a bell which hangs at the opposite end." And this action not only provides the brain with distinct impressions but also triggers muscular actions that correspond to the type of discrimination:

> The animal spirits in [the brain's] cavities begin immediately to make their way through these pores into the nerves, and so into muscles that give rise to movements in this machine quite similar to [the movements] to which we are naturally incited when our senses are similarly impinged upon. (*Treatise*, 34)

What we find, then, is the mechanical action of things on the fibrils giving rise to the entire range of sensory experience, and the physical movement of animal spirits through the nerve tubes producing all the varieties of muscular action.

(6) Remember that only a small amount of blood, "the liveliest,

strongest and subtlest parts," enters into the brain (*Treatise,* 17). In passing, Descartes adds the idea that the "strongest and liveliest" of those particles deflected away from the brain "go to the vessels designed for generation." There is a conspicuously straight vessel running from the base of the narrow vessel going to the brain, the place where the bottleneck must occur, to the reproductive organs. And Descartes suggests that he could show from the "humor" that assembles in the genitals how "another machine, quite similar to this" could be formed (*Treatise,* 18).

Descartes, then, ties that very "flame without light" which makes conscious discrimination possible to sexual generation. There is a hidden bond between the vapors giving rise to conscious awareness and the seed engendering life. Machines begetting machines, the material interaction of particles giving rise not just to *hyle* but also to *morphe,* not just to content but also to form, which, for its part, is now understood as laws regulating such particles — mechanical explanations account not only for the structure and interaction of parts but also for the generation of entire systems, matter giving rise to life. With this the circle of material explanation attempts closure.

But the third cluster of ideas, (7) through (9), in an effort to extend this account into forbidden terrain, will stop, as we will now see, one step short.

(7) For the reader of the *Meditations* and especially *The Passions of the Soul* (1645-46)[11] it is surprising to see how far the mechanical explanations of the *Treatise* reach. External perception with its five senses of touch, taste, smell, sight, and hearing is accounted for by the movement of nerve fibers.[12] "Internal" moods or "humors" and even dispositional inclinations are referred to the absence or presence of animal spirits, on the one hand, and, on the other, the quality of the blood. For example, the presence of coarser spirits produces confidence, courage, and constancy; their absence, timidity. The presence of animal spirits in a higher state of agitation gives us diligence, in an even higher state, desire. Their absence, for those who have wondered about classroom dynamics, results in tardiness. And, of course, there are any number of combinations that can produce yet other states: joy, for example, is a combination of promptness (agitated spirits) and tranquil-

---

11. In *Works,* I:331-427.
12. *Treatise,* pp. 41-67. We will handle the question of awareness in a moment.

ity (uniform spirits). In short, the whole range of passions and emotions — or at least "the movements in this machine that give evidence in us" of such "humors" and "natural inclinations" (*Treatise*, 72) — and even the operation of the will are accounted for by the actions of the body, not the mind.

(8) Significantly, Descartes also believes that he can explain memory in physiological terms. As external objects act upon us, nerve fibers are expanded and opened, and "a certain arrangement of the filaments" is produced (*Treatise*, 86). The result is a "trace" imprinted on the interior part of the brain. In a way that anticipates the development of cybernetics, Descartes tells us:

> But the effect of memory that seems to me to be most worthy of consideration here consists in the fact that without there being any soul in this machine it can be naturally disposed to imitate all the movements that real men (or many other similar machines) will make when the soul is present. (*Treatise*, 96)

The addition of memory allows Descartes to offer a fully material explanation of the *behavior* of the body. For example, the action of withdrawing the hand from a burning fire is explained entirely by the mechanical action of particles displacing the surface of the skin and thereby pulling "the little thread" that opens a pore or conduit in the brain, releasing animal spirits into the fibrils that cause the muscles to contract. Memory supplies the associations that reinforce and enhance such behavior. No feeling, no movements of consciousness, no passionate soul intervenes (*Treatise*, 34-35).

(9) As Descartes's theory of the body displaced what earlier theories thought of as the emotive and the "vegetative" functions of the soul, so the *Treatise* goes some distance toward a physiological account of our cognitive activities. This is especially true of his account of perception, where the ideas resulting from a perceptual act are actually understood as physical events. This is easy to miss, for he does tell us that in the case of a sound the physical action of the air on the inner ear "will cause the soul to conceive the idea of sound" (*Treatise*, 46). And we do read that the stimulation of the optic nerves "will enable the soul, when united with this machine, to conceive the diverse ideas of colors and of light" (*Treatise*, 49). But in the *Treatise* the notion of something "occasioning the soul to conceive the idea of X" *(conceuoir l'idée)* is usually

equivalent to the notion of something "causing the sensation or feeling of X" *(causer le sentiment; Treatise,* 70) — that is, causing a figure or pattern with differential features that can be sensed. Thus the "ideas" derived from the senses still belong to the realm of extended substances. Vision, for example, consists of various changes in the nerves such that the figure seen "traces" a figure on the back of the eye, then on the internal surface of the brain, and finally on the surface of the pineal gland, the seat of imagination and *sensus communis.* Those figures "traced in spirits on the surface of [this] gland" must be material, yet they are taken by Descartes to be

> ideas, that is to say, the forms or images that the rational soul will consider directly when, being united to this machine, it will imagine or will sense any object. (*Treatise,* 86)

They are then stored in the internal part of the brain, the seat of memory. Perceptual ideas, then, are neurophysical "impressions" or "traces," correlated to a particular pattern of the animal spirits, stored in the interior brain as "creases" or "folds" in its tissues (*Treatise,* 84-87). And the *Treatise,* rather than giving us a further mechanism for converting these corporeal traces into nonextended mental entities, seems to view them as the objects of our awareness.

One can still find a place for the soul in this account. In the *Rules,* written five years earlier, Descartes introduced a "cognitive power," which he thought of as "a single agency" that could be defined in terms of various mental operations such as sensing, remembering, imagining, and understanding (*Works,* I:38-39). Perhaps the physiological theory covers only noematic content, not noetic acts; only the seen, not the seeing; only the imagined, not the imagining. And, of course, the soul would possess the ability to form ideas of its own, purely intellectual in nature. We are not surprised to see, as a consequence, Descartes's later works splitting both the ideas and the modes of cognition into the corporeal and the intellectual, and then eventually seeing, as in the *Passions of the Soul,* the intellectual replicating the corporeal.

But the *Treatise* does not abide by such a tidy distinction between acts of awareness and content, for it generally thinks of not just the objects experienced but also the experiencing itself as explained by the movement of animal spirits. In fact, the first time the soul is introduced there Descartes uses it to explain the lived quality of experience:

according to the different ways in which the entrances of the pores
in the internal surface of this brain are opened through the intervention of the nerves, the soul will have different feelings.

The soul here is what *senses* the changes in the distribution and patterns
of the animal spirits. While the behavior of pulling the hand from the
flame requires no intervention of the soul, the physical actions involved
will themselves "cause the soul to experience a feeling of pain" (*Treatise*,
37-38). Thus the sensing itself is an effect. And this also applies to
visual perception, for the figures transmitted to the brain take on the
quality of being experienced only by virtue of the differential pressures
of the animal spirits flowing through the pores and cavities of the pineal
gland.

The end result is that Descartes's theory of the independence of the
soul from the body combines, in an unstable union, with his treatment
of both the objects experienced and the quality of experiencing as an
epiphenomenal *effect* of physiological events. For it, the notion of soul
is coextensive with the notion of consciousness, and consciousness,
while "distinct from every part of the body" (*Works*, I:38), is produced
only as the result of physical interactions. Let me call this Descartes's
psychological characterization of the soul, one that is rooted in his characterization of matter as extended substance, but one that he developed
before the ontological *opposition* between extended and nonextended
substance came to dominate his account, as drafted in the *Discourse* and
systematically presented in the *Meditations*.

II

If the usual picture of Descartes's method were correct — a thoroughly
deductive system resting on abstract yet intuitively given postulates or
axioms, transcending the medievals in its overturn of natural kinds and
syllogistic logic yet remaining bound to a notion of coherence as the
final criterion of truth — it would be impossible to understand why
after the drafting of the *Rules* we find him enthralled by the entrails of
pigs, why we, too, should take home "the heart of some large animal
which has lungs" (*Works*, I:110), and why he viewed his work not just
as a method for organizing the discourse of the sciences but as a way
of discovering the truths that are the content of the various sciences.

Perhaps by looking at the method employed in his physiological studies we can see behind this standard picture of his method into its actual working. And perhaps there we can also discover the framework, determinative of modern thought, that makes possible as it delimits the appearance of the human body.

(1) The new method carries us beyond as it belies the body in order to construct a representation that will reveal the body. Descartes proposes a model, a resemblance, which is in fact a dissemblance. He projects a set of imaginary men constructed differently from us yet fashioned in such a way that in all their behavior they resemble us.

> I assume their body to be but . . . an earthen machine formed intentionally by God to be as much as possible like us. Thus not only does He give it externally the shapes and colors of all the parts of our bodies; He also places inside it all the pieces required to make it walk, eat, breathe, and imitate whichever of our own functions can be imagined to proceed from mere matter and to depend entirely on the arrangement of our organs. (*Treatise*, 2-4)

This first step is limited, since it is only by virtue of a morphological resemblance that a comparison between an earthen machine and the body becomes plausible.

(2) In being placed in relation to what is possible, the method allows us to say in advance what could be true of the body that is disclosed. What is known in advance constitutes the body's fundamental determinations to the extent that it, like the model, is a possible body. The body, however, is not an open but a bound possibility, since it is circumscribed by the epistemic space that is opened only by the model of the machine. Descartes thinks of that space as a world, indeed, a new world. As he reflects in the *Discourse* on what he wrote in the *Treatise*, he tells us that he pictured a "new world" in which everything that exists could be explained in terms of matter in motion and "the laws" of nature. This displaced the old world with its Aristotelian forms or qualities determining the inner nature of things, different for various categories of objects. The opposition between celestial and terrestrial bodies with their corresponding difference in patterns of change and kinds of motions, so central to the scholastic tradition, is swept aside in this vision of "an imaginary space" (*Works*, I:107) in which the laws of physics uniformly apply to all of nature, even subsuming under them the laws

of physiology.[13] In this world the body as lived, as sentient presence, is rid of its difference from the things of nature in order now to comprehend how it is one of the things of nature. Not only its "pieces" but also its actions must "proceed from the merely material," and this means that any explanation of its essence employs no more than material and a modified version of efficient causation.

In Descartes's method, causal laws are independent elements, the type of item we know "in advance" of the object. What is known in advance of a field constitutes the basic principles of a science. The validity of this kind of knowledge is established "without the aid of anything outside" of it (cf. *Works*, I:25); for example, while we may not be certain that the action of heating causes the blood to circulate, we do know that circulation can be viewed as the effect of a cause, and we do know that blood, like all things, consists of the combination of basic elements that are regulated by laws of chemistry, thermodynamics, etc.

(3) The way in which the body becomes phenomenon must be commensurate with the framework established in advance. This not only determines the form of our discourse about the body but also specifies the fundamental mode in which both its structure and its functions can show themselves. For Descartes and for the entire modern era that fundamental mode is the *mathematical*. This is no "ordinary mathematics," for it is not concerned with "bare numbers and imaginary figures." "I am expounding quite another science, of which these illustrations are rather the outer husk than the constituents" (*Works*, I:11). Rather than its being a particular type of study, Descartes envisions a "universal mathematics," for as we consider the matter carefully we recognize that all empirical disciplines are "mathematical" in that "order and measurement" are investigated in them (*Works*, I:13). Mathematization is that movement of thought, absent from view, which provides the cognitive space in which scientific objects exist, that enframing of nature which allows phenomena to show themselves as admissible elements in a scientific theory. Thus the body becomes phenomenon only to the extent that it is *measurable*. As showing itself in the framework

---

13. Descartes argues that a world without forms is consistent with the infinite perfection of God (*Works*, I:108), but it is hard to escape the suspicion that his invocation of God is little more than a heuristic device designed to bolster a mechanistic view of the cosmos. At least he does not give a positive argument from the perfection of God to the structure of the world as mathematized.

of the mathematical, the body does not have hidden or concealed traits: *what* the body *is* is determined by *how* the measurable body *appears*. There is no inner nature determining its properties. Rather, its nature is derived strictly from the intersection of its quantifiable features.

Thus we can see why Descartes is convinced that what the senses — not just vision but the other senses as well — actually detect are figures. "The concept of figure is so common and simple that it is involved in every object of sense." And we can see why he must extend the idea that figure is involved in sensory perception to the thesis that all that the senses perceive of external objects is "figure" and that all the diverse traits of things — even colors, sounds, odors, and tastes — appear as figures and the differences between figures (*Works*, I:37).[14]

> And note that by "figure" I mean not only things that somehow represent the position of the edges and surfaces of objects [that is, their shape], but also everything which . . . can cause the soul to sense movement, size, distance, colors, sounds, odors, and other such qualities; and even things that can make it sense titillation, pain, hunger, thirst, joy, sadness, and other such passions. (*Treatise*, 85)

For having enframed the field of objects as measurable, this is all that *can* appear. "It is certain that the infinitude of figures suffices to express all the differences in sensible things" (*Works*, I:37). And since the body is known only as an object, it, too, is manifest only as a set of figures.

(4) The transformation of the body into a measurable object is completed at precisely that moment when geometry becomes analytic geometry and a morphology of the body is supplemented by an explanatory account of its internal and external functions. Analytic geometry introduced the ideas of constants and variables, which made it possible to express all the properties of figures and the relationship between figures in algebraic equations.[15] Because the rules of algebra are not just rules of inference but also rules of construction (*Works*, I:64), they are *sufficient* to explain the existence of figures and their ordered connection to each other.

14. Actually, Descartes views dimension, unity, and figure as three features of extended substances. While he speaks of order and measurement as constitutive of the relations of figures, it is clear that dimension and unity are defined in terms of the measurable. What we are saying of figure, then, would also apply to them. See *Works*, I:61-64.

15. Cf. S. V. Kelling, *Descartes* (New York: Oxford University Press, 1968), p. 311.

The relation of constants and variables defines for Descartes the natural relation of cause and effect in a uniform spatio-temporal matrix. The laws of nature become sufficient to explain the form, the function, and even the existence of the body, even how machines can beget machines (*Treatise*, 18). Closure is achieved. Thereby the dissembling body displaces all other appearances of the body.[16] And the soul can appear only as a "remainder," as a surd, as that thing which is no thing. It is this consequence of Descartes's psychological characterization that becomes the starting point of his epistemological project.

(5) The method that frames the possible appearances of the body is simultaneously the privileged way in which the body can be interrogated, can be articulated in theory. Inquiry drafts alternatives that are defined by measurable differences. Yet these alternatives are only possible facts, only alternative explanations. The very impetus to inquiry that carries us beyond the body returns us to an experience of it that responds to the questions posed by inquiry. This mode of experience, the authenticity of which is secured by the enterprise as a whole, is the experiment. The experiment is that mode of experience which presents the body in such a way that it can be viewed as an object, making possible a decision between alternative explanations. The truths that result from this process form science. This is the inner connection between the model of knowledge as consisting of elementary concepts expressed in a coherent system of propositions connected by rigorous rules and the privilege accorded the experimental method in the sciences.

(6) While the project of a rational understanding of the world is the source of the experimental method, the mode of analysis constitutive of the sciences is different from the mode of analysis that secures the logic of explanations employed by the sciences. Since that logic cannot be one of the topics of scientific inquiry, for it is presupposed by it, the mode of access to it must respect as it articulates that difference. The unthematized recourse to logic found in the sciences becomes the bridge to a *reflection* that apprehends those basic concepts and rules of inference (or construction) constitutive of scientific inquiry. These ideas, however,

---

16. By the time of his *Description of the Human Body*, a later work, Descartes treats the imaginary body of the *Treatise* as the human body and drops any suggestion that this is only an imaginative variation. See "Description of the Human Body," in *The Philosophical Writings of Descartes*, vol. 1, pp. 314-24.

"do not come from outside." They are themselves *reflexive* and thus present as possible modes of *thinking* per se. Descartes understands the *ego cogito* as that principle which secures the field of thinking as the ultimate *ground*.

Yet this field is no field at all, not itself a region or domain of scientific inquiry. As their ground, it is absent from all such fields. How are we to understand the difference? Descartes secures this epistemological difference between the field and its ground by an ontological difference between extended substance (the domain of the sciences) and what must lack any of its traits, a nonextended substance (the domain of the *ego cogito*).

III

While the particulars of Descartes's theory of the body were soon transcended, the field in which the body appears, and thereby its basic determinations, were set for modern thought.[17] It is my view, although I cannot even begin to document it here, that the variations of the mind-body problem throughout the modern period are circumscribed by margins that the account of the body prescribes. Interestingly, it is not the body as material and thereby mathematized that is the root conception but the body as mathematized and thereby material. With the identification of the mathematized and the material body in Descartes, the opening was established in which the mind can appear only as its opposite. The opposition between material and mental substances in turn gave rise to various theories of parallelism and occasionalism, which often invoked the Creator as the guarantee of a preestablished harmony between the two. The difficulties that attended these notions were generally settled by denying the dualism of substances, either by deriving body from mind, as we find in some of the stronger idealist versions, or by deriving mind from body, as we see in the various epiphenomenalist and materialist accounts. And even those theories which expressly rejected an account of substance for epistemological

17. Foucault has shown that the method, too, underwent paradigmatic shifts throughout the past four centuries, but this occurred in the various medical sciences and, so to speak, behind the back of philosophy's understanding of the body. See Michel Foucault, *Madness and Civilization* (New York: Vintage Books, 1965) and *The Birth of the Clinic* (New York: Vintage Books, 1973).

reasons, as in Kant, did so only by transposing the scientific characterization of nature to the phenomenal realm.

The important consequence of this was only to further secure the
mathematized body, for now it is no longer inferred or known indirectly,
in need of God to secure the claim that this is the noumenal reality to
which our phenomenal ideas correspond; rather, it is known directly,
within the realm of what is experienced, as an object that exhibits
law-governed features. In moving the body into a different register, the
mathematized body is also freed from matter and viewed in terms of
function. Yet its basic character as mathematized goes unchanged. It is
only a short step from this point to the conception of the body as a
web of S-R arcs, as behaviorism would have it, or a matrix of computational processes, as in earlier theories of cognitive psychology.

Instead of a historical account, we want to explore an alternative
theory of the body, to sketch a notion of the body that has the potential
of shifting our view of the person onto new ground. We will then
extrapolate from this, leaping over ever so many intervening steps, some
points that bear on the question of religious knowledge. The rest of
this section, needless to say, is offered only as suggestion, only as a
Leitfaden to very complex issues.

A

We will begin with Descartes's theory of perception. Descartes supported his treatment of the objects of experience as the things of physics
by means of a theory of perception in which the perceiver was likened
to a piece of wax, a passive receptor of that which is transmitted through
its neurological channels (*Works*, I:39). We have seen that this allowed
Descartes to connect mathematized things securely to their phenomenal
presence, to experience. But are experiential objects things in this sense?
Is the characterization of them in the hands of physics really a characterization of what we see?

In an effort to build a hedge against Cartesianism it is, of course,
tempting to answer in the negative and to insist that they are entirely
different. But I think a better approach is to begin by asking what we
must introduce into perception in order actually to experience such
things. We see a cluster of roses, alive with a velvet red, against a
background of green leaves and a whitewashed wall. What would we
have to do to this experience in order to see an extended surface whose

shape is geometrically defined, emitting light with a wavelength of 740 nanometers?

Establishing the cognitive space in which the rose becomes a thing for physics involves at least a fourfold reduction of experience.[18]

(1) The vital and effusive significance that ties objects and persons is reduced to a set of properties that things have; these are then thinned down to those that are physical. The subject, as Descartes correctly perceived and as Hume confirmed, is transformed into that stage on which such stripped-down objects are displayed. In this *reduction of properties,* all value predicates are suspended. Aesthetic and emotive traits, such a part of their palpable presence, are removed from things and, at best, are placed in subjects who project them upon things.

(2) This winnowing of properties and thinning of the subject are necessarily accompanied by an *environmental reduction.* The object is isolated from its ordinary context and placed in relationship to another context. And this is much more than replacing an everyday environment with that of the lab, for in this process the spatiality of things is changed. Science sees with a "fixed eye" that rules over a space lacking all depth, all thickness, all paths, and having only coordinates and quantified dimensions. The multiplicity of grounds and backgrounds are exchanged for a uniform grid. Ambient light, with its internal differentiations between below and above, near and far, is exchanged for radiant light, as uniform as it is homogeneous.

(3) The use of implements and equipment in experiments introduces a *technological reduction* in which the "incisions" of machines cause objects to stand forth and be "read" in terms of calibrated norms. Machines do not so much record as report, offering us an event that itself requires interpretation. This intervention of technology, however minimal it might be, is internal to the constitution of scientific objects. Yet the measure against which and in terms of which they appear is itself a product whose all too human origin is lost to view.

(4) The technological reduction is interwoven with a *praxiological reduction* in which varieties of embodied interaction with objects are restricted to actions upon objects, and these actions, at least as we view

18. The following account applies only to the objects of physics, Descartes's paradigm of a scientific object. Furthermore, among the objects of physics it applies only to "medium-sized" objects, not to micro- or macro-objects (quantum phenomena or astronomical systems).

them after the fact in theory, are restricted to rule-governed operations upon things. When it is not being viewed as a topic of investigation, the body can be understood as no more than another tool for carrying out these operations. The operations performed upon things are controlled by a hypothesis or theory, undergirded by the scientific interest in mastery, in gaining that comprehension of things which allows us not just to quantitatively describe things but also to reproduce them and thereby to use them.

By viewing the things of science as constituted by such a fourfold reduction, and by seeing such a reduction as a transformation of experience, we are able to understand their connection to everyday objects. Scientific things are objects, but objects as mastered by the interests of the scientific project. A scientific account gives us not the experiential but the physical structure of objects, along with the laws that explain their composition, and gives us the ability to control and utilize them. But this means that things exist against a backdrop of our everyday familiarity with objects; we cannot assume that a scientific account of things will give us a description of objects as they are actually experienced.

B

If a theory of the body-mind relationship must account for not just our knowledge of things but also our knowledge of objects, and if such a theory must account for the body both as an object and as constitutive of our experience of objects, then we can see that restricting its account to a method which is designed to bring only things to theory would be a methodological blunder of the worst kind. Why do we assume that the mathematized body, itself given only as the result of the fourfold reduction, is the body under a description that has the ability to account for our experience of objects and for our experience of the body itself with appropriate objectivity? Have we not fallen prey to a fallacy of misplaced abstractness, confusing the mathematized projection of things with the concreteness of objects?

Here I can only paint in broad strokes what an alternate account of our visual experience of ordinary objects might look like, concentrating on those aspects which call the body into play and reveal the internal relation between it and perceptual fields.

(1) All *objects* of external perception are given in and through *profiles.*

In viewing the "side" or aspect that directly faces us, we simultaneously perceive the object as a whole. Integral to this structure is yet another in which objects experienced in and through profiles are seen in a determinate manner: all objects are given *as* something — as possessing significant features or, more generally, significance for us. The *sense* of the object is what constitutes its determinate presence for us in perception.

(2) Objects given in and through profiles are always situated. Profiles constitute *perspectives*, which means that objects have a spatial organization that involves orientation. The space in which objects are given in perspectives is constituted by virtue of objects having a relation to the body. In an effort to capture the difference between the objects and that which affords them their orientation, phenomenological thinkers have spoken of the body as the "null" point from which and in terms of which the space of objects arises.

(3) As the perspectivity of objects can be understood in terms of a spatiality constituted by the body, so the determinacy of objects can be integrated into the body's relation to objects. The senses of objects are, first and foremost, not Cartesian "ideas" or concepts but bodily schemata of perceptual appropriation and accommodative action. They arise at the intersection of our perceptual and practical engagement with, not our conceptual mastery over, objects. And just as there is a mode of seeing objects that releases rather than dominates them, so there is a mode of appropriating objects that respects rather than violates their integrity.

(4) The theory of experiential objects can certainly use experimental means to discover their structure, and it will undoubtedly employ statistical notions of variables and constants in its various studies. But the crucial difference is that mathematics is not the language of objects but of "functional facts" that accompany and articulate "phenomenological facts," to provisionally employ Koffka's distinction.[19]

This account, all too brief, gives us both an account of objects and a "clue" as to how we might speak of the body "before" it becomes the mathematized things of science and modern philosophy. But we need to follow through on this clue.

---

19. K. Koffka, *Principles of Gestalt Psychology* (New York: Harcourt, Brace and World, 1935), p. 252.

C

On the one hand, we have seen that Descartes's treatment of the physical body requires a transformation of the body into a thing, which was entirely absent or concealed to modern thought. On the other hand, we have noticed that the account of ordinary experience gives us access to the body as a constitutive factor in the presence of objects. The requirement that we understand the body in terms of its experiential features drives our account further, for thus far we have only approached the body obliquely, only as the backdrop against which we can experience objects. Can it be approached directly?

(1) The body required by the presence of objects is one of free movements having a motility in terms of which perspectives arise. The change in perspectives and thereby the concrete presence of the object always arise in correlation to activities of the body. Yet the movements of our body are experienced in a way different from the movement of objects, of phenomena. There is a kinesthetic awareness — nonpropositional, nonthematic, nonreferential — that accompanies the intervention of bodily movements in the life of things. These sensations provide us with a tacit awareness of our body. In this awareness the body is constituted as enlived body, as *Leib*, as that invisible presence in terms of which the basic coordinates of lived space arise.

(2) This first moment, in which the body withdraws from the world of objects, is actually intertwined with a second, in which the body as *Leib* takes on an objectivity appropriate to it. If vision is the dominant sense in which objects become phenomena, then the tactile is the primary sense in which the body becomes present as body. If I hold my head in my hands, the hands will cradle it much as they would a ball or a melon. While the hands are touching, that which is touched is present to them as an object much like any other. Yet in this case, the head that is held introduces a reciprocity totally missing from other objects: that which is being touched is also touching. Not only do the hands feel the cheeks but the cheeks also feel the hands; in being touched they are also touching. There can be a shift or a reversal of one to the other, but there can never be a synthesis that pulls the dyad of touching and touched into a single objective whole, and thus there can never be the possibility of treating the touched as simply a string of profiles. Each touched (profile) is such that it is also touching (not a profile). The originary experience of the body is always caught between

identity and difference: in touching I *am* my body, in being touched I *have* my body. It is this reflexivity of self-touch, so different from both the receptivity of object perception and the reflection of the cogito, that introduces us to the peculiar presence that the body has to itself.

(3) The body as the locus of appropriative actions can undergo change by making its own care the goal of these actions. Appropriation has a reflexivity that further familiarizes us with the body as body. Basic needs, especially for nourishment, move the body from the margins into the field of experience. The cycles of hunger, seeking, eating, and satisfaction, for example, institute rhythms in which the body is present to us not only as corporeal scheme but also as mass, and in which objects are drawn into the circuit of its living. As the needs of the body intrude and as it reaches into the life of objects, we are brought before its material and thick existence. The materiality of the body as *Leib* constitutes the *flesh* of the body.

While the kinestheses bring to presence that body in reference to which the spatiality of objects arises, the reflexivity of touch and of appropriative actions unfolds the body as flesh. It is the body as flesh, not the body as thing, that is the field in which objects have their (basic) aesthetic qualities: as spatial scheme it secures their place and orientation; as corporeal scheme it is internally tied to their sense, their determinate perceptual presence; as the agent of appropriation and consumption it reaches into their existence and draws them into its own.

D

Once the body is thematized as flesh, we see that the body is best understood as a mode, the most elementary mode, of our incarnate existence, not as a "part" of our animal or human natures to be set in opposition to yet another "part," the mind or soul. The reason for this is that as soon as we avoid the category mistake of treating the mathematized body as the experiential body, as soon as the body is understood in those experiential terms required by the very posing of the question, it cannot be strictly divorced from what Descartes and the tradition could only speak of as consciousness. In fact, in defining for us a basic mode of being in the world, it cuts across the modern distinction between body and mind, between object and consciousness. In an effort to grasp this ontologically, we can speak of the body as a *structure* of our existence as persons. And the obvious implication of this line of approach, which we cannot pursue here, is that the soul and the spirit, too, once freed of their heavy burdens of theory, can also be understood as basic structures of our all too human being.

IV

John, the Gospel of the Word become flesh, is the Gospel of eating and drinking. It is no small surprise when we realize that John, which seems to reach behind the first three Gospels and lend them new disclosive space, consistently uses the language of the body, not the soul, to characterize the nature of the human spirit and to qualify the kind of knowledge that we find there. The dominant term for knowing in John (οἶδα) conveys the idea of having an intimate relationship with, even of seeing (e.g., John 10:14; 14:9). While the terms "word" (λόγος and ῥῆμα) and "spirit" (πνεῦμα) occur together (3:34; 6:63), the other term for knowing (γινώσκω) and the terms for understanding (νοέω and συνίημι) are never used in conjunction with spirit. Rather, the exercise of the spirit is described as if it were an action of the body. We are encouraged to "drink" the living water and to "eat" the living bread, even to "eat" the flesh and blood of Christ. Since John clearly sets the flesh, once fallen, and the spirit in diametric opposition (6:63), we easily miss the fact that it is only by a transposition of the dimensions of the flesh, apart from the fall (1:14), not those of our understanding, that we come to see what it means for a believer to know the triune God. Our direct acquaintance with the body provides a field of experience whose elements open up that type of awareness of Christ that brings us spiritual birth (3:5-8), quenches the spiritual thirst that religion will never satisfy (4:10-16, 19-24), and supplies us with the nourishment whose transforming effects outstrip the resources of correct understanding (6:47-57; 5:39-40).

I can touch on only a few features of the flesh that invite this transposition and open to view the type of experience of God that we find "before" understanding sets off in pursuit.

(1) Perceiving an object through its profiles is not an act of referring to an object through a signifier. We see objects, not semantic referents. Similarly, John presents belief, not as an indirect relationship to God mediated by an act of understanding that interprets symbols, but as receiving and beholding Christ (1:12; 14:8-9). As also for Paul, "the

knowledge of the glory of God" is to be found "in the face of Jesus Christ" (2 Cor. 4:6). We can *see* God because the Word became flesh, because God entered the field of our experience in Christ, and because his actions, his words, and his death and resurrection are "profiles" in which the "whole" Word is manifest to us. This space — on a different plane than the opposition between analogical or symbolic understanding and its negation, mystical intuition — is the space of incarnation.

(2) At the same time that the different aspects of Christ's life present God, the structure of this experience means that our awareness of God is always perspectival — that is, it is necessarily linked to us as situated beings. The "profiles" of God that we come to see are internally tied to our posture *(Einstellung)* in spirit, to the manner in which God is approached and the manner in which we respond to what is unfolded of God. Just as we can "close down" any further perceptions, and just as we can "cut off" the kind of appropriation solicited by things, so we can transform and even subvert our experience of God by refusing to open the spirit to God (blindness), by blending in other interests that change God into what he is not (idolatry), or by acting in a way that violates the integrity of what we have seen (hypocrisy). These are closures rooted not in a particular representation of God but in the basic mode of our relationship to him — in the "spirit."

(3) The spirit is being touched in touching. In insisting on the union between our spirit and the Spirit of God, John and Paul do not envision a synthesis with loss of difference. In touching, I am my spirit extended toward God; in being touched, I have a spirit that is being supplied and nourished with God's life. The cycles of need, reaching out, drinking or eating, nourishment, and release, forming the rhythms of our life "in spirit," are what draw Life into the branches and eventually produce the "fruit of the Spirit." In bearing fruit, the Word once again becomes flesh.

It may be that as the mathematized body displaced the lived body and became the uncriticized term in most accounts of the mind-body problem, this displacement left thinkers without a model of the body that had direct bearing on the question of religious knowledge. Accordingly, most theories push the body into the realm of metaphor, that is, into a grammar of understanding bodily symbols. But could it be that the body as flesh gives us not metaphors but experiential dimensions that resonate the life of the spirit? Could it be that the transposition of body into spirit is necessarily lost to those accounts immersed in the

Cartesian stream of modern thought, which find in the experience of faith only those elements which countenance our understanding of that experience? And could it be that a recovery of the flesh of the body and of the difference between spirit and soul provides us with an opening in which we can construct something like a "transcendental aesthetics" of religious experience "before" the "analytics" of religious understanding are set in play?

Contributors

William P. Alston — Professor Emeritus of Philosophy, Syracuse University

C. Stephen Evans — Professor of Philosophy and Curator of the Howard and Edna Hong Kierkegaard Library, St. Olaf College

Laura L. Garcia — Lecturer in Philosophy, Rutgers University

William Hasker — Professor of Philosophy, Huntington College

Galen A. Johnson — Chairman and Professor of Philosophy, University of Rhode Island

Alvin Plantinga — John A. O'Brien Professor of Philosophy, University of Notre Dame

Donn Welton — Associate Professor of Philosophy, The University of Stony Brook

Merold Westphal — Professor of Philosophy, Fordham University

Nicholas Wolterstorff — Noah Porter Professor of Philosophy, Yale University

Index of Names